Money, Politics, and Law

MONEY, POLITICS, AND LAW

A Study of Electoral Campaign Finance Reform in Canada

K. D. EWING

CLARENDON PRESS · OXFORD
1992

Oxford University Press, Walton Street, Oxford OX2 6DP

Oxford New York Toronto
Delhi Bombay Calcutta Madras Karachi
Petaling Jaya Singapore Hong Kong Tokyo
Nairobi Dar es Salaam Cape Town
Melbourne Auckland
and associated companies in
Berlin Ibadan

Oxford is a trade mark of Oxford University Press

Published in the United States
by Oxford University Press. New York

British Library Cataloguing in Publication Data
Data available

Library of Congress Cataloging in Publication Data
Ewing, K. D. (Keith D.)
Money, politics, and law: a study of campaign finance reform in
Canada / K.D. Ewing.
Includes bibliographical references and index.
1. Campaign funds—Law and legislation—Canada. I. Title.
KE4646.E96 1992   91-47935
ISBN 0-19-825738-4

Typeset by Best-set Typesetter Ltd., Hong Kong
Printed in Great Britain by Biddles Ltd
Guildford & King's Lynn

Wealth is almost invariably selfish and lacking in moral principle. Its interests are often diametrically opposed to sound public policy.

(*'Defunct Politician'*, *1931*)

Preface

CANADA has a reputation for bold and imaginative law reform in many fields. This seems particularly justified in public law where we invariably discover fascinating solutions to problems which are barely recognized in Britain. One example of this is the law relating to election expenditures and the funding of political parties. These matters are largely unregulated in Britain, with the existing legal framework having been constructed to deal with practices in the Victorian constitution. So British law imposes reporting requirements and expenditure restrictions on individual candidates but fails to impose similar requirements or restrictions on the political parties. Perhaps as a result of the lack of any effective national controls, there is a wide and possibly growing gulf in the electoral expenditures of the main political parties, it being estimated by one authority that the Conservatives spent £9 million on their re-election campaign in 1987 compared with the £4.7 million spent by the Labour Party and the £1.75 million spent by the Liberal–SDP Alliance (Pinto-Duschinsky, 1989). Such differences give rise to the not unreasonable concern that high-spending parties have an unfair advantage over their rivals, a concern which has led to calls from time to time for an overhaul of the legal machinery for the regulation of both the financing and the campaign expenditures of political parties.

An initiative worthy of consideration was in fact taken by the Canadian Parliament in the Election Expenses Act 1974. In some of the chapters which follow steps are taken to trace the origins, analyse the content, and assess the impact of the Act with an eye always on the question of whether it is desirable or practicable to introduce controls of this kind in Britain. But apart from an examination of the Canadian federal law on election expenditures, a concurrent interest pursued in this essay relates to the movement in Britain for the introduction of a Bill of Rights or for the incorporation of the European Convention on Human Rights into domestic law. At first sight

vii

this appears to have little direct relevance to the legal regulation of campaign financing. Further enquiry suggests, however, that a Bill of Rights could be a major obstacle to the effective introduction and implementation of campaign finance law. This is because there is a potentially irreconcilable conflict between the goal of equality pursued by election expenditure controls and the protection of liberty expressed in constitutional documents. This tension between equality and liberty has become an important issue in Canadian public law, following the introduction of the Charter of Rights and Freedoms in 1982. These developments provide a flavour of the problems likely to arise in a political system which promotes both electoral equality and the constitutional protection of civil liberties.

On the assumption that not all readers will be familiar with the Canadian scene, Chapter 1 provides a brief introduction to the constitutional, political, and historical context of the issues under discussion. Apart from thus providing necessary background information, this chapter may help to explain how uniquely relevant the Canadian developments are for a British audience, for Canada has not only adopted the Westminster system of government, but is also largely a two-party system at federal level, with a third trying hard to break the conventional mould. Chapter 2 considers the case for the legal regulation of campaign financing and election expenditures, dealing with arguments from equality but also introducing the tension referred to in the previous paragraph, a tension created by such constitutional guarantees as the right to freedom of expression. Chapters 3, 4, and 5 are concerned respectively with the origins, content, and operation of the Election Expenses Act 1974, as amended in 1977 and 1983. Chapter 5 is concerned mainly with developments up until 1984, which was the year of the most recent general election at the time much of the study was written. However, the opportunity has been taken to integrate into the conclusion some of the implications of the parliamentary cycle culminating in the general election of 1988. It will be seen that not a great deal has changed and that little has happened to invalidate any of the conclusions or judgments in Chapter 5.

Chapters 6 and 7 are concerned directly with the constitutional problems created by the Charter which has enabled the courts already to threaten the very survival of the legislation. Here we consider cases which have questioned the right of governments to introduce public subsidies for political parties, to permit trade unions to use their funds to support political parties, and to impose election spending limits on the activities of potentially influential pressure groups. Chapter 7 is a detour into American law in this area, justified not only because the US case-law has been influential in the Canadian courts, but also because, being much more highly developed, it provides a pointer to the possible roads down which the Canadian courts might go. The American material is useful also because it exposes even more sharply the tension which is a central theme of this essay. Finally, in Chapter 8 the different strands are pulled together with consideration being given to current proposals to deal with the problems created by the Charter. Some attention is given in particular to the work of the Royal Commission on Electoral Reform and Party Financing which was established in 1989 with wide terms of reference, under the chairmanship of Mr Pierre Lortie, a Quebec businessman.

Before concluding, it should be stated that the research and writing of this book have taken longer than I care to admit. One reason for the long gestation period is the difficulty in trying to write sensibly about another legal system. This is a problem which all comparative lawyers much face, but it does seem particularly acute in public law, where a proper understanding requires a fairly detailed knowledge and sensitive appreciation of the history and political structure of the jurisdiction under consideration. Having said this, however, the task has been made much easier by the generous support, encouragement, and advice which has been provided by a large number of people in both Britain and Canada. In particular I should like to record my thanks to the staff of the Chief Electoral Officer and his predecessor who willingly submitted themselves to interviews and who freely sent me information and material about the operation of the Act. Christine Jackson, Director of Communications, and Bud Slattery, Director of the Election Financing Branch, were especially helpful. At the same time I should also record my debt to Leslie Seidle, Senior Research Co-ordinator of the Royal Commission on Electoral Reform and Party Financing, as well as to senior officials of the three main

Preface

parties who were willing to see me at short notice on the occasion of several visits to Ottawa to discuss the finances of their parties. I am also indebted to the University of Cambridge; King's College, London; and the British Association for Canadian Studies for financial support to enable these visits to be made. Finally, it gives me great pleasure to record my enormous debt to Osgoode Hall Law School and the Faculty of Law at the University of Alberta. By appointments to visiting teaching positions both gave me the opportunity to live and work in Canada without which it would not have been possible even to contemplate research of this kind. Some of the fruits of that research have already been published and are reproduced here with the kind permission of the editors of *Public Law* and the *Cambridge Law Journal*.

K. D. E.

September 1991

Contents

List of Tables

List of Tables

Abbreviations

CBC   Canadian Broadcasting Corporation
CCF   Co-operative Commonwealth Federation
CEO   Chief Electoral Officer
CIO   Congress of Industrial Organizations
COPE   Committee on Political Education
CRTC   Canadian Radio-Television Commission
FEC   Federal Election Commission
FECA   Federal Election Campaign Act
NCC   National Citizens' Coalition
NDP   New Democratic Party
OPSEU   Ontario Public Service Employees' Union
PAC   Political Action Committee
RCMP   Royal Canadian Mounted Police

Table of Cases

Table of Cases

UNITED STATES CASES

Table of Cases

1

Introduction

THE Canadian framework for the regulation of political finance has undergone considerable change since the publication of the first major academic study of the subject (Paltiel, 1970). At that time the system was largely unregulated, with the modern framework in the process of development. These movements in the direction of reform were encouraged by Watergate, a political earthquake which rocked North America, the tremors being felt as far north as Ottawa and the Canadian provincial capitals. Detailed federal legislation was introduced in Canada in 1974, and this in turn has been revised and amended on several occasions, most notably in 1983. In addition, the provincial legislatures have also introduced comprehensive campaign finance legislation, Quebec leading the way in 1963, with most of the provinces having followed suit. The main focus of this study, however, is the Canadian federal legislation of 1974, though it will be necessary to refer to provincial developments from time to time. But before beginning our consideration of these and other issues it is appropriate to look at the constitutional, political, and historical contexts in which the modern legislation operates.

I. The Constitutional Context

The legal basis of the modern Canadian state can be traced back to the British North America Act 1867,[1] an Act of the British Parliament, since renamed the Constitution Act 1867.[2] This created the federal structure, the essential features of which survive to this day. Thus the Act provided for executive power to be vested in the Queen, the functions of the monarch being performed by the Governor-General.[3] The Act also

[1] 30 & 31 Vic., c.3.
[2] Canada Act 1982, c.11 (UK).
[3] 1867 Act, s.10.

1

created the Canadian Parliament, which consists of the Queen, the Senate, and the House of Commons,[4] thereby reflecting the goal in the preamble to the Act that the new Canadian constitution should be 'similar in principle to that of the United Kingdom'. Yet despite the institutional similarities between the British and the Canadian constitutions, there are nevertheless important differences of substance which are material for the purposes of the present study. The first relates to the division of powers between the federal and provincial governments. In addition to the federal government, there are now in Canada ten provinces (Ontario, Quebec, Nova Scotia, New Brunswick, Manitoba, British Columbia, Prince Edward Island, Alberta, Saskatchewan, and Newfoundland) and two territories (the Yukon Territory and the Northwest Territories), and the federal Parliament has power to act only in the areas of activity in respect of which authority has been conferred by the Constitution Act 1867. This provides in fact that the federal legislature, in addition to the items expressly listed in s.91 of the Act, has authority 'to make Laws for the Peace, Order, and good Government of Canada, in relation to all Matters not coming within the Classes of Subjects by this Act assigned exclusively to the Legislatures of the Provinces'.[5]

The federal Parliament clearly has authority to regulate the procedure for federal elections and the funding of campaigns and political parties who compete in these elections. But equally, the provincial legislatures have the authority to regulate the procedure for provincial elections, since one of the subjects reserved exclusively for them is 'Property and Civil Rights in the Province'.[6] Many of the features of campaign finance law would fall under this general head, including such restrictions on 'civil rights' as the duty of parties to disclose financial information about their affairs; limits on the amount which individuals, corporations, or trade unions may donate to political parties; and limits on how much money candidates and parties may spend in an election campaign. This is not to

[4] 1867 Act, ss.17–57.
[5] 1867 Act, s.91.
[6] 1867 Act, s.92.

say, however, that the allocation of power between federal and provincial legislatures is always straightforward and uncontroversial. In *McKay* v. *The Queen*[7] householders were prosecuted and convicted under a by-law which prohibited the display of lawn signs. The accused had displayed signs in support of candidates for federal election several weeks before the day of the election. By a narrow majority the Supreme Court of Canada held that this particular application of the bylaw was unlawful. The regulation had been made under the authority of a provincial statute, and the province had no power to prohibit 'political activity in the federal field'. In the famous *Oil Workers'* case[8] the Supreme Court was called upon to determine whether the British Columbia legislature had the powers to restrict by legislation the right of trade unions to use their funds to finance the NDP (at both federal and provincial levels). On this occasion, however, the Court upheld the legislation (again by a narrow majority) on the ground that it was an exercise of the labour law power which, since 1925, had been regarded as a provincial matter relating to 'Property and Civil Rights'. This is despite the fact that 'a prohibition of union contributions has a more serious, and more biased, impact on the federal electoral process than a prohibition of residential lawn signs' (Hogg, 1986: 329).

The other major difference between Canada and the principles of government under the British constitution is the Charter of Rights and Freedoms of 1982. The effect of this document is to make the Canadian constitution more like the American than the British, particularly in the extent to which the supremacy of Parliament has been limited. This supremacy is perhaps the fundamental principle of the British constitution: it means that there are no legal limits to the power of Parliament; that Parliament can make and unmake any law it chooses; and that one Parliament cannot bind its successors by fettering the power of the legislature (Wade and Bradley, 1985). In Canada that doctrine (which *did* form part of the indigenous

[7] [1965] SCR 798.
[8] *Oil, Chemical and Atomic Workers' International Union, Local 16-601* v. *Imperial Oil Ltd.* [1963] SCR 584.

constitutional law at least until 1960)[9] no longer prevails because under the Charter, governmental action, including Acts of Parliament,[10] must not violate any of the fundamental freedoms which the constitution now protects. This applies to governmental action taken after its introduction. So the Charter not only authorizes the judges to review the substance of pre-1982 Acts of Parliament, it also authorizes them to question (on an application by an interested person) the legal validity of Acts passed after 1982. The Canadian Parliament is thus now subject to a higher law, enforced by the judges. For the purposes of this study, the principal features of this are to be found in sections 1 and 2 of the Charter. Section 2 provides:

Everyone has the following fundamental freedoms:
(a) freedom of conscience and religion;
(b) freedom of thought, belief, opinion and expression, including freedom of the press and other media of communication;
(c) freedom of peaceful assembly; and
(d) freedom of association.

Like many other provisions of the Charter, section 2 is, however, subject to section 1, which provides that the rights and freedoms protected by it are subject 'to such reasonable limits prescribed by law as can be demonstrably justified in a free and democratic society'. A question now for both federal and provincial legislatures is whether campaign finance legislation

[9] In 1960 Parliament passed the Canadian Bill of Rights, SC 1960, 8–9 Eliz. II, c.44. Among other things this provided for freedom of speech, assembly, and association, and freedom of the press (s.1). It also provided that 'Every law of Canada shall, unless it is expressly declared by an Act of the Parliament of Canada that it shall operate notwithstanding the *Canadian Bill of Rights*, be so construed and applied as not to abrogate, abridge or infringe . . . any of the rights or freedoms herein recognized and declared . . .' (s.2). The expression 'law of Canada' in s.2 was defined to mean 'an Act of the Parliament of Canada enacted before or after the coming into force of this Act' (s.5(2)). The Bill of Rights applied, however, only to federal (and not provincial) matters though there are provincial equivalents. But it was never as enthusiastically adopted by the judicial branch as the Charter has been.

[10] By s.32 of the Charter, it is provided that: '(1) This Charter applies (a) to the Parliament and government of Canada in respect of all matters within the authority of Parliament including all matters relating to the Yukon Territory and Northwest Territories; and (b) to the legislature and government of each province in respect of all matters within the authority of the legislature of each province.'

4

TABLE 1. *Outcomes of general elections since 1945*

Election	Governing Party
1945	Liberal
1949	Liberal
1953	Liberal
1957	Progressive Conservative
1958	Progressive Conservative
1962	Progressive Conservative
1963	Liberal
1965	Liberal
1968	Liberal
1972	Liberal
1974	Liberal
1979	Progressive Conservative
1980	Liberal
1984	Progressive Conservative
1988	Progressive Conservative

(or parts of it) violates section 2, and if so whether it can be saved by section 1.

II. The Political Context

Under the Canadian constitution, Canada is to be governed in a manner similar in principle to the United Kingdom. Like the United Kingdom, Canada is a parliamentary democracy, with political parties playing a key role in the electoral and governing processes. Also like the United Kingdom (now) Canada effectively has a three-party system; for an account of the purposes, aims, and principles of these parties see the Appendix. The Liberal Party of Canada dominated post-war politics at least until 1984, winning nine of the fifteen elections held since 1945, the other six being won by the Progressive Conservative Party of Canada. Details of general election outcomes since 1945 are shown in Table 1. But although Canada is a three-party state, the third party, the New Democratic Party (founded in 1961 and inheriting a role performed in Canadian politics earlier by the Co-operative Commonwealth Federation (CCF)), has thus not yet succeeded in winning a general election. Yet this is not to deny that the NDP has a considerable measure of support. In 1979 the Party polled 2 million votes in contrast to the 4.1 million polled by the Conservatives and the 4.6 million polled by the Liberals (Chief Electoral Officer of Canada, 1979*a*: 37). In 1980 the vote of the NDP rose to 2.1 million while that of the Tories fell to 3.5 million and that of the Liberals increased to 4.8 million (Chief Electoral Officer of Canada, 1980*a*: 32). 1984 saw another steady increase to 2.3 million while the Tories almost doubled their support to 6.2 million votes, Liberal support falling back to 3.5 million votes (Chief Electoral Officer of Canada, 1984: 69). In the years 1979, 1980, and 1984 the Liberals won 40%, 44%, and 28% respectively of the votes cast; the Tories won 36%, 32%, and 50% of the votes cast; and the NDP won 18%, 20%, and 19% of the votes cast.

Traditionally both the Liberals and the Progressive Conservatives looked 'almost exclusively to business for the supply of their campaign funds' (Paltiel, 1970: 42). Although both had tried 'with varying degrees of enthusiasm to widen their base of financial support', these efforts had been a failure (ibid.). So far as the Liberal Party is concerned, in 1953, '50 per cent of its campaign funds were derived from commerce and industry, 40 per cent from businessmen linked to particular firms, and only 10 per cent from private individuals'. One party official reported that 300–400 contributors donated the $7.5 million raised in 1957 at the national level (Paltiel, 1970: 34). This at once distinguishes these parties from the New Democratic Party which, as a democratic socialist organization, is not supported by big businesses, but by the organized labour movement, to the extent that organized labour takes an active part in party politics in Canada. As we shall consider in Chapter 5, the unions assist the party in a variety of ways, but partly by the payment of annual affiliation fees (thereby ensuring resources 'on a regular and continuing basis' (Paltiel, 1970: 56)) and by the donation of funds to help with campaign budgets. But unlike the other two parties, the NDP has never been the party of federal government, though it has held power in a number of provinces, namely British Columbia, Saskatchewan, and Manitoba, and most recently in Ontario. And although it has never been the largest party in the federal Parliament, it helped to sustain the minority Liberal government in 1974. This is of more than passing interest, for it was in 1974 that the Election Expenses Act—the modern campaign finance legislation—was crafted by the Liberals. The NDP was, however, in a position to influence the shaping of the legislation and to gain concessions on content as a condition of support.

Although federal politics have been dominated since 1945 (at least until 1984) by the Liberals, the domination is not reflected in provincial government. Indeed, until 1985, Ontario had had an unbroken Conservative administration for 42 years. Also, while the Liberals held office in Ottawa in 1983, they formed the government in not a single provincial capital. Indeed out of 698 seats in the ten provincial legislatures, the Liberals had captured only 130, with the Progressive Conservatives being the governing party in all provinces except British Columbia, Manitoba, and Quebec where the largest parties were Social Credit, NDP, and Parti Québécois respectively. Two factors help to explain this phenomenon of Canadian politics. The first is that the federal parties are sometimes regionally polarized, with no party having effective representation across the country. Thus, in 1980 the Liberal Party won 52% of the seats in Canada, but only two seats in western Canada, and both of these were in Manitoba. In contrast the minority Conservative government of 1979 won three-quarters of its seats in western Canada, and only two in Quebec (D. S. MacDonald, 1985: 3, 76). A second factor helping to explain the differences between federal and provincial governments is that 'irrespective of whether federal and provincial parties of the same name are simultaneously strong in both areas, they have become increasingly autonomous: they are often supported by different organisations, are financed by different sources and aim at different goals' (D. S. MacDonald, 1985: 3, 77). But whatever the explanation, federalism has important implications for the present study to the extent that provincial autonomy has led to a rich variety of campaign finance laws in the different jurisdictions in Canada. The essentials of the federal system of control were adopted initially in only one jurisdiction while both Quebec and Ontario introduced rather different measures to suit peculiar political problems, or in the case of the latter to accommodate the convenience of a political party with a long-established domination of the political process.

III. The Historical Context

Apart from the constitution and the political framework, a third factor which has a bearing on the modern campaign finance legislation in Canada is the experience of similar legislation in the past. Canada is in fact a country (like its great southern neighbour) where scandal has never been far from the electoral process (Seidle and Paltiel, 1981: 227). Indeed, the first major incident—the Pacific Scandal of 1873—occurred within five years of confederation. Here the government party of Sir John A. MacDonald 'had received large sums of money from an entrepreneur vitally interested in a government contract and subsidy; the party, moreover, had gone on to win' (Barbeau, 1966: 13–14). As is often the case, scandal was the midwife of reform, on this occasion the reforming measures being enacted in the Dominion Elections Act 1874.[11] As has been pointed out, however, the 1874 Act was useful but inadequate. It introduced the doctrine of agency, thereby investing legal responsibility for the use of money by a candidate in a single agent,[12] with both the candidate and the agent responsible for providing a statement of the candidate's expenditure, and the items of expenditure.[13] But as has also been pointed out, if the legislation had been in force in 1872 rather than 1874, it would have had no bearing on the Pacific Scandal (Barbeau, 1966: 15). The problem there related to 'the *source* of the money involved' (ibid.) not the way in which money was *spent* by candidates for office. Yet under the 1874 Act 'no candidate or party would have been legally compelled to state that money had been received from anyone, including persons involved in government contracts. After the legislation of 1874,

---

[11] SC 1874, 37 Vic., c.9.
[12] 1874 Act, s.121.
[13] 1874 Act, s.123.

8

the source from which candidates received their money remained as free from publicity as before' (ibid.). It was not until 1920 that candidates were required to disclose details of contributions as well as expenditures.

But despite this and many other criticisms of the 1874 Act (including the lack of any effective enforcement machinery), it took another scandal to induce further reform, and even then the reforms were modest and ultimately meaningless. The McGreevy Scandals 'disclosed a system operating in federal elections in Quebec whereby contractors gave kickbacks on government contracts to finance government candidates' (Barbeau, 1966: 17). The government responded with legislation which made it unlawful for anyone to assist any candidate at an election in return for money or any valuable consideration, or for the promise of any office, place, or employment.[14] But predictably neither this measure (described by Barbeau (ibid.) as a 'legal platitude' incapable of enforcement) nor the Act passed earlier in 1874 succeeded in preventing other unsavoury incidents, it being claimed, for example, that the 'parliamentary sessions of 1906 and 1907 were among the most scandal-ridden on record' (ibid. 18). This led to further reform in the Dominion Elections Act 1908[15] which by s.36 prohibited corporations (other than those incorporated for political purposes alone) from contributing to candidates and political parties, a similar measure having been introduced in the United States in the previous year.[16] In 1920 the prohibition was extended to all companies and associations, whether or not they were legally incorporated (unless the body in question had been incorporated for political purposes alone).[17] The effect of the 1920 amendment was to extend the legislation to trade unions, which had previously been excluded. The American legislation was also extended from corporations and banks to labour unions, though not until 1943[18] (the wartime measures being re-enacted in 1947[19]), which was in fact some

[14] Dominion Elections Act, SC 1891, 54–55 Vic., c.19, s.14.
[15] Dominion Elections Act, SC 1908, 7–8 Edw. VII, c.26.
[16] Act of 26 Jan. 1907.
[17] Dominion Elections Act, SC 1920, 10–11 Geo. V, c.46, s.10.
[18] War Labor Disputes Act of 1943, s.9.
[19] Labor Management Relations Act of 1947.

thirteen years after restrictions on both corporate and union contributions in Canadian law had been repealed.[20]

Why should 'the most radical and audacious attempt at legislative control over election expenses ever advanced' (Barbeau, 1966:18) in Canada survive on the statute book only twenty-two years? In the United States, in contrast, the modern (detailed and complex) legislation on campaign financing has a direct and unbroken descent from the Act of 1907, becoming more sophisticated with the passage of time and the eruption of fresh scandals. The answer lies in the claim that the 1908 Act 'turned out in actuality to be only the most ridiculous chapter in an uninspiring story of ineffective legislation' (Barbeau, ibid.). According to Barbeau, the law had no impact, in the sense that there were no prosecutions after 1908 and no evidence of business contributions having fallen. Indeed they may even have increased. And Barbeau (1966: 20) continued:

The main point is that, even supposing zealous enforcement on the part of the government (which, considering the needs political parties have for money, was a dubious assumption) businessmen willing to contribute would have little difficulty classing corporate funds as, say, 'personal expenses' or even salary; nor would a corporate executive meet any difficulty in giving 'bonuses' to employees, who would then give, as individuals, to a political party. Nor do these in any way exhaust the list of devices which might be so employed. The law was once again only a legal platitude, this time made even more empty by virtue of its pretension.

Perhaps even more significant is the fact that there was no enforcement machinery nor, astonishingly, any penalty provided in the Act for those who contravened its terms. At best it was a pious statutory declaration, an optimistic statement of good political behaviour, the optimism proving eventually to be misplaced. The restriction was repealed in 1930, and few, it seems, lamented its passing, with one legislator having remarked in Parliament some five years earlier not only that 'it is violated by all concerned in every election', but that 'to retain a section in an act which cannot be enforced—no; worse than

---

[20] Dominion Elections Act, SC 1930, 20–21 Geo. V, c.16, s.9.

that, which invites its own violation—is to bring law itself into disrepute' (Barbeau, 1966: 20).

IV. Conclusion

The year after the removal of the ban on corporate contributions was the year of yet another scandal, the Beauharnois Scandal, it being 'revealed that $700,000 to $800,000 had been given by the Beauharnois corporation to the previous Liberal Government and that an extremely valuable government contract had been given to the corporation' (Barbeau, 1966: 22). Yet although this was 'in many ways one of the worst scandals in Canadian history', on this occasion 'not even another legal platitude was called in to mollify public opinion' (ibid.). The scandal had 'turned the law, in retrospect, into a joke' (ibid. 21). Barbeau continued:

Indeed, after 1920, whatever innovating spirit Parliament had once possessed concerning election expenses seemed to disappear altogether. Not a single new law of any significance has been brought down since that time. Campaign funds have been the subject of a good deal of public comment; newspapers and magazines have, often enough, contained articles on the matter, usually accompanied by pleas for reform. Parliament itself, in committees and in discussion of private members' bills, has considered a number of ideas; the Provincial Legislatures have, on occasion, passed far-reaching and even radical legislation. Yet for almost a half-century nothing of significance to election expenses has changed in the federal statutes. (ibid. 22).

It was not in fact until 1964 that the matter was revived in any serious way, with the Liberal government appointing a Committee 'to advise on the best practicable way to set enforceable limits to expenditures in election campaigns' (ibid. 5), thereby responding to a promise given at the election in 1962 to 'legislate a limit on election campaign expenditures and a system of election subsidies out of public funds' (Wearing, 1981: 62). On this occasion, however, it seems that the pressure for legislation was a response to internal rather than external stimuli. That is to say legislation was stimulated not by public scandal but by the bureaucratic concerns of the governing party, which was not only troubled by rising campaign costs, but which also found continued dependence on a few large donors to be unacceptable in a modern democracy (Wearing, 1981).[21] The recommendations of the Barbeau Committee, and the implementing legislation, are considered in Chapter 3. But first it is necessary to consider why campaign financing should be controlled, if necessary by legislation. It is to a consideration of that question that we now turn.

[21] See also Seidle, 1980: 176.

2

The Function of Campaign Finance Reform

IN this chapter we consider why law should regulate the funding of political parties, and the possible forms which such regulation may take. In Canada many jurisdictions have in place sophisticated statutory provisions on the subject[1]—in sharp contrast with the largely unregulated British position.[2] The different Canadian jurisdictions reveal, however, many different approaches to the control of party finances, with some preferring to intervene mainly through contribution limits,[3] others through spending controls,[4] and still others (such as Quebec) by government funding of the parties.[5]

I. The Function of Control

The case for control starts with the principle of political equality, the principle which may be said to lie at the heart of the system of government in the liberal democratic tradition. Formal political equality is regarded as an essential requirement in any system which lays claim to being democratic. Indeed any other premiss of government is rightly regarded as repugnant. This means not only that all people should have a right to vote—as is recognized by section 3 of the Charter of Rights and Freedoms—but also that people's votes should be of equal value. Thus, in *Reynolds* v. *Sims*[6] the US Supreme

---

[1] See nn. 3, 4, and 5 infra. See also Election Finances Act, SO 1986, c.33; Elections Finances Act, RSM 1970, c.E32; Political Process Financing Act 1978, c.P-9.3 (NB).

[2] For which see Ewing, 1987*a*.

[3] See Election Finances and Contributions Disclosure Act, RSA 1980, c.E-3.

[4] See the Election Act, RSS 1978, c.E-6.

[5] See Election Act, SQ 1989, c.1.

[6] 377 US 533 (1964).

Court displayed a willingness to monitor electoral boundaries to ensure that they were fairly apportioned and in the course of so doing Chief Justice Warren said: 'representative government is in essence self-government through the medium of elected representatives of the people, and each and every citizen has an inalienable right to full and effective participation in the political processes of his State's legislative bodies'.[7] The principle of political equality means also that the right to vote should not be conditional on arbitrary, irrational, or unnecessary criteria or conditions. Thus, in striking down a poll tax in *Harper* v. *Virginia State Board of Elections*,[8] Mr Justice Douglas in another purple passage in the US Supreme Court said:

Wealth, like race, creed, or color, is not germane to one's ability to participate intelligently in the electoral process. Lines drawn on the basis of wealth or property, like those of race ... are traditionally disfavored ... To introduce wealth or payment of a fee as a measure of a voter's qualifications is to introduce a capricious or irrelevant factor.[9]

But the doctrine of political equality embraces more than the right to vote. It embraces also the right to participate in government on equal terms with one's fellow citizens. This means the right to stand for election equally with others. In *Bullock* v. *Carter*,[10] for example, the US Supreme Court declared unconstitutional a requirement of Texas law that candidates must pay high fees as a condition of standing for election. In the view of the Court such a requirement tended to exclude potential candidates who lacked personal wealth or affluent backers 'no matter how qualified they might be, and no matter how broad or enthusiastic their popular support'.[11] But we may go further still and argue that the right to political equality, and the right to participate, mean more than the right to *stand* for election equally with others. They must mean also the right of equal opportunity to *secure* election. The problem which arises here, however, is a particularly serious one for governments

[7] 377 US 533 (1964), at p. 565.
[8] 383 US 663 (1966).
[9] Ibid., at p. 668.
[10] 405 US 134 (1972).
[11] Ibid., at p. 143.

14

in market economies. It is simply that the political freedoms which these societies seek to guarantee operate against a backcloth of deep-rooted economic inequality. It may be, of course, that Tocqueville (1946: 137) was right when he wrote that 'Democratic institutions awaken and foster a passion for equality which they can never entirely satisfy'. Nevertheless, the integrity of these institutions as instruments of liberal forms of government demands that control of economic resources should not permit domination of the political process on the simple expedient of unrestrained liberty for all in the political arena. It is widely accepted that wealth and power should not be used directly as a corrupting influence on elections or legislatures and for this reason most jurisdictions have enacted legislation designed to curb corrupt and illegal practices. Campaign financing raises equally sensitive questions, and indeed the line between corrupt practices and indulgent financing has long been regarded as a fine one. Controls on campaign spending were introduced in Britain as early as 1883, partly because 'extravagant expenditure was so near alien to corruption that it was almost the very father of corruption'.[12]

Unregulated political financing presents two problems for the doctrine of political equality. The first, and most obvious, is that it fails to guarantee that candidates who compete for political power do so on equal terms. More significantly it also fails to ensure that the political parties compete on equal terms. In the parliamentary system, electors may participate in government through membership and support of political parties. All things being equal, they are entitled to expect that their party will be given the same opportunity for government as any other. That opportunity may not be secured by unregulated political financing. It would be like inviting two people to participate in a race, with one participant turning up with a bicycle, and the other with a sports car. While both have the right to participate, it can hardly be claimed that they are doing so on equal terms, that is to say with a reasonable prospect of success. A chasm separates the quality of the right of the rival candidates in the race. And so it is in the context of a campaign. It can hardly be claimed that party A, and

---

[12] CCLXXIX Parl. Debs. (3rd ser.) 1697 (Sir Henry James).

correspondingly its members and supporters, are competing on equal terms with party B which spends twice as much as party A. This is not to say, of course, that the citizen on the bicycle has no chance of success: the sports car might break down, or the driver might lose the way. But equality of opportunity does not depend on such fortuitous circumstances. Unregulated financing may thus create inequality of opportunity between those who compete, thereby undermining the right to equal participation by candidates, political parties, and the members and supporters of the parties.

Unregulated funding does not only affect the right of everyone to be elected on equal terms. It also affects the influence which individuals will have on those who are elected. Thus, large financial contributions undermine political equality by enabling wealthy individuals to have a disproportionate influence in the political process, in the sense that they have more ready access to legislators. As one commentator has remarked:

It is widely acknowledged . . . that at the very least [the large contributor] gains access to the office-holder; such access is usually denied to the average voter. But it would be naive to contend that the influence ends with access. The actual effect upon public policy apparently covers a spectrum from the most blatant purchase of legislation to influences which are so subtle that the officeholder may not be aware he or she is being biased. (Nicholson, 1974: 820)

And unregulated funding does not simply allow disproportionate influence by the wealthy. It also facilitates access by and the representation of interests which are beyond the immediate duties of the legislators, who become responsible to groups such as corporations which clothe them with neither legitimacy nor authority, but only with money. In the liberal form of government, the legislators' primary duty is to the electorate: 'Legislators represent people, not trees or acres. Legislators are elected by voters, not farms or cities or economic interests.'[13] This is not to say that legislators should be

---

[13] *Reynolds* v. *Sims*, 377 US 533 (1963), at p. 562. See also *Oil, Chemical and Atomic Workers' International Union, Local No. 16-601* v. *Imperial Oil Ltd.* (1962) 30 DLR (3d) 657 where Whittaker J. said: 'The political party serves or should serve, the voter, not the corporation . . .' (at p. 661).

unresponsive to the demands of interest groups. Indeed, many political scientists have argued that the functional representation of interests in the political process is the only effective way of securing democratic self-government in contemporary Western societies where representatives may be elected on a minority of the popular vote. It is, however, difficult to see how the representation and influence of interest groups remedies the defects of the electoral system. It is true that policy-making will take place only in conjunction with the powerful pressure groups, that their aspirations will thus be taken into account, and that by membership of those groups the individual citizen has some opportunity to direct the policy of the group and perhaps the government. But ultimately, this is the politics of the pig trough, with the swill being appropriated by those with the biggest snouts. Money and power are the basis of pressure-group influence and to that extent functional representation merely encourages disproportionate access to government and legislators.

II. Equality of Opportunity

The doctrine of equal participation in the political process thus has two essential requirements. The first is to ensure as far as possible that those who compete in elections, whether candidates or political parties, do so on equal terms, and the second is to ensure as far as possible the elimination of financial influence by the economically strong on those who exercise political power. So far as the first of these issues is concerned, there are three specific goals. The system should guarantee the following.

1. Each of the candidates or parties representing major strands of opinon should have enough money effectively to fight an election campaign, and to maintain an adequate organization between campaigns.

2. Each of the candidates or parties representing major strands of opinion should have access to the major instruments of communication for the dissemination of its message. This means not only that they must have the necessary finance, but also that those who control scarce resources—particularly the

broadcasting companies—are regulated to ensure that they do not use their strategic position to control scarce resources as a means of excluding political views of which they disapprove.

3. Although candidates and parties may be endowed with different sums of money, no candidate or party should be permitted to spend more than its rivals by a disproportionate amount. Otherwise the market-place will be monopolized by the sound of one voice and there may be no healthy competition for office.

As to the first of these concerns, states in the West have dealt with the problem by subsidizing the political parties in a variety of ways. By this means the state ensures a measure of equality of access to the electorate by the different parties by providing a floor from which serious participants may fight their campaigns. The least generous response of this kind is that which operates in Britain, where the state has assumed responsibility for some (though not all) of the expenses which the political actors themselves might otherwise incur. These include the registration of electors, political broadcasting, and the costs incurred by the returning officer (Ewing, 1987a). A second, and a more favourable, arrangement is to reimburse the candidates and the parties for some items of expenditure which they have incurred. In practice this normally means the reimbursement of all or some election expenses of parties and candidates, a device which has been adopted in Australian federal elections where a party is entitled 'to claim public funding in respect of its endorsed candidates . . . who gained 4% of the first preference votes in the elections in which they stood' (Australian Electoral Commission, 1984: 1). A third device is more favourable still, involving a state subsidy not just for election expenses, but for all the other operational costs of the parties. So we find in Sweden (Ewing, 1987a), and also in Quebec, that government makes a generous annual payment to the parties to be used for any purpose whatsoever. In Quebec, though not in Sweden, the money is accompanied by a prohibition on the receipt by the parties of corporate and trade union contributions.[14] Finally, the most generous arrangement is for total public funding, that is to say, state

[14] Election Act, SQ 1989, c.1, s.87.

money to the exclusion of all other funding. This option has been adopted in a few jurisdictions, though is difficult to justify not only because of the obvious expense but also because of its negative impact on the democratic process in the sense that it takes away an important incentive to the political parties to recruit members and organize fund-raising drives.

So far as the second issue is concerned, the major problem relates to access to the media, and to the broadcasting media in particular. This problem is twofold: the facility is expensive and it is a scarce but powerful resource, so it is necessary to ensure that candidates and parties are not denied the opportunity of access either because of insufficient funding or because of exclusion for what may be overtly partisan reasons on the part of the owners or controllers. The case for intervention was recognized by the US Supreme Court in *Red Lion Broadcasting Co. v. Federal Communications Commission*[15] where a broadcasting corporation challenged the fairness doctrine of the Commission, which requires broadcasters to give a right of reply to people who are the victims or targets of political criticism. The corporation argued that this violated the First Amendment to the US Constitution[16] protection of the right to free speech in the sense that the broadcaster was denied a measure of control over what could be transmitted. In rejecting this argument, Justice White for the majority said that the right of free speech of a broadcaster does not include the right to snuff out the free speech of others, and that 'It is the purpose of the First Amendment to preserve an uninhibited market-place of ideas in which truth will ultimately prevail, rather than to countenance monopolization of that market'.[17] In France, recognition of the same problem led to the following regulation of presidential election contests:

Pendant la durée de la campagne électorale, le principe d'égalité entre les candidats doit être respecté dans les programmes d'information de la radiodiffusion-télévision française en ce qui concerne la reproduction ou les commentaires des déclarations et écrits des candidats et la présentation de leur personne.

[15] 395 US 367 (1969).
[16] The First Amendment provides that 'Congress shall make no law ... abridging the freedom of speech, or of the press ...'.
[17] 395 US 367 (1969), at p. 390.

Chaque candidat dispose sur les antennes de la radiodiffusion-télévision française au premier tour de scrutin de deux heures d'émission télévisée et de deux heures d'émission radiodiffusée. Compte tenu du nombre de candidats, la durée de ces émissions pourra être réduite par décision de la commission prévue à l'article 10 du présent décret. Cette décision devra être prise dans les vingt-quatre heures de la publication au *Journal officiel* de la liste des candidats.

Les heures d'émission sont utilisées personnellement par les candidats. Toutefois, chaque candidat peut demander que les partis ou groupements politiques dont l'action s'étend à la généralité du territoire national et désignés par lui participent à ses émissions, après y avoir été habilités par la commission nationale de contrôle qui vérifiera que ces partis ou groupements répondent aux exigences prévues au présent alinéa.

Le ministre chargé de l'information fixe le nombre, la durée et les horaires des émissions. L'aménagement de chaque tranche d'émission est fixé par la commission prévue à l'article 10 de telle sorte que soit assurée l'égalité d'audience de chaque candidat. L'ordre d'attribution des temps de parole est déterminé par voie de tirage au sort effectué par ladite commission.

Chacun des deux candidats, au second tour de scrutin, dispose dans les mêmes conditions de deux heures d'émission radiodiffusée et de deux heures d'émission télévisée sur les antennes de la radiodiffusion-télévision française.[18]

---

[18] Décret No. 64-231 du 14 Mars 1964 (modifié) portant règlement d'administration publique pour l'application de la loi no. 62-1292 du 6 novembre 1962 relative à l'élection du Président de la République au suffrage universel. Article 10 provides:

Art. 10. Conformément aux dispositions organiques de l'article 3-IV de la loi du 6 novembre 1962, tous les candidats bénéficient de la part de l'État des mêmes facilités pour la campagne en vue de l'élection présidentielle.

Une commission nationale de contrôle de la campagne électorale veille au respect desdites dispositions. Elle exerce les attributions prévues aux articles suivants. Elle intervient, le cas échéant, auprès des autorités compétentes pour que soient prises toutes mesures susceptibles d'assurer l'égalité entre les candidats et l'observation des règles édictées au présent titre.

Cette commission comprend cinq membres:
—le vice-président du Conseil d'État, président;
—le premier président de la Cour de cassation;
—le premier président de la Cour des comptes;
—deux membres en activité ou honoraires du Conseil d'État, de la Cour de cassation ou de la Cour des comptes désignés par les trois membres de droit.

Les membres de droit sont, en cas d'empêchement, remplacés par ceux qui les suppléent normalement dans leur corps; les deux autres membres de la

So far as the third issue is concerned (that the parties would raise different amounts) the need here is to impose some limit on expenditure in order to ensure equal access to the electorate. One way in which this might be done is to require the publicity of election expenses, in the hope that the full glare of such publicity would induce the parties to moderate their activity. This may, however, be of rather limited value given that publicity is not likely to occur until after rather than before the election, and given that it tends to obscure the function of elections which should be about issues and not tactics. An alternative, then, is to impose a ceiling on the amount which parties and candidates may spend in an election campaign. Indeed, legislation for this purpose is in force in many jurisdictions in Canada. In adopting such an approach it is possible to apply a limit to all the election expenses of a candidate or party (as in the case of Nova Scotia,[19] Quebec,[20] Ontario,[21] Manitoba,[22] and Saskatchewan[23]). On the other hand, it is possible to apply a limit only to a particular item or a segment of election expenditure, such as broadcasting or advertising expenses. This in fact was the position in Ontario until 1986,[24] and it is interesting to note that Manitoba now imposes a total limit on election expenses generally, while also imposing a limit on advertising expenses as a portion of the total.[25] But although preferable to disclosure as a means of

commission sont, le cas échéant, remplacés par des suppléants désignés dans les mêmes conditions qu'eux.

La commission peut s'adjoindre des rapporteurs pris parmi les membres du Conseil d'État, de la Cour de cassation ou de la Cour des comptes.

Elle est assistée de quatre fonctionnaires:

—un représentant du ministre chargé des Départements et Territoires d'outre-mer;

—un représentant du ministre de l'Intérieur;

—un représentant du ministre des Postes et Télécommunications;

—un représentant du ministre chargé de l'Information.

La Commission nationale de contrôle est installée au plus tard 48 heures avant le jour de l'ouverture de la campagne électorale.

For an account of contemporary French law, see Doublet, 1990.

[19] Elections Act, RSNS 1967, c.83, s.164A.
[20] Election Act, SQ 1989, c.1, s.426.
[21] Election Finances Act, SO 1986, c.33, s.39.
[22] Elections Finances Act, RSM 1970, c.E32, s.50.
[23] Election Act, RSS 1978, c.E-6, s.208.
[24] Election Finances Reform Act, RSO 1980, c.134, s.39.
[25] Elections Finances Act, RSM 1970, c.E32, s.51.

controlling election expenses, a campaign limit is not a complete answer to the problem in the sense that it fails to deal with the potentially important expenditures which may take place in the precampaign period. Many are aware of this problem, but few jurisdictions seem prepared to deal with it. One which does, however, is New Brunswick where in addition to controlling the amount of election expenses, the legislation also provides that expenditure for 'advertising or broadcasting undertakings or in newspapers, periodicals or other printed matter' must not exceed annually $25,000 in the case of a provincial party, $2,000 in the case of a local party, and $2,000 in the case of independent candidates.[26]

III. Equal Representation

As already suggested, the second essential requirement of the right to equal participation is to eliminate the dependence on economic interests by those who wield political power. Again, there are three specific goals.

1. Electors should be encouraged to contribute to the political parties in order to reduce and ultimately perhaps eliminate the dependence of the parties on institutional money.

2. Those who contribute to the parties and candidates should be publicly accountable for their contributions. So far as possible policy should not be developed as an inducement to financial interests for contributions to party funds or as a reward to those interests in return for funds.

3. The influence of the economically powerful should be restricted by controlling the amount of money which they contribute to the candidates or the political parties. Related to this is the need to control the advocacy of these groups in a campaign, advocacy which may be conducted in support of, but without the consent of, one of the parties or candidates.

So far as the first of these goals is concerned, the normal means of stimulating contributions is by the use of the income tax system to give tax relief of some kind in consideration for

---

[26] Political Process Financing Act 1978, c.P-9.3 (NB), s.50(1).

political donations. This may take the form of an expense which may be deducted from the income assessable for tax purposes. Or it may be more generous in the sense that it may take the form of a tax credit whereby electors are permitted to donate part of their assessment directly to the party of their choice. The concept of a tax deduction (the first method) has been criticized on the ground that 'its impact would be inequitable and that such an incentive would not be likely to effect the desired increase in political donations'.[27] Thus, 'In a progressive taxation system ... the deduction would result in a greater relative and absolute saving for those in an upper income level than those in the lower. It therefore favours those political parties appealing to the wealthier classes' (Ontario Commission on Election Contributions and Expenses, 1978b: 23). Canadian jurisdictions have avoided these problems by opting for the tax credit (the second method). Electors under federal law (as we shall see in Chapter 4) and in many provinces benefit from a tax credit for political donations, the credit being constructed in order to encourage the giving by many of small contributions. The most favourable stimulus to donations is a tax credit in the form of an income tax check-off where each taxpayer simply allocates a portion of his or her assessed tax to the support of a political party or candidate. This contrasts with the schemes typically in force where the taxpayer makes a contribution and is given a receipt which is then submitted to the income tax authorities.

So far as the second of these goals is concerned, the typical response is to require the reporting and disclosure of contributions. This may take one of several forms. In Britain, for example, candidates (but not political parties) must submit a return to the returning officer in which they disclose their expenses and also the names of donors to campaign funds (Ewing, 1987a). In Australia, in contrast, federal election law provides that within twenty weeks after polling day in a general election, party agents must furnish returns to the Australian Electoral Commission with 'details of gifts received by the party in the period from the day after polling day in the

---

[27] Ontario Commission on Election Contributions and Expenses, 1978b: 23, quoting Alexander, 1961: 11.

previous . . . General Election until polling day in the current election' (Australian Electoral Commission, 1984: 5). Party agents must also submit returns 'showing electoral expenditure incurred or authorised by the party. Returns must be furnished within 20 weeks after polling day in an election, including a by-election' (ibid. 12). Most Canadian jurisdictions are even more demanding, requiring disclosure annually, and separately after a general election. In Alberta, for example, the Election Finances and Contributions Disclosure Act, as amended, provides that

Every registered party and registered constituency association shall file with the Chief Electoral Officer within the period during which an annual financial statement must be filed, a return setting out
(a) the total amount of all contributions not exceeding $40 received during the year,
(b) the total amount of all contributions received during the year that exceeded $40 but did not exceed $375 in the aggregate from any single contributor, and
(c) the individual amounts contributed and the name and address of each contributor when the contributions of that contributor during the year exceeded an aggregate of $375.

Similar information must be provided in election returns, which must be filed separately.[28] In the USA, the Federal Election Campaign Act goes even further, requiring disclosure of contributions on a six-monthly basis in a non-election year, and more frequently during a campaign.[29]

The third goal is to be met either by a prohibition or a restriction on the source of funding. By far the most radical position is that taken by Quebec where the Election Act provides that 'Only an elector may make a contribution'.[30] This means that contributions by both corporations and trade unions are unlawful. In the USA there is a similar ban on corporate and union donations to parties and candidates, though this is undermined by the fact that both corporations and labour unions may set up political action committees to solicit voluntary contributions from stockholders and em-

---

[28] RSA 1980, c.E-3, s.26(4).
[29] On U.S. reparting and disclosure requirements, see chapter 7, *infra*.
[30] Election Act, SQ 1989, c.1, s.87.

ployees in the case of the former, and members in the case of the latter. The money so collected may then be used for partisan political purposes, either as contributions to candidates, parties, or other political action committees (in which case there is a limit of $5,000 from each political action committee to each recipient); or independently in favour of a political cause (in which case there is now no financial limit).[31] The most common method of regulation in Canada is in fact not to ban donations from any source, but to impose a limit on the size of a donation, from whatever source. This is done in Alberta,[32] New Brunswick,[33] and Ontario.[34] In Alberta, the legislation provides:

Contributions by any person, corporation, trade union or employee organization to registered parties, registered constituency associations or registered candidates shall not exceed
(a) in any year,
    (i) $15,000 to each registered party, and
    (ii) $750 to any registered constituency association, and $3,750 in the aggregate to the constituency associations of each registered party,
and
(b) in any campaign period,
    (i) $30,000 to each registered party less any amount contributed to the party in that calendar year under clause (a)(i), and
    (ii) $1,500 to any registered candidate, and $7,500 in the aggregate to the registered candidates of each registered party.[35]

The Alberta statute in this regard was modelled on the Ontario Act of 1975,[36] which has since been revised. The contribution limits have been increased in Ontario,[37] though they are still less than the limits laid down in Alberta. The maximum donation to a party in any non-election year by a single contributor is $4,000 rather than $15,000.[38]

---

[31] On U.S. contribution limits, see chapter 7, *infra*.
[32] Election Finances and Contributions Disclosure Act, RSA 1980, c.E-3, s.15.
[33] Political Process Financing Act 1978, c.P-9.3 (NB), s.39, as amended.
[34] Election Finances Act, SO 1986, c.33, s.19.
[35] Election Finances and Contributions Disclosure Act, RSA 1980, c.E-3, s.15, as amended.
[36] Election Finances Reform Act, RSO 1980, c.134, s.19.
[37] Election Finances Act, SO 1986, c.33, s.19.
[38] Ibid.

IV. Democracy and Liberty

It has been argued, then, that the unregulated use of money in political campaigns violates the goal of political equality, first because it does not guarantee equality of opportunity by those who compete for office, and secondly because it tends to permit disproportionate access to government by those who make large contributions to party funds. There are, nevertheless, problems associated with intervention in the manner prescribed, and very major problems at that. For the fact is that liberal democratic forms of government stand on two pillars. One is equality, but the other is liberty or freedom. And one of the essential freedoms of democratic government is freedom of speech, which has rightly been described as 'the rock on which . . . government stands' (Meiklejohn, 1965: 77). In a similar vein, the US Supreme Court has remarked:

The maintenance of the opportunity for free political discussion to the end that government may be responsive to the will of the people and that changes may be obtained by lawful means, an opportunity essential to the security of the Republic, is a fundamental principle of our constitutional system.[39]

The fundamental question which arises concerns the extent to which the freedom of speech is to be protected. One view, that promoted by Meiklejohn (ibid. 37), is that the First Amendment to the US Constitution represents an 'unlimited guarantee of the freedom of public discussion'. It is a public right which 'springs from the necessities of the program of self-government. It is not a Law of Nature or of Reason in the abstract. It is a deduction from the basic American agreement that public issues shall be decided by universal suffrage' (ibid. 27). Meiklejohn (ibid. 59) also contended that

intellectual freedom is the necessary bulwark of the public safety. That declaration admits of no exceptions. If, by suppression, we attempt to avoid lesser evils, we create greater evils. We buy temporary and partial advantage at the cost of permanent and dreadful disaster. That disaster is the breakdown of self-government. Free men need the truth as they need nothing else. In the last resort, it is only the search for and the dissemination of truth that can keep our country safe.

---

[39] *Stromberg* v. *California*, 283 US 359 (1931), at p. 369.

But although there may be a strong case for respecting freedom of speech, the freedom cannot be unlimited. Meiklejohn's arguments are persuasive as a means of ensuring that there should be no interference with the circulation of ideas. But the crucial point about his argument is his assertion that the freedom of expression is derivative of the right of self-government. In other words freedom of expression is a principle which exists to foster that right. The difficulty is that the principle cannot be absolute, for in a society which operates on the basis of inequality of wealth, absolute freedom would be the very antithesis of democratic self-government. It would become a device which would threaten the functional basis of the franchise and would be inconsistent with the values which the franchise is designed to foster. Moreover, it would become the means of legitimizing the domination of the political process by institutions which are denied any part in our system of responsible self-government yet which could threaten its very existence. So there is the dilemma: unrestrained liberty would undermine political equality, while the pursuit of equality will restrict freedom to some degree. And the problem is as acute in Canada as it is in the United States given that the Charter expressly protects freedom of expression, though it is to be noted that the concept was deeply ingrained in the Canadian legal system long before 1982. In *Switzman* v. *Elbling and Attorney-General of Quebec*,[40] for example, Rand J. said that democratic self-government 'means ultimately government by the free public opinion of an open society' which in turn 'demands the condition of a virtually unobstructed access to and diffusion of ideas'.[41] The difference between 1957 and now, however, is that then Parliament was sovereign (within its own sphere of legislative competence) and could strike its own balance between liberty and equality in this as in other fields. Now the final say in determining how the balance will be struck is to be made by the judges. And it is to be noted that although the Charter protects and promotes liberty, it does not protect or promote equality save to the extent that section 15 offers guarantees against discrimination on grounds such as race, religion, and sex.

[40] [1957] SCR 285.
[41] Ibid., at p. 306. See also *Re Alberta Legislation* (1938) 2 DLR 81.

The Charter is thus institutionally predisposed towards liberty rather than equality. This is not to say that libertarian concerns cannot be qualified or overcome by considerations of equality. Considerable opportunity is provided by section 1 of the Charter, which permits the guaranteed freedoms to be subject to 'reasonable limits prescribed by law as can be demonstrably justified in a free and democratic society'. What is reasonable is a question for the judges, and more importantly so is what is meant by a free and democratic society. So it is for the courts to determine the essential priorities of the political system under which the Canadian people live. The dilemma (between liberty and equality) is, of course, not one which is confined to Canada. As we have seen the problem arose in the United States in *Red Lion Broadcasting Co.* v. *Federal Communications Commission*[42] where the Supreme Court upheld the fairness doctrine of the FCC partly to enable competition rather than monopoly in the market-place of ideas. *Red Lion* is, however, a rather exceptional decision, for the Court has not otherwise shown any desire to abridge First Amendment rights in order to keep open the avenues of discussion or to ensure a greater degree of political equality in the voting system. Perhaps a more typical example of the court's response is *Miami Herald Publishing Co.* v. *Tornillo*[43] where a Miami statute required newspapers to give free space for the opportunity of a reply by political candidates who had been attacked in the newspaper. In holding the statute unconstitutional, the Court wrote:

A newspaper is more than a passive receptacle or conduit for news, comment, and advertising. The choice of material to go into a newspaper, and the decisions made as to limitations on the size and content of the paper, and treatment of public issues and public officials—whether fair or unfair—constitute the exercise of editorial control and judgment. It has yet to be demonstrated how governmental regulation of this crucial process can be exercised consistent with First Amendment guarantees of a free press as they have evolved to this time.[44]

[42] 395 US 367 (1969).
[43] 418 US 241 (1974).
[44] Ibid., at p. 258.

In reaching this conclusion the Court rejected the argument that the statute was necessary because of the monopolization of the newspaper industry, as a result of which a few people now have the power to inform the American people and shape public opinion. The monopoly of the means of communication, it was claimed, denied individuals the ability to respond or to contribute in a meaningful way to public debate and allowed for little or no critical analysis of the media except in professional journals of very limited readership.

More recent cases have adopted an equally robust attitude to attempts to secure a measure of political equality at the expense of political liberty. Two cases—*Buckley* v. *Valeo*[45] and *First National Bank of Boston* v. *Bellotti*[46]—are particularly relevant. *Buckley* was concerned with the constitutionality of legislation passed in the aftermath of Watergate in an attempt to dredge the corporate sludge from American politics. The legislation was comprehensive in scope and included contribution limits imposed on individuals, corporations, and labour unions; spending limits; public financing of presidential candidates; and the reporting and disclosure of campaign contributions. The Supreme Court effectively neutered the package by striking down the three main spending limits. These were, first, a limit of $1,000 on so-called independent expenditures, that is, expenditures for example by individuals, corporations, or unions 'relative to a clearly identified candidate'; secondly, a restriction on the amount of private resources which candidates could use to finance their campaigns; and thirdly, a total spending ceiling on candidates for election to federal office. In reaching this decision the Court was strongly influenced by First Amendment considerations and was concerned that the limits heavily burdened First Amendment expression. The Court was not persuaded that the controls were necessary to equalize the relative ability of individuals and groups to influence the outcome of elections. In the case of the independent expenditures the Court held:

the concept that government may restrict the speech of some elements of our society in order to enhance the relative voice of others is wholly

---

[45] 424 US 1 (1976).
[46] 435 US 765 (1978).

29

foreign to the First Amendment, which was designed 'to secure the widest possible dissemination of information from diverse and antagonistic sources' and 'to assure unfettered interchange of ideas for the bringing about of political and social changes desired by the people.' . . . The First Amendment's protection against governmental abridgement of free expression cannot properly be made to depend on a person's financial ability to engage in public discussion.[47]

In the case of the overall spending limits by candidates the Court said:

Given the limitation on the size of outside contributions, the financial resources available to a candidate's campaign, like the number of volunteers recruited, will normally vary with the size and intensity of the candidate's support. There is nothing invidious, improper, or unhealthy in permitting such funds to be spent to carry the candidate's message to the electorate.[48]

In view of the decision in *Buckley*, the approach which would be followed in *Bellotti* was not unpredictable. At issue in that case was a Massachusetts statute which prohibited certain corporations from incurring expenses in any election or in influencing or affecting the vote on any question submitted to the voters, other than one materially affecting any of the property, business, or assets of the corporation. The Court by a majority held the provision to be unconstitutional, as abridging the expression which the First Amendment was designed to protect. The Court noted that if the speakers had been individuals and not corporations, no one would have suggested that the Legislature could silence their proposed speech. It continued by saying that the corporate identity of the speaker does not deprive the speech of what otherwise would be its clear entitlement to protection. In reaching this decision, the Court rejected two important arguments for the state. The first was that the legislation was necessary to preserve the integrity of the electoral process, prevent corruption, and sustain the active, alert responsibility of the individual citizens for the wise conduct of government. To this the Court replied:

---

[47] 424 US 1 (1976), at pp. 48–9.
[48] Ibid., at p. 56.

According to appellee, corporations are wealthy and powerful and their views may drown out other points of view. If appellee's arguments were supported by record or legislative findings that corporate advocacy threatened imminently to undermine democratic processes, thereby denigrating rather than serving First Amendment interests, these arguments would merit our consideration . . . But there has been no showing that the relative voice of corporations has been overwhelming or even significant in influencing referenda in Massachusetts, or that there has been any threat to the confidence of the citizenry in government . . . Nor are appellee's arguments inherently persuasive or supported by the precedents of this Court. Referenda are held on issues, not candidates for public office. The risk of corruption perceived in cases involving candidate elections . . . simply is not present in a popular vote on a public issue. To be sure, corporate advertising may influence the outcome of the vote; this would be its purpose. But the fact that advocacy may persuade the electorate is hardly a reason to suppress it . . .[49]

The second state argument was that the legislation was necessary to protect shareholders by preventing the use of corporate resources in furtherance of views with which some shareholders might disagree. This was dismissed on several grounds, one of the most important being that:

Ultimately shareholders may decide, through the procedures of corporate democracy, whether their corporation should engage in debate on public issues. Acting through their power to elect the board of directors or to insist upon protective provisions in the corporation's charter, shareholders normally are presumed competent to protect their own interests.[50]

V. Conclusion

We have seen that there is a conflict between two central tenets of modern liberal democracy. On the one hand, there is a need to secure political equality, which does not mean simply the right to vote, but means also the right to stand for election and to secure election on equal terms with one's fellow citizens. It means also that groups or individuals should not have

[49] 435 US 765 (1978), at pp. 789–90.
[50] Ibid., at pp. 794–5.

disproportionate access to legislators simply by reason of their financial resources. On the other hand, we have seen that there is a need to secure political liberty, particularly liberty or freedom of expression, in this context for political purposes. Without the free expression of ideas and opinions there can be no competition for office. But as we have also seen, unrestrained liberty can be as dangerous for democracy as restrictions on liberty in the sense that it allows the economically powerful to compete on more favourable terms than the economically deprived. The need is clearly to strike a balance between the two so that both equality and liberty serve the same democratic mission. The striking of that balance is, however, no longer in the hands of the people or their democratic representatives in Canada, with the Charter having given the last say on political questions to the courts. The US courts have shown themselves unwilling to surrender liberty to the ideal of political equality. At best the courts will anxiously preserve *formal* political equality (the right to vote and the right to be a candidate for office) from the effects of economic inequality. But they are either unwilling or unable to go further and protect effective political equality by recognizing the impact of the unequal distribution of resources on the content of that formal equality. The success of Canadian legislation designed to promote political equality will thus depend on the extent to which Canadian judges are prepared to depart from American precedents in their interpretation of the Charter.

3

The Origins of Federal Legislation

IN this chapter we pick up the themes which we left at the end of Chapter 1. Having considered the function of campaign finance legislation we now consider the background to the enactment of the Election Expenses Act 1974, the source of the present legal regulation of federal elections in Canada. We begin by examining the law in force before 1974—legislation which has its origins in the Dominion Elections Act 1874.[1] We then move to consider some of the major proposals which were made to reform the law, proposals which increased with intensity in the late 1950s and early 1960s. The major developments, however, were the appointment by the federal government in 1964 of the Barbeau Committee to examine the question of election expenses, and the appointment by the House of Commons of a Special Committee on Election Expenses in 1970 under the chairmanship of the Progressive Conservative member, Mr Hyliard Chappell. The Barbeau Committee reported in 1966, and the Chappell Committee reported with its recommendations in 1971. A consideration of the work of these Committees forms the basis of the later parts of this chapter. It will be seen that many of the proposals for reform made by backbenchers were made also by Barbeau and Chappell and that the reports of both Committees were influential to a considerable degree in shaping the form of future legislation.

I. The Statutory Background

As we saw in Chapter 1, Canada had an unhappy experience with campaign finance legislation. The Dominion Elections Act 1908[2] prohibited corporations from giving money to political

---

[1] SC 1874, 37 Vic., c.9.
[2] SC 1908, 7–8 Edw. VIII, c.26.

parties.[3] But this was repealed in 1930,[4] having been openly evaded yet never once enforced. Thereafter there was virtually no legal regulation of political party funding, there being no requirement that the parties should disclose their income and expenditure, no regulation of the source of financing, and no regulation of how much money might be spent in a campaign. This is not to say that the law abstained completely from the conduct of campaigns. Although the political parties were free from any direct legal controls, there remained in force a measure of statutory regulation of campaigns by individual candidates. These measures were introduced as long ago as 1874[5] and were similar in many respects to the statutory framework adopted in Britain,[6] though with one crucial difference to which we shall come in due course. The starting-point of this early Canadian (and British) approach to control is the doctrine of agency, a doctrine which was to play a crucial part in the recommendations of the Barbeau Committee and in the legislation finally introduced in 1974. So by a remarkable coincidence the doctrine which was the basis of candidate accountability in 1874 was to become the basis of party accountability exactly one hundred years later.

Under the Canada Elections Act,[7] every candidate was required to appoint an official agent, whose name, address, and occupation were to be declared to the returning officer.[8] As a general rule, no payment was to be made before, during, or after an election by a candidate or by any person other than the agent if the expense was incurred 'on account of or in respect of the conduct or management of such election.'[9] Moreover, any donations by third parties to help meet election expenses were to be paid to the agent, and not otherwise.[10] This requirement that all funds should be channelled through

---

[3] s.36.

[4] SC 1930, 20–21 Geo. V, c.16, s.9.

[5] Dominion Elections Act, SC 1874, 37 Vic., c.9.

[6] For an account of British Law, see Ewing, 1987*a*.

[7] SC 1960, 8–9 Eliz. II, c.39. This was the statute in force at the time of reform.

[8] s.62.

[9] s.62(4).

[10] Ibid.

the agent was subject to qualifications for payments by a candidate of personal expenses and for payments by any person out of his own money for any small expenses legally incurred.[11] Otherwise, any person who made payments by any other means than through the agent was guilty of an illegal practice and of an offence against the Act.[12] In addition, any contract whereby expenses were incurred on account of or in respect of the conduct or management of an election was not enforceable against a candidate unless made by the candidate or his agent.[13] The major sanction against improper spending, however, was the risk that a candidate might be unseated if he won the contest. Improper spending could lead to the election being voided by an election court unless it was 'proved by a candidate that any payment made by an official agent in contravention of this section was made without the sanction or connivance of such candidate'.[14]

Apart from the agency principle, the other major feature of the law in operation for the century before the Election Expenses Act 1974 was the duty of disclosure.[15] Within two months of the election, the official agent of every candidate was under a duty to transmit to the returning officer a return respecting election expenses. This should detail

- all payments made by the agent, together with bills and receipts;
- the personal expenses paid by the candidate;
- any unpaid and disputed claims;
- all money, securities, and equivalent of money received by or promised to the agent by the candidate or any other person for the purpose of election expenses;
- the name of every person from whom money, securities or the equivalent of money may have been received or by whom a promise was made, showing the amount of each sum.[16]

---

[11] s.62(4)(a) and (b).
[12] s.62(5).
[13] s.62(6).
[14] s.62(13).
[15] s.63.
[16] s.63(1).

The duty of disclosure was thus rather detailed. The prescribed form for this purpose[17] required the agent to 'accurately set out . . . the name and occupation of every person (including the candidate) and of every club, society, company or association, from whom any money securities or the equivalent of money was received . . .'. Here the agent was to list the name, address, and occupation of the contributor, together with the amount of the contribution. The agent was also required to detail money promised but not received, the names and addresses of those from whom premises were hired, to whom money was paid for services rendered, to whom money was paid to meet travelling expenses or the hire of vehicles, to whom money was paid for any goods supplied, and to whom money was paid for advertising.

The return so submitted was to be accompanied by a declaration of the agent made in the presence of a notary public or a justice of the peace.[18] Also important is the fact that a summary of the agent's return was to be published at the candidate's expense in one newspaper published or circulated in the constituency where the election took place.[19] A form was prescribed by the Chief Electoral Officer for this purpose. A further safeguard was the fact that a successful candidate could not sit or vote in the House of Commons until a return was transmitted[20] and that it was a criminal offence to submit a false return or to fail to submit a return at all.[21] There was, however, a procedure whereby a candidate could apply to a court for relief in the event of any failure to file or in the event of a wrong filing.[22] So,

Where the return and declarations respecting election expenses of a candidate at an election have not been transmitted as required by this Act or, being transmitted, contain some error or false statement, then,
(a) if the candidate applies to a judge competent to recount the votes given at the election and shows that the failure to transmit such

---

[17] Form No. 61.
[18] s.63(2).
[19] s.63(5).
[20] s.63(7).
[21] s.63(8).
[22] s.63(12).

return and declarations or any of them, or any part thereof, or any error or false statement therein, has arisen by reason of his illness, or of the absence, death, illness or misconduct of his official agent or of any clerk or officer of such agent, or by reason of inadvertence or of any reasonable cause of a like nature, and not by reason of any want of good faith on the part of the applicant; or
(b) if the official agent of the candidate applies to the said judge and shows that the failure to transmit the return and declarations which he was required to transmit, or any part thereof, or any error or false statement therein, arose by reason of his illness or of the death or illness of any prior official agent of the candidate, or of the absence, death, illness or misconduct of his clerk or officer of an official agent of the candidate, or by reason of inadvertence or of any reasonable cause of a like nature, and not by reason of any want of good faith on the part of the applicant;

the judge may, after such notice of the application in the electoral district and on production of such evidence of the grounds stated in the application and of the good faith of the application, and otherwise as to the judge seems fit, make such order for allowing an authorized excuse for the failure to transmit such return and declaration, or for an error or false statement in such return and declaration as to the judge seems just.[23]

Where relief was given in this way it could be tied to an obligation to make 'the return and declaration in a modified form or within an extended time, and upon the compliance with such other terms as to the judge seems best calculated for carrying into effect the objects of [the] Act.'[24]

So two key features operated in Canadian law before the 1974 reforms. The first was the doctrine of agency and the second was the duty of disclosure, even though both were confined to candidates and did not apply to the political parties. There was, however, no restriction on the sources of funding, a point recognized in Administrative Instructions prepared by the Chief Electoral Officer. Thus, 'There is no prohibition against the receipt of campaign contributions from any source. Consequently, the source of campaign contributions is not material, and all contributions, no matter what their source,

[23] s.63(14).
[24] Ibid.

may be treated in the same way.'[25] In these respects the Canadian federal law was very similar to that operating (still) in Britain. But as already pointed out, there was one crucial difference. As well as recognizing both the principle of agency and the duty of disclosure, British law also imposed a limit on the amount of election expenditures permitted by candidates, the amount being based on a formula which distinguished between rural and urban constituencies and which determined the limit according to the number of voters in the constituency.[26] In Canada, in contrast, apart from bribery which was a corrupt practice, as a general rule 'there [was] no limitation upon the amount which a candidate may lawfully disburse in good faith, or any restriction . . . upon the objects of such expenditures'.[27] So candidates could spend as much as they could raise, and there was no limit on how much of their budgets could be used for items such as broadcasting or other expenditures. British law also imposed and still imposes restrictions on the amount of money which might be spent by pressure groups on behalf of specific candidates.[28] If any such group wished or wishes to promote the election of a specific candidate or candidates, it must first have the approval of the candidate or candidates and any expenditure incurred by the group would form part of the candidate's maximum permitted expenses and would have to be accounted for as such.[29] Again there was no parallel in the Canadian legislation, though it is strongly arguable that such expenditure was unlawful anyway in view of the requirement that all expenditure be made by the agent,[30] a point which arose forcefully in the only major case before the 1974 reforms.

In *Johnson* v. *Yake*[31] the appellant was returned as member for Moose Jaw. The election was challenged on two grounds:

---

[25] Administrative Instructions Prepared by the Chief Electoral Officer, para. 354.

[26] This was introduced in the Corrupt and Illegal Practices Prevention Act, 1883, s.8.

[27] Administrative Instructions Prepared by the Chief Electoral Officer, para. 355.

[28] This was introduced in the Representation of the People Act 1918, s.34.

[29] Ibid., now Representation of the People Act 1983, s.75.

[30] Canada Elections Act, *supra* n. 7, s.62(4).

[31] (1923) 2 DLR 95.

first that 'agents' of the candidate paid election expenses other-wise than through the official agent; and secondly that the candidate and his official agent were guilty of making a false return of election expenses. According to the information pro-vided in the judgment of Duff J., the 'funds on which the appellant was at liberty to draw for election expenses were in part in the hands of an association organized in part at least for the purpose of financing the canvass of the Progressive Party under whose auspices the respondent was conducting his candidature'.[32] The association had a local committee in Moose Jaw, which received money from the central committee for the purpose of defraying the expenses of the Moose Jaw election, the money being deposited in a bank account under the control of the president and secretary of the local committee. With the consent of the candidate, but without the knowledge or con-sent of the official agent, the local officials wrote cheques on behalf of the candidate. Apart from being irregular, the agent's declaration alleged that these payments were made with his authority, whereas in fact they were not. In addition the state-ment failed to declare all the expenses incurred by the candi-date. One of these payments was for sandwiches provided for scrutineers on election day, and the other was for the services of the Great War Veterans' Association for performing in the celebration of the candidate's victory on the night of the elec-tion. In order words, both principles were violated—the obligation to make payments through an agent, and the duty to disclose all expenditures—with the result that the election was set aside.

II. Proposals for Reform

The legal framework remained in this shape from 1930 until 1974, when the Election Expenses Act was passed. This is not to say that there was complacency during this period about the state of the law, though, as pointed out in chapter one, until the 1960s there was only sporadic concern about the need for reform, the basic philosophy being one of *laissez-faire* (Barbeau,

---

[32] At p. 96.

1966: 23). One problem with the existing law was that, despite the possible sanctions which supported it, it was not effectively enforced. Indeed, some provisions were not enforced at all. The failure to provide an official statement was never punished, despite the fact that between 1962 and 1974, as many as one-quarter of all candidates did not submit statements of expenditure in the relevant general elections (Seidle, 1980: 148). In fact, *Johnson* v. *Yake*[33] is the only case in which the Act was used—there to punish, as we have seen, improper payments and incomplete as opposed to no disclosure. And it has been pointed out that in *Johnson* v. *Yake* the defendant was a member of a newly formed political party, whereas no prosecution had been initiated against a member of one of the established parties. Barbeau (1966: 23) felt unable to explain this failure, 'involving as it does certain judgments about the motives of political parties' (ibid.). It was noted, however, that '1. the established parties have been unwilling to initiate action against each other; 2. the trouble and cost of contesting an election suit about election expenses is prohibitive to the private citizen; 3. no organized, nonpolitical group has ever undertaken to bear the cost of a suit; 4. no governmental agency has felt itself responsible, or been made responsible, for prosecuting candidates violating the law on election expenses' (ibid.).

The law under discussion thus suffered from two defects. The first was the limited nature of the obligations imposed, and the second was the lack of enforcement of these limited obligations. Attempts at reform were made as early as 1938 when C. G. Power, the Minister of Pensions and National Health, introduced a Political Expenditures Bill,[34] which contained a number of sweeping proposals. The first object was to identify and keep a public record of all receipts and expenditures for political purposes. Political expenditures would be incurred only by special corporate bodies constituted simply on request.[35] Political contributions would be made only to such bodies and contributions would be deposited in a bank with

[33] (1923) 2 DLR 95.
[34] House of Commons Debates, 3rd session, 18th Parliament, vol. ii, 5 Apr. 1938, pp. 2023–36.
[35] Ibid. 2024.

duplicate deposit slips.[36] Power explained that 'A return of expenditures and contributions will thus automatically be made by the transmission to [an] officer appointed by this house of the duplicate deposit slips and cheques'.[37] This officer, who would be known as the inspector general of elections, would have the duty of setting up corporations on request and of making an annual return to Parliament of all receipts and expenditures of the corporations. The second object of the bill was to limit expenditures which could lawfully be incurred in promoting the election of members of Parliament. The amount of expenditures permissible in a particular district would depend upon the number of electors in the constituency. The limits would apply to the 'corporations', and the national expenditures of the political parties would be distributed amongst the different candidates of the party in question. And in addition to these general limits, there would be ('in the interests of the public') 'a limitation on the amount to be expended on radio broadcasting',[38] this limit again to be based on the number of electors. But as startling as these measures were sweeping were the very wide definitions employed in the bill. Thus 'the definition of a political expense [was] so drawn as to include all outlays designed to affect public opinion or governmental action other than such action as is consequent upon judicial or semi-judicial procedure'.[39] And 'political purpose' was defined to mean:

The purpose of promoting or opposing the selection of candidates or of any person as a candidate for membership in the House of Commons, the return of any such candidate, the enactment or repeal of any legislation either by parliament or affecting its legislative jurisdiction, the adoption of any resolution by either house of parliament or the adoption of any policy or the taking of any action by the governor general in council, and extends to and includes all and any analogous purposes.[40]

Mr Power explained, without understatement, that

---

[36] Ibid.
[37] Ibid.
[38] Ibid.
[39] Ibid. 2024–5.
[40] Ibid. 2025.

This definition will at once appear to the house to be pretty broad. Certain associations and corporations who do not, generally speaking, consider themselves to be of a political character will inevitably when they engage in their normal activities be embraced within this definition. I could say, for instance, that if such an association existed as a civic reform league which wished to engage counsel for the purpose of promoting the passage of this bill, it would itself probably be the first to come under its provisions. But may I point out to the house that it is essential that all who take part in or undertake any political action must come under the provisions of this act. Otherwise there will be loopholes left for individuals and organizations, and it might be that the effectiveness of the legislation would be destroyed. We must, if this bill is to be of any effect whatsoever, take all precautions to prevent any evasion of its provisions.[41]

As might be expected, the bill failed[42] and a similar fate met a modified version of the bill when it was reintroduced in 1949.[43] Subsequent bills and proposals for reform were much less ambitious. One bill, introduced in 1958[44] and 1959,[45] proposed that political parties should be required annually to disclose the sources of their income.[46] The sponsor of the bill, Mr Frank Howard, claimed that this was necessary essentially for two reasons. In the first place, it was necessary in order to ensure that the duty of disclosure on candidates was rendered effective and not so easily out-manœuvered. Many candidates revealed that the major source of their income was the national party, but there was no obligation on the national party to disclose for its part where its money came from.[47] Secondly, it

---

[41] House of Commons Debates, 3rd session, 18th Parliament, vol. ii, 5 Apr. 1938, pp. 2023–36.

[42] The Bill was, however, given a Second Reading, although strong reservations were expressed by the Leader of the Opposition. See House of Commons Debates, 3rd session, 18th Parliament, vol. ii, 7 Apr. 1938, p. 2105.

[43] House of Commons Debates, 5th session, 20th Parliament, vol. i, 2 Feb. 1949, p. 161.

[44] House of Commons Debates, 1st session, 24th Parliament, vol. iii, 22 July 1958, pp. 2541–7.

[45] House of Commons Debates, 2nd session, 24th Parliament, vol. ii, 13 Mar. 1959, pp. 1953–7.

[46] In 1961 a different private members' Bill proposed the disclosure of party income and expenses after each election. See House of Commons Debates, 4th session, 24th Parliament, vol. viii, 15 Sept. 1961, pp. 8444–52.

[47] House of Commons Debates, 1st session, 24th Parliament, vol. iii, 22 July 1958, p. 2541.

was argued that as a matter of principle the national parties should in any event be required to disclose the sources of their income:

if political parties are to operate to the best interests of the general public then there must be an accounting to the general public as to the source of campaign fund contributions. If it is equitable that a candidate must declare the names of individuals or companies from whom he receives contributions and the amount of such contributions, then it is equitable that the national party itself should make a similar declaration to the general public as to the source of its income.[48]

A second bill was also introduced on several occasions, for the first time in February 1964, sponsored by Mr Andrew Brewin.[49] In moving the Second Reading of his bill, Mr Brewin contended:

But it is my view that we have in Canada today only a half democracy or what might be called the caricature of a democracy, and one of the reasons for this situation is that in our election of representatives to parliament we do not give either the candidate or the electors a fair choice or a fair chance. We allow the scales to be weighted heavily in favour of candidates and parties who can secure large campaign funds. I suggest that if we were discussing a game we would not tolerate the fixing of the handicaps in a way which would ensure the victory of one side or the other by favouring those who could lay their hands on the most money. But we do this with respect to something far more important than any game, that is, in the choosing of the people who will be our representatives in parliament.[50]

He proposed that a limit should be imposed on the election expenses of both candidates and political parties. The agents of candidates would be permitted to spend up to 20 cents per elector (giving a maximum of $10,000 in an average constituency of 50,000 voters) and the parties would be permitted to spend up to 10 cents per elector in the constituencies in which they had candidates (allowing the major parties $600,000 each). In order to police the limits, the parties (like candidates)

[48] Ibid.
[49] Bill C-38, 2nd session, 26th Parliament, 13 Eliz. II, 1964.
[50] House of Commons Debates, 2nd session, 26th Parliament, vol. vi, 31 July 1964, p. 6274. See also House of Commons Debates, 1st session, 27th Parliament, vol. i, 4 Feb. 1966, p. 759, *re* Bill C-5, 1st session, 27th Parliament, 14 Eliz. II, 1966.

would be required to submit a return of election expenses, detailing the sources of income and the persons to whom money was paid.

The Howard and Brewin bills thus embraced the central features of the Power Bill several decades earlier, namely disclosure and a limit on permitted election expenses. Another proposal was quite different. This was for tax relief for individuals who wished to make donations to political parties. In 1964 the following resolution was moved in the House of Commons by J. E. Lloyd, the member for Halifax:

That, in the opinion of this house, the government should consider the advisability of amending the Income Tax Act to permit taxpayers to deduct from taxable income contributions to registered national political parties, providing such deductions do not exceed a stated maximum percentage of taxable income.[51]

This was proposed on the ground that the parties need funds, and that if the people 'are not encouraged to make contributions to political parties, with a high sense of service as democratic citizens, we encourage undemocratic influences upon those elected to office'.[52] The purpose essentially was to 'broaden the base of contributions from . . . Canadians',[53] and it was proposed by Lloyd that this could be done while also maintaining the anonymity of contributors. But like the private members' bills before and after it, this proposal also failed, being attacked on a number of grounds. One of the most interesting criticisms was from the member who claimed:

The only taxpayers who I believe would take advantage of this deduction would probably be those earning in excess of $15,000; because those who earn less than that amount are probably on a budget and cannot afford to make a contribution of any sizeable amount to assist political campaigns. This would make political parties completely dependant [*sic*] upon the people in the upper income brackets.[54]

The same member continued by pointing out forcefully that

---

[51] House of Commons Debates, 2nd session, 26th Parliament, vol. iv, 20 May 1964, p. 3416.
[52] Ibid. 3417.
[53] Ibid. 3418.
[54] Ibid. 3422.

According to the report of the chief electoral officer on the 26th general election there were a shade under 10 million registered voters in Canada. According to the 1963 taxation statistics there are some 4,500,000 taxpayers in Canada. Of this number approximately 22 per cent pay tax on incomes of $15,000 and over, and simple arithmetic shows that less than 10 per cent of the voting population of this country would be the main contributors to election funds. If this were the case it would mean that political parties would be conscious of their electoral responsibilities vis-à-vis the 10 per cent who were supplying all the money. It would also mean that persons in the upper income brackets would be able to make contributions to political parties in off election years; and in certain instances people in the higher income brackets, in order to become taxable in a lower bracket, would make contributions to political parties even in off election years.[55]

In his view 'the government should provide election funds for political parties', and an 'equitable basis should be provided whereby the government would supply the money to political parties in election campaigns'.[56]

So by the early 1960s three major proposals were circulating amongst federal parliamentarians. These proposals were, however, all from backbenchers and were not sponsored by government. The first major step by government in the direction of reform was the announcement from the Throne on 18 February 1964 that it intended 'to institute an inquiry to advise on the best practicable way to set enforceable limits to expenditures in election campaigns'.[57] In the previous year provincial Liberals had gone one better by legislating in a bold and imaginative way. The Quebec Election Act contained a number of important initiatives:[58]

1. During an election only the official agent of a candidate or of a recognized party could incur election expenses.
2. Election expenses of parties were limited to 25 cents for

---

[55] Ibid.

[56] Ibid. A similar proposal had been made by Mr Pickersgill in 1960. See House of Commons Debates, 3rd session, 24th Parliament, vol. vi, 12 July 1960, p. 6125.

[57] House of Commons Debates, 2nd session, 26th Parliament, vol. i, 18 Feb. 1964, p. 2.

[58] Election Act, SQ 1963, c.13.

each elector in the aggregate of electoral districts in which the party had candidates.

3. Election expenses of candidates were limited, the limit depending on the number of electors in each constituency.

4. Candidates would be reimbursed from provincial funds for election expenses paid and incurred by agents on their behalf. The reimbursement would be up to 15 cents per elector, payable to those candidates polling at least 20% of the votes cast.

5. The official agents of both candidates and parties were required to file a return of election expenses to the chief returning officer, with details of advertising and other expenditures. There was, however, no requirement to disclose the details of contributors.

As we shall see, similar measures were to find their way into federal law.

It was inevitable perhaps that the Quebec experience should influence the deliberations of the federal inquiry. But whether or not they agreed with the details of the Quebec legislation, leading federal politicians appeared to support the decision to appoint an inquiry, which as we saw in chapter one was partially a response to the financial problems of the Liberals in a period of spiralling election costs. Indeed the other parties were by all accounts much less well financed than the Liberals and must have been encountering even greater difficulties. But whatever the reason for the consensus, the Prime Minister contended that 'the financing of campaigns is becoming more and more unsatisfactory. Television and the increased scale and cost of communications methods generally have enormously increased this problem. To set effective, enforceable limits to campaign expenditures obviously is the first step, on which other steps would depend. There is no point in attempting anything else unless we can first make sure of establishing limits that will be entirely genuine.'[59] Action was in fact taken when on 27 October 1964 the government announced in the House that an advisory committee had been established to 'inquire into and report upon the desirable and practical

---

[59] House of Commons Debates, 2nd session, 26th Parliament, vol. i, 20 Feb. 1964, p. 57.

measures to limit and control federal election expenditures'.[60]
The Committee of five was to be chaired by Mr François Nobert,
the other members being M. J. Coldwell (former national leader
of the CCF); Gordon Dryden (Secretary-Treasurer of the Liberal
Federation of Canada); Arthur Smith (a businessman and a
former Progressive Conservative member of the House); and
Professor Norman Ward of the University of Saskatchewan. At
an early stage, illness prevented Nobert from serving and he
was replaced as chairman by Alphonse Barbeau (a lawyer from
Montreal) in January 1965.

III. The Barbeau Report

In its report, the Barbeau Committee was influenced by several
underlying themes. The first was the need of political actors for
money. Thus, 'candidates have legitimate electoral expenses,
and must have means sufficient to enable them to explain to
the electorate what Canada's domestic and international problems are, and their proposed solutions' (Barbeau, 1966: 28). In
a similar vein, the Committee claimed that 'The elector cannot
make a sensible choice unless he is well informed. Keeping the
electorate well informed means using the great communications media: radio, television, newspapers, printed flysheets,
billboards etc. If these media are to be used well, parties and
candidates must spend very considerable sums of money. The
sums are essential expenditures incurred in informing the
public' (ibid. 29). But if there is a need for money, so also is
there a need 'to have good legislation on political finances if
democratic government is to be effective' (ibid. 28). Thus, 'the
source of income must not be such as to prevent parties and
legislators from adopting legislation that is in the public
interest' (ibid. 29); 'measures should be taken to limit the
expenses of parties and candidates that are too lavish in their
expenditure' (ibid.); and measures should also be taken 'to
encourage the development of new sources of money for those
who have not enough, so that they, too, may be able to use the

---

[60] House of Commons Debates, 2nd session, 26th Parliament, vol. ix, 27
Oct. 1964, p. 9457. The Minister making the announcement stated that the
terms of reference were 'general' and that the government expected the
Committee to give them a wide interpretation (ibid.). The announcement was
approved by the leaders of the Progressive Conservatives (J. G. Diefenbaker)
and the NDP (T. C. Douglas).

informational media to the full' (ibid.). In particular, 'electors should be encouraged to bear a heavier burden of the expenditures occasioned by political campaigns' (ibid. 34). The Committee was concerned that candidates generally 'have never made much effort to gather modest contributions from a large number of electors' but, on the contrary, 'attempt to get large contributions from a few sources' (ibid.). In proposing reform to give effect to these principles, the Committee made seven principal recommendations.

1. *Political parties should be legally recognized and, through the doctrine of agency, made legally responsible for their actions in raising and spending funds* (ibid. 37). The Committee had noted that the Parliament of Canada had never granted legal recognition to political parties, and only indirectly acknowledged their existence. Yet the 'development of the Canadian democratic system seems . . . to require that legal recognition be extended to political parties' (ibid. 31). It was thus proposed that each national political party intending to contest federal elections should be required to register formally with a new Registry of Election and Political Finance. The parties would be required to register details such as their names, addresses, leaders, and chief financial agents. Failure to comply would not lead to any criminal penalty, but to the denial or withholding of the benefits recommended later in the Report.

2. *A degree of financial equality should be established among candidates and among political parties, by the extension of certain services and subsidies to all who qualify* (ibid. 37). Here the Committee anticipated extending subsidies to both candidates and parties. So far as candidates are concerned, it was proposed that they be reimbursed for media expenses, with a sum equal to 2 cents for every elector on the list of electors. So far as the parties are concerned, the Committee was satisfied 'that the increasing use of broadcasting media constitutes the greatest contributing factor to rising costs of campaigning', and of the view that political parties should not assume the broadcasting costs for their national campaigns (ibid. 43). With this in mind Barbeau concluded that a total of six hours of prime broadcast time in the four weeks preceding polling day should be allocated among the duly registered national parties on each public and

private network. This would be free of cost to the parties. The time would be allocated between the parties after negotiation with the Canadian Broadcasting Corporation, with an appeal in the case of dispute to the Board of Broadcast Governors, whose decision would be final and binding. The costs of this time would be met equally by the broadcasting authorities and the federal government, and no time beyond the six hours would be available for purchase by the political parties (ibid. 43–5).

3. *An effort should be made to increase public participation in politics, by broadening the base of political contributions through tax concessions to donors* (ibid. 37). The Committee was concerned about the fact that financial support for the political parties by the public was minimal, and that the parties depended heavily on institutional sources for their funding. It was claimed that 'the greater the number of people involved in a party's financing, the less the dependence on a few big interests, and the greater a party's freedom of action in pursuit of what its members conceive to be the public interest' (ibid. 46). One factor which helped to explain the low level of public support was that donations to campaign funds were not recognized as legitimate deductions under income tax law (ibid.). This is despite the fact that Parliament had recognized a multitude of other worthy causes as deserving of public support. The Committee thought it strange that a contribution to a political party— 'which goes to the root of our democratic practice' (ibid.)—was not also recognized in this way and recommended that the anomaly should be rectified. Thus, it was proposed that there should be introduced a graduated income tax credit for personal income taxpayers. The credit would vary with the size of the donation, with a ceiling on donations of $300 as an incentive to encourage small donations. Thus a donor would be entitled to a tax credit of 50% of the contribution between $1 and $20; of 40% for the contribution between $21 and $100; and of 30% for the contribution between $101 and $300. No credit would be available for corporate or non-resident taxpayers, the Committee taking the view that the tax credit should be 'an encouragement to the individual to involve himself in political activity, as well as a fund-raising device' (ibid. 47).

4. *Costs of election campaigns should be reduced, by shortening the campaign period, by placing limitations on expenditures on mass media by candidates and parties, and by prohibiting the payment of poll workers on election day* (ibid. 37). Here the Committee proposed that there should be no restriction on the size or source of political contributions, rejecting arguments that unusually large contributions should be prohibited on the ground that 'limitation in size is simply and easily evaded; a large donation, for example, can be divided among a number of token contributors, thus defeating the principle' (ibid. 48). The Committee did propose, however, that campaign periods should be shortened in order to reduce expense, and that a limit should be imposed on the media expenditures of candidates. The Committee opposed general limits on candidates' expenditures on the ground that a 'total dollar limitation is inviting by its simplicity, but meaningless in practice. A total dollar limitation appears hopelessly inadequate in evaluating volunteer support in work or services. It is also the Committee's contention that any attempt to place such a limitation could be easily circumvented' (ibid. 49). So far as the parties were concerned, the Committee was cautious in its approach here too, proposing that spending would be kept under control by prohibiting any broadcasting publicity outside the six hours of free time. But again the Committee rejected a total limit on spending, suggesting instead that 'as a first step, reports on expenditures, and the attendant publicity, (provided the system adopted is rigorous enough) would oblige parties to put wise limits on their expenditures. Should political parties incur exaggerated expenditures, the electorate will be in a position to reach its own conclusions' (ibid. 32).

5. *Public confidence in political financing should be strengthened, by requiring candidates and parties to disclose their incomes and expenditures* (ibid. 37). The Committee was easily convinced by the arguments in favour of disclosure.

The arguments in favour of disclosure generally appeared convincing. Disclosure would assist in educating the public on the need for involvement in the financing of the legitimate, though high, campaign expenses required in an increasingly complex political system. Disclosure also has a cleansing effect in politics, and acts indirectly to reduce campaign expenditures. The Committee was told that no candidates or parties would attempt to buy an election if the public were made aware of their tactics. The Committee also heard that the fear of public disapproval as a result of disclosure would reduce the possibility of a wealthy candidate overpowering his opponents by the sheer weight of money. Disclosure, the Committee was urged, would reduce the mystery surrounding political influence, and perhaps elevate the image of political parties and politicians. (ibid. 53)

Although the Committee also heard arguments against disclosure (that it was an invasion of privacy and a violation of the principle of the secret ballot), on balance the Committee concluded that meaningful reporting and disclosure were vital if any controls were to be introduced, for 'limitations could not be policed if no one could audit and check the income and expenditures of those to be restricted' (ibid. 54). In addition, 'if public funds are to be spent in support of political parties and candidates, the public has the right to know if the recipients needed the funds, and if the funds were expended for legitimate election purposes' (ibid.). So it was proposed that each party should be required to disclose details of income and expenditure, both annually and within sixty days of an election. Each candidate would be required to disclose campaign income and expenses within thirty days of the election. The Committee did not, however, propose pre-election reporting, as in the case of some US jurisdictions, taking the view that post-election reporting would be onerous enough for both parties and candidates until they had become accustomed to the more refined standards of bookkeeping which would be required.

6. *A Registry under the supervision of a Registrar should be established to audit and publish the financial reports required, and to enforce the provisions of the proposed 'Election and Political Finances Act'* (ibid. 37). The first proposal in this context was for the creation of a Registry of Election and Political Finance to be separate from the offices and duties of the Chief Electoral Officer. The Registrar would have unchallenged qualifications of impartiality and integrity, his appointment and removal being the sole prerogative of the House of Commons. The Registrar would have a right of access to party premises in order to inspect financial records and would be responsible for ensuring the publication of financial data. He would be

required also to report annually to Parliament through the Speaker of the House of Commons. The other duties of the Registrar would be the keeping of the legislation under review, and the payment of subsidies to those candidates who qualified. In addition to all of this, the Registrar would have the responsibility for enforcing the legislation, the Committee expressing concern 'about electoral legislation which leaves the right and opportunity to commence action for an infraction solely to private citizens', having found that 'under such circumstances nobody takes action' (ibid. 61). Consequently, it was proposed that 'The Registrar, on his own initiative and discretion and at public expense, may on his own authority institute and maintain an action against a candidate, political party, or third persons involved in any breach of the requirements of the proposed [Act]' (ibid.).

7. *Miscellaneous amendments to broadcasting legislation should be enacted to improve the political communications field* (ibid. 37). Several recommendations were made under this general head. One related to the ability of the parties to appeal for funds on the air. Regulations then in force appeared to prohibit such appeals for funds, 'a fact which struck the Committee as paradoxical' (ibid. 63–4), it having received no evidence to suggest that the community gained from regulations which inhibited the promotion of efforts to raise money for democratic purposes. It was recommended that the regulations should be revoked. It was also recommended that restrictions on the right of candidates to use foreign broadcasting stations in federal elections should be continued and extended to apply to political parties.

IV. The Chappell Committee

Seidle (1980: 185) has pointed out that no immediate action was taken on the Barbeau Committee's recommendations. Although the Committee reported in 1966, and although the Prime Minister said that it would be given 'top priority', in fact the government appeared to do nothing until the introduction of Bill C-211 in 1972, the details of which we discuss in Chapter 4. Indeed, the first real step towards legislation did not take place until October 1970 when a Special Committee on Election Expenses was set up by the House of Commons under the chairmanship of Mr Hyliard Chappell 'to consider the question of the limitation and control of election expenses in Canada and to report from time to time its observations and opinions thereon' (Chappell, 1971: 5). In the course of its work, the Committee held 49 sessions during which it took evidence from provincial legislators in Ontario, Nova Scotia, and Quebec; government officials; representatives of the three principal political parties; the Canadian Broadcasting Corporation; and the Canadian Labour Congress. The Chappell Committee had, however, initiated its study by considering the Barbeau Committee's proposals of 1966, and much of its analysis and presentation were concerned with an affirmation or rejection of them. The report of the Chappell Committee consisted of 53 recommendations, which it invited the government of Canada to incorporate in a bill 'to be presented for consideration of the House at the earliest possible date' (ibid. 9).

Chappell agreed with Barbeau about the need for the recognition and registration of parties (ibid. 11), which in any event had since been implemented by an amendment to the Canada Elections Act.[61] There was also agreement about the doctrine of agency, it being proposed also by Chappell that both candidates and political parties should appoint agents. The duties of the agent would include the receiving of all contributions, the payment of bills, the keeping of financial records, and the reporting of details of the candidate's or party's finances (ibid. 19). Reporting would not, however, be to a specially created Registry of Election and Political Finance, a proposal of Barbeau which Chappell rejected, recommending instead that the Chief Electoral Officer be solely responsible for the administration of any legislation in this area. Chappell explained that the 'two subjects, namely the conduct of elections, and the expenses of elections, are like the lyrics and music of a song, inseparable and inextricably intermingled' (ibid. 9), and continued by pointing out that if there were two officers, 'each . . . would in the first instance be constrained

---

[61] Canada Elections Act, RSC, c.14 (1st supp), s.13. Now Canada Elections Act, RSC 1985, c.14 (1st supp), s.24.

from acting exclusively on his own but would have to refer to the other; this would be a disadvantage in itself, without more. Further, notwithstanding their desire to co-operate, a genuine and intractable conflict of opinion could arise (for example, over the appropriateness of a new party's name . . .)' (ibid.). In the absence of a higher authority, asked Chappell, 'how would these conflicts of opinion be resolved?' (ibid.).

So far as Barbeau's second recommendation is concerned, Chappell endorsed the need for financial reimbursements of candidates' election expenses. A candidate would qualify for assistance if he or she was elected; or if he or she received 50% or more of the valid votes cast for the winning candidate; or if he or she received at least 20% of the total valid votes cast. Chappell was, however, more generous in its proposals than Barbeau, recommending a reimbursement not only for media expenses, but for all proven campaign expenses with a sum of 5 cents for every elector in the constituency up to 25,000 plus 3 cents for every elector over 25,000 (ibid. 25). So far as the parties are concerned, Chappell endorsed the proposal of free broadcasting time for the parties, but recommended $6\frac{1}{2}$ hours in place of Barbeau's 6. It was also recommended that the time would be allocated by the CBC, and that the broadcasting corporations would be entitled to a reimbursement of 50% of the costs, with the rest to be met by the companies themselves as a condition of their licence (ibid. 23). Like Barbeau, Chappell did not recommend any additional funds for the parties, but proposed that the possibility of other subsidies to parties should stand over for consideration at some later date (ibid.). So Barbeau's second recommendation met a broad measure of agreement, as did the third (the need to broaden the base of political contributions). Here, however, Chappell was more cautious. While agreeing that there should be no limit on the sources of funding, Chappell rejected a tax credit for donors on the ground that it would give political contributions an advantage over charitable contributions and would thus meet public resistance (ibid. 29). In its place, the Committee recommended that individuals and corporations should be able to claim as tax-deductible expenses annual and campaign contributions 'up to a maximum of 2% of their net income or One Thousand Dollars whichever is less' (ibid.). It is to be noted that unlike

Barbeau's report, which had proposed a tax credit for individual donors only, Chappell's proposed a tax-deductible expense for both individual and corporate donors.

A more serious disagreement between the two Committees took place on the fourth of Barbeau's recommendations, relating to the reducing of campaign costs. Chappell agreed that the parties should not spend money on broadcasting (ibid. 23), but disagreed strongly that there should be no general campaign spending limits. Barbeau had proposed that the only cash limits should be a limit on the media expenses of candidates. Chappell argued that 'imposing limitations on candidate's [*sic*] expenditures would not be as effective if limitations were not also imposed on parties' expenditures' (ibid. 21). Chappell thus proposed not segmental limits on candidates, but general limits on both candidates and parties. Thus, for candidates, the Committee recommended a limit of $1.00 per elector for the first 15,000 electors; 50 cents per elector from 15,001 to 25,000 electors; and 25 cents per elector over 25,000. For parties, the Committee recommended that a registered party should be allowed to spend only 30 cents per elector in the aggregate of the electoral districts in which the party had candidates (ibid.). In making these proposals, Chappell pointed out that total limits on election expenses had been imposed in Quebec and Nova Scotia. So far as the danger of evasion is concerned, Chappell argued that spending limits could be enforced by requiring candidates to supply reports audited by their own auditors. A candidate who wished to spend above the legal maximum and avoid penalty would have to deceive his auditor, deceive his agent, deceive the electorate in his constituency, and deceive his opponents in the electoral district. Nevertheless, the question of enforcement was one which had troubled Barbeau, and it is to be noted that Chappell had nothing to say about how the problems of evasion by the political parties could be monitored, and controlled.

Another major area of disagreement related to Barbeau's fifth principle. It is true that Chappell agreed with the need for reporting, recommending that the agents of candidates and parties should send to the Minister of National Revenue after an election all donors to whom a receipt for income tax purposes had been given. Unlike Barbeau, however, Chappell also proposed that this information should not be made public on the ground that public disclosure of the names of individual donors either to parties or to candidates would be counter-productive:

(1) it would discourage donors who would fear business or community repercussions;

(2) it would discourage business based donors who would anticipate that the published list would be used by other parties as a canvassing list and thus lead to requests for several times as many contributions. Eventually it would diminish rather than increase contributions;

(3) it would breach the principle of the secret ballot, since by extension a donor will be presumed to vote for the candidate or party he supported financially;

(4) if it is wrong, as the Barbeau Committee concluded, to disclose the name of individual donors to parties, then to require such disclosure of individual donors to candidates would upset the balance between parties and candidates because donors would naturally contribute to the parties rather than to the candidates;

(5) it would be an invasion of privacy;

(6) we believe that it is fallacious to require disclosure of the name of donors only above a specified limit, as for example $100. The reason is that such a scheme, as in the United States, inevitably invites circumvention. Using his wife a donor could double the contribution without disclosure, using his children he might quadruple it, and using his friends he might multiply it many times. Circumvention of such a limit is so simple that the scheme would easily be brought into ridicule. (ibid. 31)

Apart from this proposed duty to communicate with the Minister of National Revenue, Chappell also recommended an additional duty to report to the Chief Electoral Officer: after elections in the case of both parties and candidates as well as annually in the case of the parties. There would be, however, no duty to identify the individual donors, but otherwise the information required would be very similar to that which Barbeau recommended should be disclosed. In the case of political parties, for example, reporting of the following was recommended:

Receipts
(a) The total number of dollars received from private individuals.
(b) The total number of dollars received from private corporations.
(c) The total number of dollars received from public corporations.
(d) The total number of dollars received from trade unions and associations.
(e) The total number of donors in each category.
(f) The total number of dollars received from all sources.

Disbursements and Expenses
(a) Total financial assistance given by the national party to all candidates.
(b) Total financial assistance and value of other assistance given by the national party to provincial and regional party organization.
(c) The total amount expended by the national party in each of the mass media, radio, television and press, and printed brochures, etc.
(d) Total costs of travel for party leader and other officials.
(e) Total of administration costs.
(f) Total expenditures for all purposes. (Chappell, 1971: 31, 33)

It is presumed that Chappell had no objections to the public disclosure of this information, though the point is not clear.

As already pointed out, Chappell disagreed with Barbeau's sixth principle, the formation of a specially created Registry, with the view being taken that any new statute could properly be monitored and enforced by the Chief Electoral Officer. Apart from the arguments already considered, other practical considerations weighed heavily with Chappell. First, it was suggested that a second Act would have to incorporate many of the existing provisions of the Canada Elections Act, either by reference or by a repetition thereof. Secondly, it was pointed out that since Barbeau, the Canada Elections Act had been amended to require the parties to register with the Chief Electoral Officer. A new Registrar would require the parties to register with him too, and this would be bureaucratically unnecessary. The parties would have to register twice, on different forms, and the 'cumbersomeness' of such an arrangement 'could cause both administrative chaos and political criticism' (ibid. 9). The Committee recognized that there might, nevertheless, also be difficulties with an integrated procedure in the sense that 'it would be difficult for the Chief Electoral Officer to maintain the appearance of impartiality to candidates and parties if at the same time he is called upon to police the accuracy of their financial reports' (ibid. 13). It was believed, however, that this difficulty might be overcome by requiring the parties and candidates to file their own audited reports. These would be prepared and certified in the usual way by a chartered accountant or other licensed public accountant. The agents of the candidates and parties would be required to make available to their respective auditors all their vouchers, receipts, cheques, and other relevant documents relating to receipts and expenditures. Barbeau (1966: 58) had recommended that the proposed new Registrar should have responsibility for auditing financial reports, and had suggested the need for a new office on the basis that there was 'a clear division of duties and responsibilities between the office of Registrar and that of Chief Electoral Officer. The Chief Electoral Officer is responsible for the arrangements, the management and control of the official election machinery and procedure. The Registrar . . . would supervise the financial activities of the contending parties and candidates and their supporters as these bear on election campaigns.'

V. Conclusion

The two major developments in the preparation of legislation were thus the reports of the Barbeau and Chappell Committees. But although both recommended major reforms, the proposals differed in key respects. On some issues Barbeau was more radical, whereas on others this was true of Chappell. They agreed about the need for recognition and registration of political parties; about the doctrine of agency; and about the provision of free broadcasting time for the parties in election campaigns. But they disagreed on the form of tax incentives for political contributions, with Barbeau favouring a tax credit and Chappell a tax-deductible expense. They disagreed on disclosure, with Barbeau supporting full disclosure of donors, but Chappell recommending reporting of this information only to the Minister of National Revenue, the information not to be made public. And, apart also from disagreement on questions of enforcement, they disagreed on spending limits in election campaigns. This time, however, Barbeau was the more cautious, proposing only that there should be a limit on broadcasting expenses of candidates in contrast to the more sweeping recommendation of Chappell that there should be limits on the total permitted expenditure of both candidates and parties. In the end both of these documents proved influential, with the government being bound by neither but adopting parts of both. It is to a consideration of the form which the legislation took that we now turn. The influence of both Barbeau and Chappell will be readily apparent.

4

The Election Expenses Act 1974

BY June 1971, proposals for the reform of Canadian election finance laws were rather detailed, even if there were major differences between the competing reform packages. Political events dictated that one or other, or a combination of both, of these major packages would be implemented sooner rather than later, with the government eventually losing control over the pace of events. Thus, Flora MacDonald, a leading Progressive Conservative, was to claim that legislation was introduced, not because the government had voluntarily decided to clean up the Augean stable, but because politicians had been 'overtaken by events which have threatened the credibility of our political system'.[1] Pressure for reform was maintained by legislative activities in the provinces. Since the appointment and reporting of the Barbeau Committee in 1966, Nova Scotia,[2] Manitoba,[3] and Saskatchewan[4] had introduced reforms of their campaign finance legislation. The reforms included disclosure, limits on candidate and party campaign expenditures, and the reimbursement of candidate expenses. But pressure for reform was dictated by scandal, never far from the arena, with allegations that the Ontario Progressive Conservatives had given favours to corporations which had made substantial donations to party funds.[5] The allegations were serious enough to induce the Provincial Premier to refer the matter for investigation to a commission under the chairmanship of Dalton Camp.[6] More important perhaps was Watergate. Although it had nothing to do with Canada, it did not leave Ottawa untouched and appeared to contribute markedly to the alleged

---

[1] House of Commons Debates, 1st session, 29th Parliament, vol. v, 12 July 1973, p. 5563.
[2] An Act to amend Chapter 83 of the Revised Statutes, 1967, the Elections Act, NS, 18 Eliz. II, 1969, c.40.
[3] An Act to amend the Election Act, SM, 19 Eliz. II, 1970, c.150.
[4] Election Act, SS, 19 Eliz. II, 1971, c.10.
[5] See Ewing, 1989.
[6] Ibid.

public demands for legislation in Canada.[7] So to some extent Canadian federal politics were a vicarious victim of scandal elsewhere.

I. Bill C-211

The first major parliamentary initiative was the introduction of Bill C-211 on 18 May 1972 by Mr Allan MacEachen, the President of the Privy Council. The bill drew on both Barbeau and Chappell for its inspiration, though it disappointed many members of the House of Commons by making only a modest gesture in the direction of reform. In fact Bill C-211 was not passed, as the intervention of a general election frustrated its progress. It did, however, form the basis of the 1974 Act, though as we shall see the Act differed in crucial respects from what had been originally proposed by the Liberal government. This is because after the election the Liberals depended on NDP support in the House, with the result that the NDP was able to secure some concessions as the price of that support. It may be, however, that some if not all of the subsequent improvements would have been made anyway, as Mr MacEachen made it clear from the outset that the government was 'keeping an open mind in respect of the details of [the] bill'.[8] He conceded also that if 'persuasive arguments can be made and if gaps can be revealed in the bill', then he would be ready to accept changes to it.[9] And although the 1974 Act departed to some extent from Bill C-211, it did not depart from the basic principles of that bill, namely 'the limitation of election expenses, the disclosure of sources of contributions and the need for financial assistance by candidates and political parties',[10] while recognizing that in 'the modern world very large amounts of money are required to conduct election campaigns and to communicate effectively with the electorate'.[11]

---

[7] Seidle and Paltiel, 1981: 232. The authors also give an account of the other factors inducing reform.

[8] House of Commons Debates, 4th session, 28th Parliament, vol. iii, 18 May 1972, p. 2404.

[9] Ibid.

[10] Ibid. 2404–5 (Mr Allan MacEachen).

[11] Ibid. 2405.

So far as the limitation of election expenses is concerned, the government accepted that 'money and financial resources in the hands of any individual or any party should not be the deciding factor in elections', yet did not propose in Bill C-211 to assert full equality, but only 'to bring us closer to the objective of equality among candidates competing for public office'.[12] Thus, the bill was limited in two respects. First the term 'election expenses' was defined to mean only the cost of paid broadcasting time, paid press advertising, and other forms of paid advertising. The definition did not cover travelling expenses, the costs of nomination meetings, or the renting of halls, those being excluded because they were 'relatively static in nature and . . . have not been inordinate consumers of election campaign funds'.[13] The limit proposed was the same as that suggested by Chappell,[14] that is to say $1 per elector for the first 15,000 electors, plus 50 cents per elector for every elector over 15,000 and 25,000, and 25 cents per elector for each elector over 25,000. In other words, the limit would be $20,000 for the first 25,000 electors plus 25 cents for each elector over 25,000. But apart from limiting the range of expenses to which it applied, the bill proposed also to restrict its operation by confining the limits to candidate expenditures, not applying them to political party expenditures. The bill did, however, propose limits on the use of the broadcast media by political parties during an election campaign, the area where 'campaign spending by registered parties has escalated most notably in recent years'.[15] Thus, registered parties would be limited to $6\frac{1}{2}$ hours on any broadcast outlet during the election campaign. Mr MacEachen explained that this was not '$6\frac{1}{2}$ hours for each political party; the total $6\frac{1}{2}$ hours is to be shared by the registered parties' with the Canadian Radio-Television Commission (CRTC) to adjudicate any disputes as to the allocation of time.[16] The time would be paid time rather than free time as proposed by Barbean and Chappell. Beyond this limit, political

[12] House of Commons Debates, 4th session, 28th Parliament, vol. iii, 18 May 1972, p. 2404.
[13] Ibid.
[14] Though Chappell proposed that the limit would apply to all of a candidate's expenses and not only to advertising expenses.
[15] See 2406 n. 8.
[16] Ibid.

parties would not be permitted to buy time, but broadcasters who so wished could contribute additional time provided that it was offered to all parties on the same basis as the allocation of the prescribed $6\frac{1}{2}$ hours.

So far as disclosure is concerned, the government proposed that political parties should be obliged to disclose their sources of funds by category, that is to say, by corporations, trade unions, private individuals, and so on. There would, however, be no obligation to disclose the names of any individual donors; the government accepted the advice of both Barbeau and Chappell, yet contended also that

in obliging political parties on an annual basis and after an election to disclose by source their contributions in total dollars, by obliging the chief agent of the party to make a report to the Chief Electoral Officer, by obliging the party to have its accounts audited and confirmed that in the opinion of the auditor the accounts had been kept in accordance with the law, and by obliging the Chief Electoral Officer to make these accounts public we are going a long way in putting a searchlight on the activities of political parties. We are taking a very important step and I hope that members of all parties will realize its implications for the future of all political parties and the operation of their financing.[17]

Under the bill registered parties would be required to submit annually a return showing the amount of contributions made to it in that year by each of the different categories, together with the amount of money provided by the parties to provincial and regional organizations; the amount of money spent in operating expenses; and the total of all other expenditures. After an election campaign the parties would be required to submit a similar return with respect to contributions and expenditures made by the party during the election.

The third underlying principle of the bill was the provision of financial assistance to candidates and parties. This would be done in a number of ways. One would be by a rebate to candidates of a part of their permitted election expenses. So any candidate receiving 20% of the valid votes cast in the constituency would be entitled to 25% of 'proven and allowable election expenses defined in the act and certified in the audited report'.[18] The candidate would also receive a lump

[17] Ibid. 2407.
[18] Ibid. 2408.

sum of $250 to help meet the cost of the auditor's report. According to Mr MacEachen,

These payments are directed to assisting candidates for parliament to meet the basic requirements of communicating with the public, and since modern election campaigning is heavily dependent on the mass media with their very high costs, it becomes desirable that candidates should receive a degree of assistance in meeting these costs.[19]

Candidates would be assisted further by a requirement (which applied also to the parties) that broadcasters should charge the normal commercial rate and not raise their charges during an election campaign. In other words, 'the media [would] have to provide candidates with the lowest commercial rate'.[20] There would be a limited rebate for the expenses of political parties in the sense that one half of broadcasting expenditures would be met by the Chief Electoral Officer. It was also anticipated that the parties would be helped by the tax incentives for contributions to their funds. Thus, an individual or a corporation would be eligible annually for a tax credit of up to $500, or one-third of a maximum annual contribution of $1,500. This, it was hoped, would broaden the base of support and reduce the dependence on the large donors. The government preferred the Barbeau proposals for a tax credit rather than Chappell's suggestion for a tax deduction on the ground that 'it was in the interest of equality among taxpayers and better for our political system'.[21]

Although these principles found widespread support in the House, there was also considerable criticism of the government for the delay in introducing legislation[22] (Barbeau having been appointed in 1964). More significantly perhaps there was also considerable criticism of the proposals themselves for not going far enough, as a result of which many members were unable to support the bill. Indeed criticism came from all directions, including from Mr Hyliard Chappell, who argued for improvements to bring the bill into line with the recommendations contained in the Report of his Committee. Opposition came from

[19] House of Commons Debates, 4th session, 28th Parliament, vol. iii, 18 May 1972, p. 2404.
[20] Ibid.
[21] Ibid. 2409.
[22] Ibid. 2412.

other Progressive Conservatives, with the leader of the Opposition (Robert L. Stanfield) supporting 'with great zeal' the case for public subsidies for candidate expenses, but unable to support such a proposal which was not tied to a ceiling on the total permitted expenses of candidates. The principal Conservative critic, Mr Heath Macquarrie, was troubled by the fact that there was not yet 'anything like a limitation on what the parties will be spending' and also by the fact that the bill failed to 'take advantage of present day advances in the mass media and transportation which would provide for a shorter election period and thereby, amongst other things, substantially reduce election expenses'. The Social Credit criticism was perhaps more fundamental. Mr René Matte contended that the candidate spending limits were too high, contrasting the low expenditure of Social Credit candidates with that of Liberals, and suggesting that no member of the House should be elected because 'money made up for his lack of personal qualities'.[23] Secondly, he argued that broadcasting time should be allocated equally or almost equally between the parties, and that similar restrictions should be extended to the press. Concern about the broadcasting allocation was expressed also by Mr Roland Godin, who objected to allocation of time by the CRTC and argued for equality between the parties, anticipating that the government's proposals would lead to the Social Credit Party of Canada being unable to get more than half an hour of broadcasting time—a 'blatant injustice' in his view.[24] The third concern of the Social Credit Party, as expressed by Matte, also related to broadcasting. In his view, 'when election time comes, all of [the broadcasting stations] should make free air time available to the candidates. If those periods cannot be had free of charge, then they should be reimbursed fully and not only to the extent of 50 % as provided for in the bill.'[25]

The most wide-ranging criticism was left, however, to the several NDP speakers in the debate. Essentially, this party's comments tended to cluster around three issues. The first was the failure to propose a limit on the general expenses of

[23] Ibid., 19 May 1972, p. 2435.
[24] Ibid., 25 May 1972, p. 2577.
[25] Ibid., 19 May 1972, p. 2435.

political parties, as had been proposed by Chappell. According to Mr Les Benjamin, this omission 'nullifies the whole purpose of legislation to limit and control election expenses',[26] while Stanley Knowles asked 'What earthly use is there in saying that a candidate in an election can spend only so much money, if the provincial or national party behind that candidate can spend on his behalf without limit?'[27] Andrew Brewin attacked in similar terms, asserting that everyone 'knows that major expenditures in an election are made by political parties and not individual candidates. Everybody knows that the major scandals in the history of Canada in this field are related to political parties and not individual candidates. I suggest this is a gap which must be filled if parliament is to be able to say it has grasped the subject and dealt with it adequately.'[28] The party leader, David Lewis, also joined the fray, arguing that 'There is no reason why we cannot enforce a limit on party expenditures, unless we assume that the political parties in this country are thoroughly dishonest, will not obey the law and will find ways of evading it when they can.'[29] NDP spokesmen were equally scathing in their criticisms of the disclosure provisions. Thus, while accepting the difficulties associated with full disclosure, Stanley Knowles argued 'very strongly' that 'in terms of the effective working of democracy those problems are minor compared with the problems that are created by a situation in which powerful corporations can make sizeable contributions to the parties of their choice, knowing that there need be no public disclosure of those contributions'.[30] He continued by asserting that proper disclosure requirements would ensure that the people of the country were 'much more free and able to make their decision as to which party should be given support at election time'.[31] John Burton went even further, claiming that one active corporate participant in a provincial Liberal Party was coincidentally a major beneficiary of federal treasury support. This led Burton to claim that until

[26] House of Commons Debates, 4th session, 28th Parliament, vol. iii, 18 May 1972, p. 2413.
[27] Ibid., 25 May 1972, p. 2569.
[28] Ibid., 19 May 1972, p. 2439.
[29] Ibid., 7 June 1972, p. 2950.
[30] Ibid., 25 May 1972, p. 2570.
[31] Ibid. 2570–1.

'we deal with the problem of identifying contributions, no matter by whom they are made, to political campaigns and political parties I suggest that we will not obtain effective legislation in the field of election expenses'.[32] He wanted it 'made known what contributions are made by corporations and the role they are playing behind the scenes in the electoral process'.[33]

A third target of NDP criticism was the reimbursement proposal, the attack being led chiefly by Les Benjamin, who had been on the Chappell Committee. In his view the government's proposal would be of more benefit 'to the well-heeled candidate; the poor candidate benefits least'. In the first place, he argued that the requirement that a candidate poll 20% of the vote as a condition of eligibility was too high, though it was consistent with the Chappell recommendations. Benjamin had unsuccessfully tried to persuade that Committee to reduce the threshold to 10% on the ground that such a candidate 'is not a nuisance candidate and should be entitled to some reimbursement'.[34] Secondly, Benjamin was concerned also with the nature of the scheme proposed by the government and the manner of its deviation from the Chappell recommendations. Under the Committee's proposals, it would have been possible for a candidate without means to have claimed a full rebate of election expenses provided he or she received 20% of the vote and kept within the limit of the rebate. For under the Committee's proposal a qualifying candidate would be entitled to 5 cents per elector (plus 3 cents for those in excess of $25,000) provided only that he or she actually spent this amount.[35] The effect would be to reward low-spending candidates by providing them with what could well be a 100% rebate. In contrast the government's proposals effectively rewarded the higher-spending candidate to the extent that no more that 25% of permitted expenses would be rebated, regardless of how frugal the candidate may have been. Benjamin commended the Committee's proposals over those of the government on the ground

[32] Ibid., 19 May 1972, p. 2443.
[33] Ibid. 2442.
[34] Ibid. 2414.
[35] Ibid.

67

that the former maximize 'fair play' and equalize 'the fight between candidates who have little or no financial resources and those who have all the resources they need'.[36]

II. Election Expenses Act 1974

Bill C-211 died on the order paper when the 28th Parliament was dissolved in September 1972. A year later, however, the minority Liberal government had another go, in Bill C-203, introduced after negotiations with the NDP, on whose support the new government relied to stay in office. Bill C-203 contained many of the proposals contained previously in Bill C-211, though it also incorporated major changes. Chief amongst these were the requirement for full disclosure and the imposition of a ceiling on campaign spending by political parties—both of which had previously been demanded by the NDP. There was thus some substance in the MacEachen's claims that Bill C-203 represented 'probably the most comprehensive attempt at the reform of electoral expenditures undertaken so far in Canada',[37] and indeed that it would give Canada 'one of the most democratic and open electoral systems in the world'.[38] So why had the government embraced radical new ideas which it had appeared to eschew only twelve months earlier? According to Mr MacEachen,

There are several reasons for the significant changes between the old and the present bill. The discussion of election spending which took place during the last Parliament produced worthwhile suggestions from all parties which the government accepted in drafting the new bill. In addition, public demand for greater disclosure of the financial affairs of political parties has increased since the original bill was introduced.[39]

So the government was responding to proposals made in Parliament by opposition speakers, and also to the weight of

[36] House of Commons Debates, 4th session, 28th Parliament, vol. iii, 18 May 1972, p. 2414.
[37] House of Commons Debates, 1st session, 29th Parliament, vol. v, 10 July 1973, p. 5476.
[38] Ibid.
[39] Ibid.

public opinion. Mr David Lewis, the leader of the NDP, had a different explanation.

Mr Lewis had no doubt that the contents of the bill were a direct result of the composition of the House in the new Parliament:

The vast improvements in the present bill cannot be due to anything but the fact that the government is not a majority government, that it has to pay attention to the opposition parties and their views on this matter, and that the government knew and the President of the Privy Council knew from conversations with me throughout the last number of months . . . that the kind of things which at least my party would insist on in any such bill were the elements which I . . . am happy to find in this legislation.[40]

(He was referring here particularly to disclosure and to the limits on elections expenses.) But although it appeared to win the battle of principle, this is not to say that the NDP was satisfied with all aspects of the detail. Lewis himself expressed objections about the proposal that there should be full disclosure only for donations in excess of $100, the NDP taking the view that there should be full disclosure regardless of the amount of the contribution. Similarly, he was concerned that the limit on expenditures was set too high, with a party and its candidates being permitted to spend in total between $7 million and $8 million, the party alone being permitted about $4.5 million. And thirdly, the NDP renewed its concern that the conditions for claiming a rebate of election expenses by candidates were still too high, the government not having moved from its original position that a rebate should be paid only to those candidates who polled 20% of the votes. In the view of Mr Lewis, the only logical and moral justification for saying that not every candidate is entitled to this privilege is to keep out 'freak and nuisance' candidates—people who are candidates only because they want to get their names in the newspaper or on a ballot.[41] But if money is to be paid from the public treasury to serious candidates, then it should be paid to all serious candidates, and 10% of the vote was a sufficient indication of a candidate's merit, in view of the fact that this

[40] Ibid., 12 July 1973, p. 5553.
[41] Ibid. 5555.

means the candidate would be attracting 3,000 to 4,000 votes depending on the size of the constituency.

Despite these reservations, the NDP supported the bill and sought its speedy passage. The bill also had the support of the Conservatives, whose leading spokesman said that its principles were 'acceptable' and that they too hoped for a speedy passage, emphasizing that the measure was not the 'particular and private preserve'[42] of the NDP. The Conservatives appeared annoyed by the successes of the NDP. Thus, Flora MacDonald, who also spoke in the debate, referred to 'the mood of euphoria which [had] characterized [the] debate so far',[43] the 'self-congratulatory mood, evident on all sides of the House, almost smug in its assertion of virtue', this nowhere 'more evident'[44] than in the remarks of David Lewis. But although the Conservatives also accepted the principles of Bill C-203 they too had questions and reservations. One related to the disclosure requirements, a similar concern being expressed by the NDP. As already pointed out, it was proposed that disclosure should be limited to donations of $100. It was claimed that 'a corporation wishing to make a major donation to a political party could easily evade the disclosure provision by acting at arm's length and making lesser donations to a number of people'.[45] The same spokesman asserted that 'contributions could be funnelled through employees, through subsidiaries of the company or through national associations. Indeed, there are a number of ways in which the disclosure provisions could be evaded.'[46] In fact, the Conservatives were concerned with questions of enforcement generally, contending strongly that the bill must be capable of effective enforcement, effectively administered, with loopholes blocked. For this reason the party appeared attracted to the idea of enforcement by a registrar of election finances 'whose functions would be somewhat similar to those of the Auditor-General: he would police election financing'.[47]

[42] House of Commons Debates, 1st session, 29th Parliament, vol. v, 10 July 1973, p. 5479.
[43] Ibid., 12 July 1973, p. 5563.
[44] Ibid.
[45] Ibid., 10 July 1973, p. 5480.
[46] Ibid.
[47] Ibid.

This concern about enforcement was expressed most strongly by Flora MacDonald, who said:

There is one final matter I would like to raise. Our sincerity as members of parliament in this matter will be judged by our willingness to enforce this legislation. Surely none of us is so naïve as to think that the spirit and letter of the present bill will be universally adhered to unless extraordinary ways are devised for enforcing them. The history of successful violations of many important features of income tax legislation, or in the field of industrial relations—and notably by the more powerful and affluent sections of the population—suggests that the best legal and accounting minds could be utilized to enable those who can afford them to ingeniously evade the intent of this legislation. It is therefore essential, if we are really serious about this undertaking, that we create at once a mechanism for the automatic, continuous and free review of the implementation of these measures.

At the same time—and the two tasks could be performed by the same person and his staff—we ought to establish an electoral ombudsman responsible directly to parliament to whom breaches, irregularities or simply actions contrary to the spirit of the act will be reported. This official should have powers to investigate and report on any developments or incidents deemed by him to impede the full implementation of the basic intentions of Bill C-203. The field of inquiry should be so defined as to permit investigation into areas not explicitly covered by the present act, such as, for example, the unfair use of government advertising, or activities by business, industries or unions constituting, in effect, electioneering although technically outside the scope of the proposed measures.[48]

So here we have a wide agreement between the three principal parties as to content, with debate about points of detail. On these the government gave little away. It is to a consideration of some of the more significant aspects of the bill that we now turn. Amending legislation was introduced in 1977 and 1983 and this will be taken into account where appropriate.

1. DISCLOSURE

The first principle of the 1974 Act is 'full and complete disclosure of revenues and expenditures of political parties and

---

[48] Ibid., 12 July 1973, p. 5564.

candidates'.[49] In fact, all the Canadian jurisdictions which have legislated on campaign funding have adopted some system of mandatory disclosure of funds by the parties. The federal legislation requires the chief agent of a registered political party to transmit to the Chief Electoral Officer each year a return of the party's receipts and expenses[50] (other than election expenses for which a separate return must be made[51]). The return must set out the amount of money and the commercial value of goods and services provided for the use of the party by way of loan, advance, deposit, contribution, or gift by each of the following classes of donors: individuals, businesses, commercial organizations, governments, trade unions, corporations without share capital, and unincorporated associations. In addition, the agent must disclose the number of contributors in each of these categories, and perhaps more importantly, the name of every contributor of more than $100 in the contribution period. So far as candidates are concerned, a similar obligation lies on the official agent of the candidate, to transmit to the Returning Officer a copy of the election receipts and expenses, again with the names of those who donated more than $100.[52] All the information is open to public inspection.[53]

2. GOVERNMENT ASSISTANCE

The second principle of the 1974 Act is 'government assistance in meeting the cost of election campaigns'.[54] This has taken three forms. One was to use the income tax system to stimulate donations to the parties. Attempts to encourage donations by

[49] House of Commons Debates, 1st session, 29th Parliament, vol. v, 12 July 1973, p. 5478.
[50] Election Expenses Act, SC 1973–4, c.51, s.4, amending the Canada Elections Act, RSC, c.14 (1st Supp), by inserting a new s.13.4. Now Canada Elections Act, RS 1985, c.14 (1st Supp), s.44.
[51] Election Expenses Act, ibid., s.4, inserting a new 13.5 of the Canada Elections Act, ibid. Now Canada Elections Act, RS 1985, c.14 (1st Supp), s.46.
[52] Election Expenses Act, SC 1973–4, c.51, s.9, amending the Canada Elections Act, RSC, c.14 (1st Supp), s.63. Now Canada Elections Act, RS 1985, c.14 (1st Supp), s.228.
[53] Ibid., s.6, amending the Canada Elections Act, ibid., s.60(7). Now Canada Elections Act, RS 1985, c.14 (1st Supp), s.197.
[54] House of Commons Debates, 1st session, 29th Parliament, vol. v., 10 July 1973, p. 5478.

using the income tax system are now a common feature of party financing legislation throughout Canada. In adopting this device in federal law the drafter of the 1974 Act favoured an approach based on the Barbeau recommendations in preference to the more cautious approach of Chappell. As enacted, the 1974 Act amended the Income Tax Act[55] to permit a taxpayer to deduct from tax otherwise payable the following amounts in respect of political contributions:

- 75% of the value of the donation, if the donation does not exceed $100;
- $75 plus 50% of the amount by which the donation exceeds $100 but does not exceed $550; and
- $300 plus $33\frac{1}{3}$% of the amount by which the donation exceeds $550.

The maximum relief permitted in any one year was $500. For the purpose of calculating the amount of a donation, it is the aggregate of all contributions in the year which is taken into account rather than each individual donation. In order to prevent abuse, the Act also provides that all donations must be made through an agent. Moreover, every agent (of parties and candidates) shall keep records and books of account, including duplicates of all receipts for contributions. Agents are then required to submit returns to Revenue Canada, together with duplicates of all receipts of contributions held by them.

A second form of government assistance in the 1974 Act is the reimbursement of candidates' election expenses, the Act adopting the Chappell recommendation of reimbursement for all election expenses rather than the Barbeau proposal for a reimbursement of media expenses only. The Act was, however, rather more generous than Chappell in several respects. First, entitlement would depend on polling 15% of the valid votes cast, and not 20% as proposed by Chappell and indeed by the government in its earlier Bill C-211. And secondly, the amount of the rebate was larger than anticipated by the Commons Committee. Thus, a candidate would be entitled to the aggregate

[55] Election Expenses Act, SC 1973–4, c.51, s.19 amending Income Tax Act, RSC 1952, c.148 by inserting a new s.126.1. Section 126.1 was repealed by Income Tax Act, SC 1974–1975–1976, c.26, s.84(1). A similar measure was reintroduced by the same Act (s.85(2)), this becoming s.127(3) of the Income Tax Act.

of (i) the postage costs of mailing one item (not exceeding one ounce) by first class mail to each person appearing on the list of electors in the constituency; (ii) 8 cents for each of the first 25,000 names appearing on the list; and (iii) 6 cents for each name in excess of 25,000 appearing on the list.[56] If, however, the candidate spent less than this aggregate amount, he or she would be entitled to be reimbursed only for the amount actually spent. A slightly varied procedure operated for candidates in large isolated constituencies where electoral costs are correspondingly greater. In 1983 the method of calculating the rebate was changed. Under the law as it now stands, a candidate who polls at least 15% of the vote is entitled to a rebate of 50% of his or her election expenses, provided that this does not exceed the maximum permitted expenses under the Act. The payment is made to the candidate's agent by the Receiver General. A payment is also made direct to the candidate's auditor, the payment not to exceed the lesser of $750 and 3% of the candidate's election expenses.

3. REGULATING A SCARCE RESOURCE[57]

As originally passed, the 1974 Act introduced a number of important reforms to political broadcasting.[58] In the first place, it required the broadcasting authorities to set aside $6\frac{1}{2}$ hours of prime broadcasting time for allocation between the parties in the period one month or so before the date of the election. The time would be allocated between the parties following agreement with the Canadian Radio-Television Commission. If the parties were unable to agree, the Commission would impose an allocation of time. The time so allocated would be paid time, but it would be an offence for a television company to charge more than the normal commercial rate for each of the participants. Moreover, and very importantly, the parties would

---

[56] Election Expenses Act, SC 1973–4, c.51, s.10, amending Canada Elections Act, RSC 1970, c.14 (1st Supp) by inserting a new s.63.1. Now Canada Elections Act, RS 1985, c.14 (1st Supp), ss.241–7.

[57] For a fuller analysis of the broadcasting arrangements, see LaCalamita, 1984.

[58] Election Expenses Act, SC 1973–4, c.51, s.14, amending Canada Elections Act, RSC, c.14 (1st Supp) by inserting a new s.99.1.

be entitled to a rebate of 50% of the cost of the broadcasting time.[59] In addition to the $6\frac{1}{2}$ hours allocated and regulated in this way, the Act also imposed a duty on every broadcaster carrying on a network operation to make available free broadcasting time to the parties, the time being allocated on the basis of the agreement or imposition worked out for the paid time.[60] The amount of time in aggregate to be devoted for this purpose was to be determined after consultation between the registered parties and the CRTC. The use of the free time facility (unlike the expenses on the $6\frac{1}{2}$ hours allocation) would not constitute an election expense for the purposes of the limit on election expenses discussed below.[61]

This general framework is still in force, though the legislation so far as it relates to broadcasting was the subject of important and far-reaching reforms in the 1983 amendments.[62] The major change introduced by the 1983 Act was the creation of a Broadcasting Arbitrator, to be appointed by the Chief Electoral Officer. In making this appointment, the CEO must convene a meeting of the representatives of the parties represented in the House of Commons and if the representatives are unanimous as to the choice of arbitrator, the person in question must be appointed by the CEO. The first arbitrator was Mr Charles Dalfen of Ottawa, appointed with the unanimous approval of the representatives of the parties (Chief Electoral Officer of Canada, 1984), and given the task by statute to allocate broadcasting time, taking over the work done initially by CRTC. This means that if the parties are unable to agree on how time is to be allocated, the Arbitrator must make the allocation between them. In making this provision, the arbitrator is required to have regard not only to the number of seats which any party has, but also to the share of the popular vote which it attracted at the previous general election.[63] The first allocation under the 1983 amendment was made in 1984 in respect of the general

[59] Election Expenses Act, ibid., s.14, inserting a new s.99.2 to the Canada Elections Act.
[60] 1974 Act, s.14, inserting a new s.99.1(18) to the Canada Elections Act.
[61] Ibid., inserting a new s.99.1(20).
[62] An Act to amend the Canada Elections Act (No.3), SC 1980–1981–1982–1983, c.164, s.17. Now Canada Elections Act, RS 1985, c.14 (1st Supp), ss.303–22.
[63] Ibid.

election of that year and was unanimously agreed by the parties (Chief Electoral Officer of Canada, 1984: 82), though it did not strictly follow the guidelines, which would otherwise have led to a rather different outcome. The time was in fact allocated as follows: Liberal Party of Canada (183 minutes); Progressive Conservative Party of Canada (129 minutes); NDP (69 minutes); Parti Rhinocéros (8 minutes); Communist Party of Canada (5.5 minutes); and Libertarian Party of Canada (5.5 minutes) (ibid. 86).

Apart from the creation of the Broadcasting Arbitrator, the 1983 Act introduced three other amendments of considerable importance. The first is the provision of broadcasting time for new political parties, which are entitled to either 6 minutes or a lesser amount equal to the lowest allocation of an established party.[64] In 1984 this meant that new parties (of which there were five including the Green Party of Canada and the Pro-Life Party of Canada) were entitled to 5.5 minutes, the same as had been allocated to the Communist Party and the Libertarian Party (Chief Electoral Officer of Canada, 1984: 86). The second change related to the reimbursement for broadcasting expenses. Under the old arrangements, as we have seen, the parties were entitled to half of their costs. Under the new arrangements— which will exclude many small parties from the subsidy—a party will be eligible for reimbursement only if it spends more than 10% of its permitted maximum under the Act. If it does spend above this level, it will be entitled to a rebate of 22.5% of its total election expenses rather than 50% of broadcasting expenses.[65] The third change relates to the free broadcasting time, the major feature of the new law being the fact that the discretion under which the facility is to be made available is slightly more closely structured. Under the 1983 Act, the broadcasters are to make available in total at least the same amount of time as they made available at the previous election. At least two minutes must be allocated to any party which did not want any allocation of the paid time, with the remainder being allocated to those parties requesting paid time.[66] The allocation

[64] An Act to amend the Canada Elections Act (No.3), SC 1980–1981–1982–1983, c.164, s.17. Now Canada Elections Act, RS 1985, c.14 (1st Supp), ss.303–22.
[65] Ibid.
[66] Ibid.

TABLE 2. *Allocation of free broadcasting time in the federal election, 1984* (minutes)

Federal Party	Television	Radio
Liberal	87.0	49.7
Progressive Conservative	64.9	37.1
NDP	34.7	19.8
Rhinocéros	4.9	2.3
Communist	2.75	1.6
Libertarian	2.75	1.6
Pro-Life	2.75	1.6
Green	2.75	1.6
Confederation of Regions Western	2.75	1.6
United Canada Concept	2.75	1.6
L'Action des Hommes d'affaires	2.75	1.6
TOTAL*	210	120

* As given in source.

Source: Chief Electoral Officer of Canada, 1984: 89.

of the free time is to be on the basis of the principles worked out for the paid time. The allocation of free time in the 1984 general election is shown in Table 2.

4. ELECTION EXPENSES

Apart from the requirement of disclosure, and the provision of government assistance with campaign costs, the third principal feature of the 1974 Act is the 'limit on the expenditures by candidates and parties'.[67] On this point the legislation owes more to Chappell than to Barbeau. Expenses are curbed first by imposing a limit on the time within which some forms of campaigning may take place.[68] Essentially, in the period after the writ is issued (which may be up to fifty days before

[67] House of Commons Debates, 1st session, 29th Parliament, vol. v, 10 July 1973, p. 5478.

[68] Election Expenses Act (*supra* n. 50) s.4, amending Canada Elections Act (*supra* n. 50), by inserting a new s.13.7. Now Canada Elections Act, RS 1985, c.14 (1st Supp), s.48.

the election) the parties and candidates may only campaign in the broadcasting media beginning the twenty-ninth day before polling day. Secondly, during the period of a campaign (defined to run from the issue of the writ), a limit was imposed on the permitted election expenses of both candidates and parties.[69] So far as candidates are concerned, as originally enacted, they were permitted to spend the aggregate of $1 for each of the first 15,000 names appearing on the electoral roll in the constituency in question; 50 cents for each name in excess of 15,000 but not in excess of 25,000; and 25 cents for each name in excess of 25,000 electors. The limits have since been increased. The level of the increase is directed by the consumer price index, a similar device being employed for the limits on the permitted expenditure of the political parties.[70]

Here too limits were introduced in 1974—and here too they were general limits applying to all election expenditure rather than segmental limits applying to some aspects of election expenditure. The Act now provides as follows:

39(1) The chief agent of any registered party that, through registered agents acting within the scope of their authority, or other persons acting on behalf of the registered party with the actual knowledge and consent of an officer thereof, incurs election expenses on account of or in respect of the conduct or management of an election that exceed in the aggregate the product obtained by multiplying

(a) the product obtained by multiplying thirty cents by the number of names appearing on all preliminary lists of electors at the election for the electoral districts in which there is an official candidate who has the endorsement of the party,

by

(b) the fraction published by the Chief Electoral Officer pursuant to subsection (2) that is in effect on the date of the issue of the writ for the election

is guilty of an offence.

---

[69] Election Expenses Act (*supra* n. 50), s.4, amending Canada Elections Act (*supra* n. 50), by inserting a new s.13.2 (party limits) and Election Expenses Act, s.7, amending Canada Elections Act, by inserting a new s.61.1 (candidate limits). Now Canada Elections Act, RS 1985, c.14 (1st Supp), ss.39 and 208.

[70] An Act to amend the Canada Elections Act (No. 3), SC 1980–1981–1982–1983, c.164, ss.2 and 8, amending ss.13.2 and 61.1 of the Canada Elections Act respectively. Now Canada Elections Act, RS 1985, c.14 (1st Supp), ss.39 and 208 respectively.

Section 39(2) deals with the publication of the fraction which is calculated in accordance with s.39(3). This in turn provides:

(3) The fraction determined under this subsection is the fraction of which

(a) the numerator is the average of the Consumer Price Index, as published by Statistics Canada under the authority of the *Statistics Act*, for the twelve month period ending December 31 of the year immediately preceding the calendar year during which the fraction is to commence to be in effect, calculated on the basis of 1981 being equal to 100;

and

(b) the denominator is 88.9, being the Consumer Price Index, as published by Statistics Canada under the authority of the *Statistics Act*, for 1980 calculated on the basis of 1981 being equal to 100.

An important question which relates to both of these limits is to determine what is meant by an election expense. And here we find that the term is widely defined in the Act to include not only amounts paid and liabilities incurred, but also the commercial value of goods and services donated or provided (other than volunteer labour).[71] This is an important provision which prevents the limits being out-manœuvred by donors making gifts in kind to parties and candidates. Also important for this reason is the additional provision which deals with the situation where goods and services are provided at less than their commercial value. Thus, the definition of election expense is wide enough to catch any difference between the commercial value of goods and services and the amount actually charged. On the other hand, however, considerable difficulty is caused by the fact that an election expense is limited to expenses incurred only after the writ has been issued (which may not exceed fifty days before the election) 'for the purpose of promoting or opposing, directly and during an election, a particular registered party, or the election of a particular candidate'.[72] This is a measure which has caused a great deal of uncertainty and has given rise to fears that much of the potential impact of

---

[71] Election Expenses Act (*supra* n. 50), s.2, amending Canada Elections Act (*supra* n. 50). The definition was modified by the 1983 Act. Now Canada Elections Act, RS 1985, c.14 (1st Supp), s.2.

[72] Ibid.

the Act is lost by a very narrow reading of such a profoundly unhelpful definition. This is something to which we return in Chapter 8.[73]

Perhaps the most controversial question under the 1974 Act has been the problem of so-called independent expenditures. These are the expenditures incurred during a campaign, not by the parties but by individuals or organizations in support of the party or candidate, sometimes with consent and approval, sometimes not. The difficulty had been anticipated by the Barbeau Committee, which drew attention to the fact that 'many corporations, trade unions, professional and other groups take a lively interest in political activity and political education' (Barbeau, 1966: 50). Although it had no desire to stifle this activity, the Committee was troubled that if such groups were allowed to campaign actively in an election, any limits on the political parties or candidates would become meaningless. Reference was made to experience in the United States where 'ad hoc Committees such as "Friends of John Smith" or "Supporters of John Doe" commonly spring up to support a candidate or party', and concern was expressed that such Committees 'make limitation on expenditures an exercise in futility, and render meaningless the reporting of election expenses by parties and candidates'. As a result, Barbeau recommended that

No groups or bodies other than registered parties and nominated candidates be permitted to purchase radio and television time, or to use paid advertising in newspapers, periodicals or direct mailing, posters or billboards, in support of, or opposition to, any party or candidate, from the date of the issuance of the election writ until the day after polling day. (Ibid.)

It was not proposed by this to restrict normal news and public affairs reporting on television or in the newspapers.

The 1974 Act gave effect to this recommendation[74] in what became s.70.1(1) of the Canada Elections Act by providing that:

(1) Every one, other than
    (a) a candidate, official agent or any other person acting on behalf

---

[73] See pp.218–220.
[74] Election Expenses Act, SC 1973–4, c.51, s.12.

of a candidate with the candidate's actual knowledge and consent, or

(b) a registered agent of a registered party acting within the scope of his authority as such or other person acting on behalf of a registered party with the actual knowledge and consent of an officer thereof,

who, between the date of the issue of the writ for an election and the day immediately following polling day, incurs election expenses is guilty of an offence against this Act.

So it was an offence for anyone other than a candidate or party to spend money in a campaign. The section then provided (by s.70.1(4)) a very important defence to a charge under s.70.1(1):

(4) Notwithstanding anything in this section, it is a defence to any prosecution of a person for an offence against this Act that is an offence by virtue of subsection (1), if that person establishes that he incurred election expenses in the period described in subsection (1)

(a) for the purpose of gaining support for views held by him on an issue of public policy, or for the purpose of advancing the aims of any organization or association, other than a political party or an organization or association of a partisan political character, of which he was a member and on whose behalf the expenses were incurred; and

(b) in good faith and not for any purpose related to the provisions of this Act limiting the amount of election expenses that may be incurred by any other person on account of or in respect of the conduct or management of an election.

The defence was clearly an attempt to strike a balance between the need to protect the integrity of the legislation from being undermined on the one hand and the right of free expression on the other.

The attempt failed in the sense that it was very difficult successfully to use s.70.1 to regulate the activities of third parties. The leading case is *R. v. Roach*[75] where the accused was the president of local 767 of the Ontario Housing Corporation Employees' Union, which was affiliated to the Canadian Union of Public Employees. On behalf of his local, Roach hired an aeroplane to fly over the Ottawa area towing a banner which

[75] Unreported, 24 Oct. 1977 (Judge H. E. Zimmerman)

read 'O.H.C. Employees 767 C.U.P.E. vote but not Liberal'. The banner was towed on 17 October 1976, two days before a by-election for the electoral district of Ottawa–Carleton. The simple question then was whether these facts disclosed an offence under s.70.1, it being found that Roach was not acting with the consent of a candidate or a political party. The answer was equally simple, it being held by the Provincial Court, Criminal Division, that the conduct was covered by s.70.1(4). Thus, the Court accepted that the aim of the union by incurring this expenditure was to oppose the Anti-Inflation Programme and that the method employed was 'to attract publicity for the purpose of advancing those aims'. In addition, it was held that because Roach had no contact with candidates or their agents, he had incurred the expense in good faith. As a result it became unnecessary to consider whether the section violated the protection of freedom of expression in the Bill of Rights on the ground that as interpreted the Act did not limit the right of people in such circumstances to express their opinions on matters of public policy. The decision was upheld on appeal,[76] with the appeal court accepting that the defendant was clearly expressing the views of his association on an issue of public policy. The appeal court also accepted that Roach had acted in good faith, for 'while his motives [were] not entirely unassailable', the provisions of the Canada Elections Act were 'penal in character and motives cannot be given the same force and effect as intent'.[77]

This provision of the statute, as interpreted by the judges, gave rise to considerable practical difficulty. In his Statuory Report for 1979 the Chief Electoral Officer reported that at the 1979 election a large number of requests were received from people seeking interpretations of s.70.1, with twenty-one complaints regarding persons, organizations, or associations who were causing advertisements to be disseminated that promoted or opposed a particular candidate or political party (Chief Electoral Officer of Canada, 1979a: 26). Inquiries conducted by the CEO revealed that each advertisement contained a refer-

---

[76] *R.* v. *Roach* (1980) 101 DLR (3d) 736.
[77] Ibid., at p. 742.

ence to one or more issues of public policy. In addition, no evidence could be found of any collusion between the political parties or the candidates and the advertisers, who in the view of the Officer seemed to be acting in good faith. As a result the CEO had to conclude that the alleged offenders were entitled to the defence which s.70.1(4) of the Act provided so that no legal action could be taken. Indeed the CEO was moved to complain that the wide freedom permitted to third parties under the Act (when the political parties and candidates were rightly controlled) was 'anomalous and, if permitted to continue, could weaken considerably efforts to control election expenses' (ibid.). The general election in 1980 gave rise to similar difficulties, with a large number of requests again being received from persons seeking guidance on the interpretation of s.70.1 as well as a number of complaints (Chief Electoral Officer of Canada, 1980a: 19). In 1980, however, two cases of alleged violation were referred to the police for investigation, but no action was taken in any of the others because it was expected that s.70.1(4) could be successfully invoked.

The 1980 election reinforced the CEO's previously expressed views about s.70.1 of the Act, and indeed in 1980 he again invited Parliament to consider this question (ibid. 22), which it did with an amendment to s.70.1 being contained in the 1983 Act. In his Statutory Report for that year the CEO considers s.70.1 again, though it was published after the bill (Bill C-169) received the Royal Assent. The Officer pointed out, however, that 'a number of persons who were not acting on behalf of or with the knowledge and consent of candidates or registered agents of political parties have availed themselves of [s.70.1(4)] during past elections' (Chief Electoral Officer of Canada, 1983: 74). He continued by pointing out that these 'people have spent unlimited sums of money to promote or oppose a particular candidate or registered party, sums which they do not have to account for in terms of sources or amount' (ibid.). To deal with this problem, the CEO made two proposals. The first is that 'persons who are not acting on behalf of candidates or political parties should be bound by the same rules during an election as are the candidates and the political parties' (ibid.). This would mean that:

— individuals and organizations, or associations of a non-political character, would be free to contribute funds or services to official candidates and parties of their choice;
— they could register as a party and nominate candidates dedicated to the aims of their organizations;
— individuals and organizations could obtain written authority from candidates or parties to incur election expenses on their behalf, the said expenses being chargeable against the expenditures of the candidate or the party. (ibid.)

The second proposal was for the repeal of subsection 4. This would mean that:

— the right of individuals or persons acting on behalf of a non-political organization or association of which they were a member to speak out during an election in favour of or in opposition to a particular candidate or registered party would not be restricted;
— the right of individuals and non-political organizations or associations to continue with their activities related to issues of public policy or for the purpose of advancing the aims of their organization or association during an election would not be restricted;
— the only restriction would be their right to spend money to oppose or promote, directly, and during an election, a particular candidate or political party. (ibid.)

With the repeal of s.70.1(4) by the enactment of Bill C-169 in 1983, it was now an offence for anyone other than a political party or candidate to incur election expenses. Although this was calculated to make a considerable difference to the operation of the statute, it is to be noted in passing that it would not have affected the outcome in *Roach*, who would still have been acquitted. This is because another ground for his acquittal was that the expenditure incurred by him was not an election expense within the statutory definition. As we have seen an election expense is defined as meaning an expense incurred 'for the purpose of promoting or opposing . . . a particular registered party, or the election of a particular candidate . . . .'[78] In the view of the appeal court, it could 'hardly be suggested . . . that the exhibited banner *directly* did what is prohibited in

[78] Election Expenses Act, SC 1973–4, c.51, s.2, amending the Canada Elections Act, RSC, c.14 (1st Supp), s.2. Now Canada Elections Act, RS 1985, c.14 (1st Supp), s.2.

the . . . definition of *election expenses*'[79] (that is directly promoted or opposed a particular political party or candidate). A more serious problem, however, related to the legality of the new reform, a problem brought into sharp focus by the patriation of the Canadian constitution and the adoption by Canada of the Charter of Rights and Freedoms in 1982. As previously pointed out in Chapter 1, the Charter operates in a manner similar to the US Bill of Rights in the sense that it imposes a constitutional limit on the power of federal and provincial governments and legislatures. Legislation and other government practices which violate the Charter may be struck down by the courts, a power which applies to both pre-Charter and post-Charter legislation and practices. Of crucial importance is the fact that one of the several fundamental freedoms protected by section 2 of the Charter is the right to freedom of expression. This may be qualified only to the extent permitted by section 1 which provides that reasonable limits may be imposed on Charter freedoms if prescribed by law and if demonstrably justified in a free and democratic society. This is a question to which we return in Chapter 6.

5. Enforcement

The effective enforcement of legislation of this kind is clearly of the first importance. History has taught the lesson that there is little point in enacting promising legislation which is unaccompanied by the necessary administrative support. This was recognized by both the Barbeau and Chappell Committees (which were influenced by the lamentable failure of the Dominion Elections Act 1908),[80] and indeed by the drafter of the 1974 Act. In determining the form of enforcement mechanisms, the authors of one study wrote that there are three essential ingredients. The first is that 'the laws themselves must be capable of enforcement. Ease of proof is an essential requirement for a workable enforcement scheme' (Ontario Commission on Election Contributions and Expenses, 1978b: 15). The second is that the controls should be enforced

---

[79] (1980) 101 DLR (3d) 736, at p. 741. Emphasis in original.
[80] See esp. Barbeau, 1966: 16–23.

vigorously, but without bias or favouritism, the body charged with enforcement being independent and non-partisan, free from the influences of those in power. It is on this count that some concern was expressed about the Ontario scheme, where the independent Commission was empowered only to report alleged violations to the Attorney-General, who had then to decide whether or not to prosecute. It is sometimes alleged that this allows too much opportunity for law enforcement to be influenced by partisan political considerations. The third and final requirement of effective legislation is that the penalties should be severe.

Under the Act each party is required to have an agent whose name and address must be registered with the CEO. All payments to or by a party are to be made through the agent (with a few minor exceptions), and any payment by the party must be vouched for by a receipt. Each party is also required to appoint an auditor, with candidates and agents being ineligible. The auditor has a statutory right of access to all the financial documents of the party, and he is required to report to the agent of the party on the annual financial statement and on the statement of election expenses, both of which the parties are required to compile. In making this report, the auditor may make such statement as he thinks necessary where, for example, he has not received from the party all the information and explanation he required. On receipt of the auditor's report, the agent of the political party is then under a duty to send the party's financial statement together with the auditor's report to the CEO. We have already seen what information will be contained in the financial statements. An agent who fails to submit the appropriate report or who submits false or insufficient reports is guilty of an offence, as also is the political party on the behalf of which he acts. The maximum penalty which may be imposed on the party is a fine of $25,000, which is the same as the maximum offence which may be imposed on a party which exceeds the spending limits. As already pointed out, the information submitted in this way is open to public inspection.

Under the Act enforcement is the responsibility of the Chief Electoral Officer, the views of the Chappell Committee thus prevailing. This contrasts with the corresponding provisions under provincial legislation in those provinces which have also adopted campaign finance legislation. Here the normal practice is for the creation of a completely new Commission separate from the Electoral Officer in the provinces concerned. It has been explained that the roles required by the election laws and the campaign finance laws 'differ substantially in philosophy' (Ontario Commission on Election Contributions and Expenses, 1978*b*: 42) in the sense that the former 'demand that the Chief Electoral Officer maintain the appearance of impartiality to candidates and parties' (ibid.) whereas the latter 'demand that the accuracy of the financial reports be policed' (ibid.). It has also been argued that it is no substitute for effective policing and supervision by a public body to have the candidates and parties submit audited returns—as is required by the 1974 Act on the recommendation of Chappell. Thus, 'The auditor's duty in preparing the return is to ensure that the return fairly represents the information contained in the accounting records. He is not required to express an opinion as to the illegality of any transaction' (ibid. 44). The Manitoba Law Reform Commission (1977: 75) had written earlier in a similar vein that it had

serious reservations about leaving so much of the enforcement to the honesty and diligence of those auditing the various returns. If accurate disclosure and reporting is to be required of parties and candidates to substantiate compliance with limitations on expenses and contributions, and to determine the amount of state subsidies, then there is, in our opinion, a need for active enforcement—i.e. for regular investigation and where necessary, prosecution, and in this regard we think it may well be advisable to establish an independent agency, one that will be sufficiently removed from the government and the parties to earn their respect and confidence.

It is to be pointed out that although the Chief Electoral Officer is responsible for administration and enforcement, the 1974 Act also provided that the Officer 'shall appoint a Commissioner whose duties, under the supervision of the Chief Electoral Officer, shall be to ensure that the provisions of this Act in regard to election expenses are complied with and enforced'. In 1977 the role of the Commissioner was extended to all provisions of the Canada Elections Act, the title of the Office being changed to Commissioner of Canada Elections, but still responsible to the Chief Electoral Officer. The CEO explained that the policy which he established with the Commissioner was that 'all legitimate complaints would have to be investigated promptly and good judgment would have to be exercised in deciding how best to deal with the result. Charges would be laid only in those cases where we and the counsel we would have retained would be of the opinion that the evidence presented a *prima facie* case and where it was clear that the offences were committed with intent' (Chief Electoral Officer of Canada, 1979*a*: 21). Two other points about the Commissioner should be noted. First, 'it was recognized that the Commissioner required assistance in the form of persons who would represent him at strategic locations across the country' (ibid.), with the result that the services of a number of representatives are retained during campaign periods in order 'to call the Commissioner's attention to possible violations of the *Act*' and 'react promptly to requests from the Commissioner for inquiries' (ibid. 22). Secondly, the Chief Electoral Officer has pointed out, also in 1979, that

Under a departmental policy going back to 1962, the federal Department of Justice has declined to become involved in investigations or prosecutions under the *Canada Elections Act* because of the sensitive political position of the Attorney General of Canada in whose name any prosecutions would have to be conducted. It was submitted that such prosecutions should be the responsibility of the Chief Electoral Officer. Consequently, it was necessary to select members of the legal profession to act as counsel in a number of major cities across the country. The main criteria used in selecting these lawyers were that they be apolitical, experienced in criminal law and willing to represent the Commissioner of Canada Elections, acting on my behalf, in any Court proceedings. (ibid.)

These arrangements have been in operation now in four federal elections (1979, 1980, 1984, and 1988) and many complaints have been made to and have been investigated by the Commissioner. An early problem reported by the Officer related to the conduct of newspapers during elections. Thus, during black-out periods (on which see below) some candidates wrote letters to 'the Editor' or articles for specific newspapers. The Commissioner took the view that the material (there were four cases in 1979) constituted advertisements promoting the election of their respective authors. However, it was decided not to prosecute on the ground that the violations had not occurred wilfully, 'coupled with the willingness of the candidate and the media representatives to abide by the Commissioner's request to comply with the *Act*' (Chief Electoral Officer of Canada, 1979*a*: 23).[81] More controversial was the practice of newspapers of directing 'a number of questions on current issues in the campaign to all candidates in the constituencies where the newspapers were sold. Included in the lot was to be an "open-ended" question. The replies to the questions were to be printed, as received, on the day preceding polling day. The *Canada Elections Act* imposes a black-out on advertising by candidates and political parties in the print and electronic media on polling day and the day immediately preceding polling day' (ibid. 24). The concern of the Commissioner was that the 'open-ended' question would give the candidates an opportunity to 'go on at great length and, unwittingly or otherwise, structure their replies in such a manner as to constitute an advertisement for the purpose of promoting their own election' (ibid.). Although it is not clear how this matter was resolved, it did give rise to a difference of opinion between the Commissioner and the representatives of the press, and the Commissioner did consider it his duty to make an attempt to prevent candidates from violating the Act, whenever possible (ibid. 23–4). This problem was caused by the fact that two sets of rules were operational:

The *Broadcasting Act*, a federal statute, prohibits the broadcast of programs of a partisan character in relation to the election of a member of the legislature of a province or territory or the council of a municipal corporation on polling day or the day before. The rules at federal elections are different; they are less restrictive but much more difficult to administer. At federal elections, broadcasters can interview candidates and party leaders as frequently as they wish from the day the writs are issued up to and including polling day, providing responses given by the persons interviewed do not constitute advertising within the meaning of the *Canada Elections Act*. We seem to be faced with a situation which, if allowed to continue, could weaken efforts to limit and control election expenses. (ibid. 24)

---

[81] The issue arose again in 1980, but again no action was taken on the ground that the violations were not intentional (Chief Electoral Officer of Canada, 1980*a*: 18).

It was proposed that the problem should be reviewed and amended by legislation, if necessary.

A second problem, before the repeal of s.70(4), related to the independent expenditures. In 1979, as we have already seen, a large number of requests were received from persons seeking guidance on the interpretation of s.70.1 and in the same year twenty-one complaints were received regarding persons, organizations, or associations who were causing advertisements to be disseminated that promoted or opposed a particular candidate or a particular political party (ibid. 26). In each case, however, the advertisement contained a reference to one or more issues of public policy and furthermore there was no evidence of any lack of good faith. As a result no legal action was taken (ibid.). In 1980 the same section again evoked a large number of requests from persons seeking interpretation of its provisions. Again complaints of violation were received, and on this occasion two such complaints were under police investigation. In all the other cases the Commissioner concluded that the s.70.1(4) defence could be successfully invoked (Chief Electoral Officer of Canada, 1980a: 19). These police investigations led to the case against an individual being dropped for lack of evidence and a charge being laid against an advertising firm under s.70.1. The firm was convicted and fined $600 (Chief Electoral Officer of Canada, 1983: 17). In 1984, the year after the deletion of the s.70.1(4) defence, the number of complaints of a s.70.1 violation appeared to fall dramatically. In that year there was a total of 567 possible violations brought to the attention of the Commissioner. Of these only five related to s.70.1, none of which led to a prosecution or conviction (Chief Electoral Officer of Canada, 1986: 6–9). In future the matter is calculated to cause even less trouble for the Commissioner. The pressure of the Chief Electoral Officer for the repeal of the s.70.1(4) defence has led to a holding that s.70.1 as it then stood was unconstitutional, being contrary to the Charter of Rights and Freedoms.[82]

A third problem, more enduring in nature, relates to failures to submit returns of election expenses on the one hand, and to

---

[82] *National Citizens' Coalition Inc.* v. *Attorney-General for Canada* (1985) 11 DLR (4th) 481.

irregularities in these submitted on the other. In 1979, 80 candidates (out of 1,427) and their official agents failed to submit a declaration and an election expenses return within the time stipulated by the Act, though all elected candidates did comply. Many of those candidates subsequently filed late, following judicial orders where there was an authorized excuse. Consent was given to prosecute 25 candidates and their agents, though of these 12 (candidates and agents) successfully applied for judicial orders permitting late filing before the charges were heard. The charges were dropped. Of those who were prosecuted, convictions took the form of fines between $75 and $200, and indeed $200 was the penalty imposed in the only reported conviction for exceeding the spending limits. The candidate had pleaded guilty, and the judge took into account the fact the candidate was a citizen of good repute who had reported the over-expenditures and had co-operated in the investigation (Chief Electoral Officer of Canada, 1980a: 17). Modest penalties were also imposed in 1980. One candidate who reported election expenses in excess of the legal spending limits was fined $450, the judge again taking into account the fact that the candidate had reported the violation and was a citizen of good repute, the prosecution having pressed for a heavier penalty (Chief Electoral Officer of Canada, 1983: 16). Another candidate who failed to report over-expenditures was fined on conviction only $100 (ibid.), while 13 candidates and 10 agents were fined between $50 and $500 following convictions for failing to submit returns of election expenses in time, though in three cases the persons convicted preferred to spend time in jail instead of paying the fine (ibid. 17). Although many similar complaints were also made in 1984 (Chief Electoral Officer of Canada, 1986: 6–9), it is to be noted that there is not yet any report of any political party having exceeded the spending limits.

III. Conclusion

By international standards, the Canadian federal statute on campaign funding is a radical and imaginative document. Thus, we have seen how the legislation

1. requires disclosure to ensure the public accountability of political parties;
2. employs the tax system to broaden the base of party funds;
3. subsidizes the political process by partially reimbursing candidates' election expenses, and by reimbursing a proportion of the election expenses incurred by the political parties;
4. regulates in some detail broadcasting time and provides an arbitrator independent of the broadcasters and the political parties to resolve any disputes;
5. imposes financial limits not only on the amount of money which candidates may spend in a campaign (as in Britain), but also on how much the political parties may spend.

So by a combination of strategies and techniques, Canadian law seeks to restrict the influence of those with disproportionate economic power and to guarantee a measure of equality of opportunity on the part of those who compete for political power. It is to a consideration of the effectiveness and impact of this legislation that we now turn.

5

The Parties and Their Funds: The 1974 Act in Practice

IN this chapter we move to consider the impact which the 1974 Act has made on Canadian political funding. In dealing with this issue there is now a wealth of material readily available to the public, in contrast to the position before 1974 when inordinate secrecy was the order of the day. As already pointed out, the parties are now required to submit annual returns to the Chief Electoral Officer, with details of income and expenditure. On the income side the returns must contain the name of any donor who has contributed more than $100, whether the donor be an individual, a corporation, a business organization, a trade union, or a government. The information is collated by the Chief Electoral Officer in large bound volumes and copies are made available to members of the public. The amount of material available to the public expands as the number of donations to the parties continues to grow. In 1979 the information relating to the three main parties covered 416 pages. In 1984 it ran to two volumes of more than 1,000 pages in total. Indeed there were over 500 pages dealing exclusively with the contributions to the Progressive Conservatives. In drawing on this and other information the chapter essentially addresses three themes. The first is to determine to what extent the parties are financed by the contributions of individual citizens. The second is to examine the role of institutional money in Canadian political funding—to what extent do the parties rely on corporate, or (in the case of the NDP) trade union money? Finally, the third theme is to consider the effect and operation of the election expense limitations.[1]

---

[1] For earlier accounts of the implications and impact of the 1974 Act, see Coates, Cook, Malone, and Reid, 1981; G. G. Murray, 1975; Seidle and Paltiel, 1981; Stanbury, 1986; and Wishart, 1974.

TABLE 3. *Contribution income of the Progressive Conservative Party from individual donors, 1981–1984 ($)*

	(1) Total contribution income	(2) Total contribution income from individuals	(2) as % of (1)
1981	6,949,797	4,319,604	62
1982	8,193,660	5,181,016	63
1983	14,108,012	9,105,732	65
1984	21,145,920	10,142,398	48
TOTAL	50,397,389	28,748,750	57

Note: Column 1 includes contributions from individuals, business and commercial organizations, governments, trade unions, and other organizations. It does not include sources of income other than contributions. Such other sources include election reimbursements and transfers from constituencies to the central party.

Source: Chief Electoral Officer of Canada, 1985*b*.

I. Fund-Raising

Before 1974 the two largest political parties—the Progressive Conservatives and the Liberals—raised their money mainly from corporations (Paltiel, 1970). Since 1974 the position has changed remarkably, with probably the most important development being the growth in the role of the individual contributor. The tax relief provided a stimulus to the parties to extend their financial bases, in the case of the Tories in particular by the development of a large-scale direct-mail programme. In 1982 the party had a computer bank with a list of 100,000 donors, held at the national office in Ottawa. At that time the party mailed contributors about four times a year to request donations, with the mailings being followed up in some cases by telephone calls, an activity which alone could increase the return by as much as $600,000. Details of Tory income from individuals in the years 1981–4, as reported to the Chief Electoral Officer, are provided in Table 3.

TABLE 4. *Contribution income of the Liberal Party from individual donors, 1981–1984 ($)*

	(1) Total contribution income	(2) Total contribution income from individuals	(2) as % of (1)
1981	5,095,158	2,101,350	41
1982	6,104,367	3,195,283	52
1983	7,285,115	3,261,950	45
1984	10,553,316	5,181,097	49
TOTAL	29,037,956	13,739,680	47

Note: Column 1 includes contributions from individuals, business and commercial organizations, governments, trade unions, and other organizations. It does not include sources of income other than contributions. Such other sources include election reimbursements and transfers from constituencies to the central party.

Source: Chief Electoral Officer of Canada, 1985*b*.

The Liberals have also seen a large increase in the number of individual donors to party funds. But they were much slower off the mark than the Tories with direct mail, and appear to have a much less sophisticated operation, with a bank of only 8,000 names in 1982. There are several reasons for this. The first is that the Liberals misjudged direct mail, seeing it as a passing fancy, a complacency born of power which tended to suppress any initiative or willingness to explore new techniques for improving organizational efficiency. A second possible explanation lies in the claim of one senior Liberal party official that the party had a much stronger grass-roots constituency-based organization than the Tories. So while the Liberals raised much less centrally than the Tories it is claimed (without evidence) that they raised more in the constituencies. There is no way of testing this claim. Nevertheless, the level of support from individual donors remains impressive, as is shown in Table 4, which presents details of Liberal income from individuals in the years 1981–4.

TABLE 5. *Contribution income of the New Democratic Party from individual donors, 1981–1984 ($)*

	(1) Total contribution income	(2) Total contribution income from individuals	(2) as % of (1)
1981	3,534,958	2,868,724	81
1982	4,537,112	3,774,971	83
1983	5,746,066	4,998,350	87
1984	6,549,680	4,156,000	63
TOTAL	20,367,816	15,798,045	78

Note: Column 1 includes contributions from individuals, business and commercial organizations, governments, trade unions, and other organizations. It does not include sources of income other than contributions. Such other sources include election reimbursements and transfers from constituencies to the central party.

Source: Chief Electoral Officer of Canada, 1985*b*.

So far as the New Democratic Party is concerned, a greater proportion of reported income comes from individuals than is the case with the other two main parties. But it is difficult to be entirely accurate about NDP finances or to know precisely to what extent we are comparing like with like when we contrast NDP financing with that of the other two parties. This is because in its returns to the Chief Electoral Officer, the party claims to report *all revenue raised and expenses incurred* by the Party at the national, provincial, and territorial levels. In so doing, the party officials have explained that its structure is different from the other two parties, most of its money being raised in the provinces with a percentage of these funds being forwarded to finance the federal party's operations. On the income side, the entry for contributions in the annual returns of the party includes money raised directly by the federal party, for example through its direct-mail programme, as well as money raised in the provinces, only some of which will come to the federal party. But not all provincially raised contributions will appear in the contributions entry. It seems that this will apply only to those contributions in respect of which a federal income tax receipt has been issued. (All the others will be included in the separate entry for sectionally receipted revenue which is substantial and not broken down into categories of donors.) Perhaps the main point to be made is that the annual returns of the party will tend to inflate the true available income and expenditure of the federal party, so that any financial advantage which the NDP appears to have over other parties will tend to exaggerate the real position, while any financial disadvantage which the NDP appears to suffer relative to the other parties will tend to underestimate the real position. With these qualifications, we may refer to Table 5, which presents contribution income of the NDP as reported to the Chief Electoral Officer. It thus includes income which may not be available to the federal party, and it excludes sectionally receipted income, some of which may be transferred to the party.[2]

II. The Role of Corporations

Apart from donations from individuals, the other major source of income for the Conservatives and the Liberals (though not the NDP) is from corporations or business organizations.[3] But it is to be noted that in the period immediately following the passing of the Act, disclosure had a negative impact on fund-raisers. As Wearing (1981: 226) has pointed out in relation to the Liberal Party,

While disclosure has certainly reduced the fund-raising potential of the Treasury Committee [the party's fund-raising committee] it is difficult to say by how much. In the first reporting year, only seventeen corporations gave $10,000 or more. Old friends, such as Canadian Pacific and Inco at first refused to give anything and the fund raisers of both the older parties feared an organised boycott by some of the big corporations.

These fears appeared, however, to be groundless, for as Wearing has also pointed out, in subsequent years most companies

---

[2] Contrast Stanbury, 1986: 803.
[3] For a particularly valuable account of business political contributions, see Stanbury, ibid.

renewed their traditional generosity (ibid.), and only a few still hold out, including foreign-owned corporations, such as IBM and Swifts which used to make substantial contributions (ibid.). But in the case of these companies,

It is not just the disclosure requirement that has stopped them: even more, it has been the criticism levelled at American multinational corporations during the Watergate investigations. Because corporate donations are illegal in the United States and often indistinguishable from outright bribery in many other parts of the world, many multinationals have simply adopted a blanket policy against making political contributions anywhere. Canadian fund raisers are, for the most part, unable to convince them that in Canada good corporate citizens ought to support the democratic process by contributing to political parties. One of the major exceptions is Gulf Canada, which contributes commensurately with its status as a major Canadian company, in spite of complaints in the United States. Ford of Canada took the position that the party should raise money from individuals. It gradually scaled down its contributions so that by 1979 it had joined the other car manufacturers in making no political donations. (ibid.)[4]

Table 6 provides some idea of corporate giving to the Conservatives and the Liberals in the years 1981–4. The amount of donations presented in Table 6 represents an increase in the amount of corporate contributions to the parties when compared with the previous four-year period (1977–80). Then sums of $13,737,501 and $12,386,119 were donated by businesses to the Conservatives and the Liberals respectively. Yet although there has thus been an increase in the amount of corporate contributions, such contributions as a proportion of total income have actually declined. So, for example, in the four-year period 1977–80, 55% of Tory and 60% of Liberal contribution income was provided by business. Also important is not just the relative decline in corporate contributions as a source of income but the fact that the corporate base in terms of the number of donors is now so large. Thus, the parties now rely on a few large donations for a relatively small proportion of their total income. If we take donations from companies of $20,000 or more, we find that the total of such donations to the Liberals amounted to only 9% of total income in 1981 and 7%

[4] See also Wearing and Wearing, 1990. Cf. Stanbury, 1986.

TABLE 6. *Contribution income of the Progressive Conservative Party and the Liberal Party from corporations, 1981–1984 ($)*

	Progressive Conservative Party			Liberal Party		
	(1) Total contribution income	(2) Total contribution income from corporations	(2) as % of (1)	(3) Total contribution income	(4) Total contribution income from corporations	(4) as % of (3)
1981	6,949,797	2,573,208	37	5,095,158	2,705,385	53
1982	8,193,660	2,922,661	36	6,104,367	2,521,810	41
1983	14,108,012	4,819,737	34	7,285,115	3,542,895	49
1984	21,145,920	11,003,522	52	10,553,316	5,339,729	51
TOTAL	50,397,389	21,319,128	42	29,037,956	14,109,819	49

Note: Columns 1 and 3 include contributions from individuals, business and commercial organizations, governments, trade unions, and other organizations.

Source: Chief Electoral Officer of Canada, 1985b.

99

of total income in 1982 and 1983, rising to 13% of total income in the election year 1984. In the four-year period, however, the party relied on such money to provide only 10% of income. The position is very similar with the Conservatives. In 1981, they received 6%; in 1982, 6%; in 1983, 3%; and in 1984, 14% of their money from this source. But overall only 8% of income between 1981 and 1984 was provided by corporate donations of $20,000 or more.

An important feature of corporate giving is the fact that the parties have imposed a self-regulatory control on the amount which they will receive from a single company in any one year. In 1978 the Royal Commission on Corporate Concentration remarked that 'Corporate contributions may lead to some sense of obligation and conflict of interest, as well as suspicion, even though the companies involved often contribute to two or more rival parties or candidates, and neither ask nor expect any such pro quo' (Dickerson and Nadeau, 1978: 343). Yet despite the absence of any restriction on the source of funding, in 1974 the Liberals (who raised most of their money in an election year) imposed a ceiling of $100,000 on the amount they would receive from a single corporation. This normally yielded a surplus—enough to keep the party running until the next campaign. After 1974 when the Act was introduced, the Liberals kept the ceiling but sought to encourage corporations to make donations annually. So the party imposed a limit of $25,000 in non-election years, and $50,000 in election years. In 1982 the figures were doubled. The Conservatives agreed to be bound by similar limits and in fact some corporations give equally to both parties. (Indeed, it was said by one senior party official to the author that corporate canvassers may make joint trips to corporate executives to request donations for each of their parties.) But it is to be noted that the self-imposed limit does allow each of the parties to receive $250,000 from a single donor in the course of a parliamentary cycle.

Few corporations give donations approaching anything like this amount. Rather, despite the best efforts of the parties to persuade the contributors to spread their donations, there is still a tendency to donate heavily in an election year. So while the Liberals received 16 donations in excess of $20,000 in 1981, 14 such donations in 1982, and 15 in 1983, they received 39 such donations in 1984. The contrast is more striking in the case of the Conservatives where the number of donations in excess of $20,000 rose from 16 in 1982 and 1983 to 77 in 1984. The most generous donor in these years appears to have been Canadian Pacific, which gave $178,458 in four years to the Liberals, and $176,500 to the Conservatives. Other large donors include the banks. So we find that in 1981 the Liberals received $148,309 and that the Conservatives received $145,000 from the same five banks (Bank of Montreal, Bank of Nova Scotia, Canadian Imperial Bank of Commerce, Royal Bank of Canada, and Toronto-Dominion Bank). In 1982 the same five banks gave $158,861 to the Liberals and $150,000 to the Conservatives, with similar amounts being donated in 1983 ($151,706 to the Liberals, and $139,148 to the Conservatives). The amounts were increased in 1984, with $360,499 being donated by the five banks to the Liberals and $290,188 to the Conservatives, and with several large donations being made by other banks in the election year: National Bank of Canada ($30,000 to the Liberals) and Banque Nationale de Canada ($30,000 to the Conservatives). In other words five banks donated a total of $1,543,711 to the two main parties in a period of only four years. Other large donors include brewers and related companies (Molson, Labatt, Seagram, Hiram Walker, Carling O'Keefe); oil-related corporations (Canadian Occidental Petroleum, Chevron, Imasco, Husky Oil, Gulf Canada, and Ranger Oil);[5] as well as those in mining and construction (Denison Mines—$100,250 to the Tories in 1984; George Wimpey Canada Ltd; and Noranda Mines). Note also that Candor Investments gave $150,000 and Eatons $25,096 to the Tories in 1984 and that Northern Telecom gave $51,200 to the Liberals and $50,000 to the Tories in the same year.

III. The NDP and the Unions

As we have seen, the NDP raises a significantly higher proportion of its contribution income as reported to the Chief

---

[5] For an account of the support of political parties by the oil companies, see Urquhart, 1976.

Electoral Officer from individuals than do either of the other main parties. Apart from factors such as the different reporting methods, this is partly because unlike the Liberals and the Conservatives, the NDP has a very small corporate base. In 1981 business and commercial organizations donated only $109,062, in 1982 this rose to only $144,324, falling to $41,432 in 1983. In 1984 total contributions from business and commercial organizations were a mere $51,665 or 0.8% of total contribution income. Indeed for the four-year period, only 1.7% ($346,483) of the total reported contribution income of the NDP was provided by business and commercial organizations. In 1984 the party received only 86 corporate donations of $100 or more, and of these only 8 were of $1,000 or more, the largest being $2,250 followed by a donation of $1,350. In fact 19 of these donations were less than $200; 26 were between $200 and $299; 11 were between $300 and $399; 8 were between $400 and $499; 11 were of $500 each; and there was one each of $600, $700, and $750. In the main these contributions came from small businesses which, exceptionally, may include sympathetic legal firms. Notably, there were no contributions from the large corporate contributors which feed the other two parties. There are, however, recent signs of a changing relationship between business and the NDP, associated with the rising profile of the party in Canadian federal politics, but these are embryonic only.

So apart from individual donations and transfers from provincial parties, the only other main source of income for the NDP centrally is from trade unions, which help the party in a number of ways. The first is by affiliation fees. Under the constitution of the party, membership is open to trade unions, farm groups, co-operatives, women's organizations, and other groups and organizations which undertake to accept and abide by the constitution and principles of the party. An application for affiliated membership may be received from one of the following:

(a) an international, national, provincial or regional organization in respect of its membership in Canada or in the province or region concerned;

(b) a provincial or regional section of an international or national organization in respect of its membership in that province or region;

(c) a local, lodge or branch of any of the above-mentioned organizations in respect of the membership of that local, lodge or branch;
(d) a local group or organization in respect of its membership. (NDP,
1981, 1990*a*)

The process of affiliation contrasts sharply with the position in
Britain in a number of respects. Unlike in Britain, though as in
Sweden, the unions do not affiliate as national organizations.
The United Auto Workers (UAW), or the United Steel Workers
of America (USWA) do not affiliate. Rather, affiliation is by
branches and locals of these parent organizations. This form
of affiliation was adopted deliberately by the party and its
supporters in the unions, in the belief that affiliation by parent
organizations would be disruptive and would cause tension
with international unions trying to dominate or interfere with
the autonomy of the locals. In 1982, approximately 300,000
trade unionists were affiliated to the party through 400 different locals, with the decision to affiliate being taken by a ballot
vote of the members of the branch.

Also unlike Britain, trade union members in Canada have no
statutory right to claim exemption from the obligation to make
political donations, despite the fact that compulsory union
membership is not uncommon. It is to be noted, however, that
the constitution of the federal party also provides that 'Any
member of an affiliated organization may at any time officially
notify his organization that he does not wish a per capita
payment to be made to the Party on his behalf, and the organization shall forthwith cease to make such payment'. In
practice, union locals will take account of the fact that some
of their members oppose affiliation with the NDP and will
normally affiliate on the basis of 85–90% of their membership.
Affiliation fees are 20 cents per affiliated trade union member
per month and if any member objects to part of his or her dues
being used for this purpose, he or she may complain to the
secretary of his local who in turn may arrange for a rebate to be
paid to the objector, though it is not altogether clear whether
this is a regular practice. So by a system of self-regulation the
NDP seeks to ensure that no one is affiliated to it involuntarily.
It is to be noted, however, (also unlike Britain) that the party
relies on affiliation fees for a small portion of its reported

TABLE 7. *Contribution income of the New Democratic Party from trade union affiliation fees, 1981–1984 ($)*

	(1) Total contribution income	(2) Total trade union affiliation fees	(2) as % of (1)
1981	3,534,958	353,300	10
1982	4,537,112	316,106	7
1983	5,746,066	299,688	5
1984	6,549,680	417,480	6
TOTAL	20,367,816	1,386,574	7

Note: Column 1 includes contributions from individuals, business and commercial organizations, governments, trade unions, and other organizations. It does not include sources of income other than contributions. Such other sources include election reimbursements and transfers from constituencies to the central party.

Source: Chief Electoral Officer of Canada, 1985*b*.

income, the nature of this limited dependence being presented in Table 7.

But although affiliation fees are only a tiny portion of total reported income, as already indicated there are other ways by which the unions provide financial assistance for the party. In addition to affiliation fees, the unions support the NDP with donations. These donations may be made by locals, by provincial or national unions, by international unions (such as the UAW or the USWA), by trade union federations (such as the Ontario Federation of Labour), or by the Canadian Labour Congress. The decision to make a donation is normally authorized by a conference resolution and will be justified as being consistent with the wishes of the members, though in order to be lawful it would have to be made under authority of the union's constitution. It is to be noted that although dissenting members are permitted to claim exemption from the obligation to pay an affiliation fee, there is no provision in the constitution of the party (nor normally in the constitutions of the unions)

The Parties and Their Funds

TABLE 8. *Contribution income of the New Democratic Party from trade union donations, 1981–1984* ($)

	(1) Total contribution income	(2) Total donations from trade unions	(2) as % of (1)
1981	3,534,958	161,886	5
1982	4,537,112	157,033	3
1983	5,746,066	336,851	6
1984	6,549,680	1,741,575	27
TOTAL	20,367,816	2,397,345	12

Note: Column 1 includes contributions from individuals, business and commercial organizations, governments, trade unions, and other organizations. It does not include sources of income other than contributions. Such other sources include election reimbursements and transfers from constituencies to the central party.

Source: Chief Electoral Officer of Canada, 1985*b*.

to enable such members to dissociate themselves from any political contributions of this latter kind, even though such contributions are more important financially to the party than affiliation fees. The extent of the party's dependence on donations is presented in Table 8.

So although donations form a larger part of NDP income than affiliation fees, it is still a relatively small source of reported income. Indeed, in the four-year period 1981–4 the party received only 19% of its reported income from trade union affiliation fees and donations combined. This in fact represents a decline not only in the total number of dollars received from the unions when compared with 1977–80, it is also a decline in the proportion of total reported income derived from this source. Between 1977 and 1980, total income from the unions amounted to 15%, 15%, 37%, and 37% per annum, representing 28% of contribution income as reported over the period. Taking into account both affiliation fees and donations, a number of interesting comparisons are to be drawn between trade union support of the NDP and business support of the other two parties.

- Less money is provided by the unions than by corporations for political purposes. Total union affiliation fees and donations to the NDP between 1981 and 1984 amounted to only 11% of total business contributions to the Liberal and the Conservative federal parties.
- The unions provide a smaller proportion of NDP income than corporations provide for the other two parties. Thus, as already pointed out, over the four-year period 1981–4 the unions contributed only 19% of party income in contrast to the 42% contributed to Tory funds and the 49% contributed to Liberal funds by business in the same period.
- Very many fewer unions than corporations give money for political purposes. Thus, the institutional base of the NDP is tiny in comparison to that of the two business-based parties. So whereas the Liberals had 25,721 business contributions in 1981–4 and the Conservatives had a staggering 56,097 such contributions in the same period, the NDP had a mere 3,675 trade union contributions. The Liberals had more contributors than this in 1984 alone, while the Tories had twice as many business contributors in 1984 as the NDP had trade union contributions in the four years from 1981.

But not only do fewer unions than corporations donate, with one notable exception they also tend to contribute much less than the corporations. So in 1981 there were only three donations in excess of $20,000 ($21,985 from the Canadian Labour Congress; $23,985 from the UAW; and $28,457 from the Ontario Federation of Labour). In 1982 there were no such donations and in 1983 there were only five: the Canadian Labour Congress Committee on Political Education ($69,158); St Catherines District Labour Congress ($26,640); British Columbia Trades' Council ($20,000); BC Federation of Labour ($20,450); and USWA ($20,687). And in 1984, the election year, there were only eight large donations, including those from the steelworkers ($122,500); the Ontario Federation of Labour ($41,626); the food and commercial workers ($40,000); the woodworkers ($36,000); the service employees ($29,000); and the transport workers ($20,100). The published returns for 1984 are in fact astonishing. It is reported that the party received $417,480 from 730 trade unions in affiliation fees, and $1,741,575 from 217 trade unions in donations. Yet the return of the party to the Chief Electoral Officer also indicates that about two-thirds of trade union contributors and two-thirds of the value of trade union contributions is provided to the party in the form of contributions of less than $100. It is thus paradoxical that one of the largest contributions to any party in the year by a trade union or a corporate source was the $122,500 donation to the NDP by the steelworkers.

IV. Unequal Funding

So far we have seen that the parties rely for a substantial part of their income on the individual donations of electors. We have seen also, however, that (at least in the case of two parties) there is still a heavy dependence on corporate money. But having examined the principal sources of income, the next question is to determine just how much the different parties raise and how evenly or unevenly the political money falls on the beneficiaries. In the four-year period 1977–80 the total income of the parties as reported from donations was as follows: Progressive Conservatives, $24,848,818; Liberals, $20,641,575; NDP, $15,363,387. Initially the Liberals were the best-financed party centrally, raising more than the Conservatives in the period 1974 to December 1976, and having a higher income than both of the other parties in 1977. They were displaced by the Tories, however, in 1978, 1979, and 1980. As a result, in this period Liberal income was 83% that of the Conservatives; NDP income was 62% that of the Conservatives; and NDP income was 74% that of the Liberals. So there are wide differences between the parties in this first period, though so far as the Liberals and the Conservatives are concerned, the difference was one of only just over $4 million.

In the second four-year cycle (1981–4) these gulfs between the parties widened. The annual contribution income of the three parties in each of these years is presented in Table 9. It

TABLE 9. *Annual contribution income of the Progressive Conservative, Liberal, and New Democratic Parties, 1981–1984 ($)*

	Progressive Conservative	Liberal	NDP
1981	6,949,797	5,095,158	3,534,958
1982	8,193,660	6,104,367	4,537,112
1983	14,108,012	7,285,115	5,746,066
1984	21,145,920	10,553,316	6,549,680
TOTAL	50,397,389	29,037,956	20,367,816

Note: This includes contributions from individuals, business and commercial organizations, governments, trade unions, and other organizations. It does not include sources of income other than contributions. Such other sources include election reimbursements and transfers from constituencies to the central party.

Source: Chief Electoral Officer, 1985*b*.

is clear from Table 9 that in each of the four years the Conservatives raised more than the Liberals, and that both of these parties raised more than the New Democrats. Indeed in 1983 the Tories raised almost twice as much as the Liberals, a feat which they did achieve in 1984 (the election year). Also significant is the fact that the Tories did not only take twice that taken by the NDP in some years, they also trebled NDP income in 1984. In fact in 1983 and 1984 the Tories raised more than the two other parties combined. If we look at the totals for this cycle what we find is that Liberal income was 58% that of the Conservatives; NDP income was 40% that of the Conservatives; and NDP income was 70% that of the Liberals.

So the gulf between the Conservatives and the other parties has widened, reflecting the remarkable growth in the Conservatives' fund-raising capacity. If we compare the period 1977–80 with the period 1981–4 we find that Conservative contribution income increased by 103%; Liberal contribution income increased by 41%; while NDP contribution income increased by 33%. In other words, the already high Tory income rose at more than twice the rate of both of the other parties. Why? Is it

TABLE 10. *The number of individual donors to party funds, 1981–1984*

	Progressive Conservative	Liberal	NDP
1981	48,125	24,735	56,545
1982	52,694	27,968	66,665
1983	99,264	33,649	65,624
1984	93,199	29,056	80,027
TOTAL	293,282	115,408	268,861

Source: Chief Electoral Officer of Canada, 1985*b*.

because they have more donors? Or is it because they have donations of larger sums? Or is it both of these factors? In answering these questions it is helpful to distinguish between individual and corporate donors. So far as the former are concerned, details are presented in Table 10. The figures presented in Table 10 are quite remarkable in the sense that they reveal that in two of the four years the NDP had more donors than each of the other two parties; that in all years it had more donors than the Liberals; and that in every year but 1983 it had more than double the number of donors as had the Liberals. (Indeed in 1985 it had more than three times this number.) Yet as we have seen in each of the four years the Progressive Conservatives raised considerably more than the NDP. In fact the annual contribution income of the NDP was only 51% (1981), 55% (1982), 41% (1983), and 31% (1984) that of the Conservatives, despite the fact that it was supported by almost as large a number of people. Similarly, although the income gap between the Liberals and the NDP is narrower, the annual income of the NDP was only 69% (1981), 74% (1982), 79% (1983), and 62% (1984) that of the Liberals despite the fact that the Liberals had less than half the number of donors of the NDP. One explanation for this is that the size of the average individual contribution varies widely from party to party. This is shown in Table 11. It would appear, then, that the Tories are better financed than the other parties partly because they have more individual donors than the Liberals and slightly more

TABLE 11. *The size of the average contribution to the political parties by individual donors, 1981–1984 ($)*

	Progressive Conservative	Liberal	NDP
1981	90	85	51
1982	98	114	57
1983	92	97	76
1984	109	178	52
1981–4	98	119	59

Source: Based on figures made available by the Chief Electoral Officer of Canada, 1985*b*.

individual donors but who pay larger average contributions than donors to the NDP.

A second factor which helps to explain the gulf between the parties is the corporate support for the Conservatives and Liberals. It is to be noted, however, that both the number and the size of corporate contributions varies widely between the two parties. In 1983 the Conservatives had 18,067 commercial donors, contributing a total of $4,819,737. In the same year, the Liberals in contrast had 7,536 commercial donors, contributing $3,542,895. In 1984 the figures rose, with the Conservatives reporting 21,286 commercial donors who together contributed $11,003,522, which in itself was considerably more than the total income of the NDP. In the same year, 6,494 commercial organizations donated a total of $5,339,729 to the Liberal Party. But although the Liberals have many fewer corporate backers than the Tories, the amount of the average corporate donation to the Liberals is higher, a point demonstrated by Table 12. This contrasts with $41,432 donated to the NDP by 199 commercial organizations in 1983, and the $51,665 donated to the party by 280 such organizations in 1984. The average size of such donations in the years in question was $208 and $185 respectively.

The significance of corporate money as a factor in explaining the gulf between the parties can be illustrated by comparing

TABLE 12. *The size of the average contribution to the political parties by corporate donors, 1981–1984* ($)

	Progressive Conservative	Liberal
1981	352	448
1982	310	446
1983	267	470
1984	517	822
1981–4	380	548.5

Source: Based on figures made available by the Chief Electoral Officer of Canada, 1985*b*.

the differences in terms of contribution income between the parties, first by taking full account of corporate funding, and then by looking at the position where such funding is left out of account. So, in the four-year period 1981–4, with corporate and trade union funding, the Liberal contribution income was 58% that of the Conservatives; the NDP contribution income was 40% that of the Conservatives; and the NDP contribution income was 70% that of the Liberals. If, however, corporate or trade union funding is not taken into account and we look only at funding from individuals, then in the same period the Liberal contribution income would have been 48% that of the Conservatives; the NDP contribution income would have been 55% that of the Conservatives; and the Liberal contribution income would have been 87% that of the NDP. The corporate funding of the parties thus permits the Liberals to close the gap between them and the Conservatives, which would be wider if corporate funding were not permitted. Although the Liberals have many fewer corporate donors than their main rivals, this is perhaps partly explained by the fact that their average donation is higher. Corporate funding also allows the Liberals to have a greater total annual income than the NDP despite having fewer individual donors, and it allows the Conservatives to extend their financial advantage over the NDP, in a manner quite disproportionate to their support from individual donors.

If the policy goal is to encourage equality of opportunity between the parties and at the same time to reward those parties which have a large number of individual contributors, there may thus be a case for restricting or prohibiting corporate contributions. This is a matter to which we return in Chapter 8.

V. Expenditures

If we turn our attention to the expenditures of the parties, we may expect that the Tories, who have a greater income than the NDP and the Liberals, will have a greater expenditure than the NDP and the Liberals. On the other hand, however, expenditure by the parties is constrained by the 1974 Act's restrictions on election expenses. What is the point of raising so much money if the parties are not free to spend what they accumulate? The answer obviously must be that election expenditures form only a part of the needs of the political parties (but how large a part?) and that there are other items of expenditure. But what are these other items of expenditure? An analysis of the financial returns suggests that there are three major areas of expenditures by the parties: operating expenses, payments to constituency or provincial organizations, and election expenses. We look at each of these in turn.

1. OPERATING EXPENSES

The operating expenses of the parties are dealt with in Tables 13, 14, and 15. They show the major items of expenditure of the three parties in the years 1981–4. They also show that in each of the years the Conservative operating expenses were higher than those of either the Liberals or the NDP. Indeed in 1983 and 1984 the operating expenses of the Tories were higher than those of the other two parties combined. Over the four-year period the figures reveal that Liberal operating expenses were 54% of the Conservatives; NDP operating expenses were 50% of the Conservatives; and NDP operating expenses were 92% of the Liberals. In fact over the four-year period 1981–4, the combined NDP and Liberal operating expenses of $44,801,532 were only $1,560,783 more than the $43,240,749 spent by the

TABLE 13. *Operating expenses of the Progressive Conservative Party, 1981–1984 ($)*

	1981	1982	1983	1984	Total
Salaries, wages, and employee benefits	1,822,696	2,426,282	3,011,310	5,228,361	12,488,649
Travelling expenses	967,085	1,353,640	1,303,091	3,738,182	7,361,998
Party conventions and meetings	770,186	458,266	2,622,425	0	3,850,877
Rent, heat, light, and power	270,025	406,406	399,256	633,937	1,709,624
Advertising	131,563	69,795	64,049	1,148,097	1,413,504
Broadcasting	0	0	0	0	0
Printing and Stationery	1,755,399	1,787,061	2,566,045	5,245,068	11,353,573
Telephone and telegraph	369,764	408,789	471,135	1,123,570	2,373,258
Legal and audit fees	59,886	80,883	75,652	67,447	283,868
Miscellaneous expenses	653,744	316,540	464,234	970,880	2,405,398
TOTAL EXPENDITURE	6,800,348	7,307,662	10,977,197	18,155,542	43,240,749

Source: Chief Electoral Officer of Canada, 1985*b*.

113

TABLE 14. *Operating expenses of the Liberal Party, 1981–1984 ($)*

	1981	1982	1983	1984	Total
Salaries, wages, and employee benefits	1,000,032	1,308,209	1,320,118	1,267,898	4,896,257
Travelling expenses	211,151	256,653	243,367	333,206	1,044,377
Party conventions and meetings	471,226	571,259	454,958	4,357,725	5,855,168
Rent, heat, light, and power	118,984	232,878	199,687	258,638	810,187
Advertising	128,691	18,950	8,130	154,027	309,798
Broadcasting	0	0	0	0	0
Printing and Stationery	235,593	329,643	301,309	367,522	1,234,067
Telephone and telegraph	152,346	179,282	161,660	336,864	830,152
Legal and audit fees	64,355	112,864	95,803	109,633	382,655
Miscellaneous expenses	911,716	785,849	1,503,225*	2,329,414*	5,530,204
Surveys	32,644	103,742	166,970	1,435,124	1,738,480
Bank charges	101,424	208,452	160,890	255,768	726,534
TOTAL EXPENDITURE	3,428,162	4,107,781	4,616,117	11,205,819	23,357,879

*Includes fund-raising activity.

Source: Chief Electoral Officer of Canada, 1985b.

114

TABLE 15. *Operating expenses of the New Democratic Party, 1981–1984 ($)*

	1981	1982	1983	1984	Total
Salaries, wages, and employee benefits	1,938,898	2,387,559	2,549,044	2,536,516	9,412,017
Travelling expenses	627,315	708,293	654,668	554,687	2,544,963
Party conventions and meetings	527,770	93,022	571,228	615,212	1,807,232
Rent, heat, light, and power	119,391	122,335	149,887	12,704	404,317
Advertising	297,536	305,050	265,778	223,763	1,092,127
Broadcasting	0	133,955	0	226,052	360,007
Printing and Stationery	423,956	546,174	826,205	911,051	2,707,386
Telephone and telegraph	121,064	189,432	192,549	229,242	732,287
Legal and audit fees	77,956	63,131	86,533	62,291	289,911
Miscellaneous expenses	201,735	183,768	277,984	1,027,358	1,690,845
Interest and bank charges	120,279	117,357	64,866	100,059	402,561
TOTAL EXPENDITURE	4,455,900	4,850,076	5,638,742	6,498,935	21,443,653

Source: Chief Electoral Officer of Canada, 1985*b*.

115

Conservatives. In other words the combined operating expenditure of the two opposition parties was only marginally more than the operating expenses of the government party. This represents a considerable variation in the earlier period 1977–80 when the total operating expenses of the parties were $13,962,076 (Conservatives), $11,820,862 (Liberals), and $12,361,156 (New Democrats).

Three points of comparison may be made between the two periods. The first is the extent to which the operating expenses of all the parties have increased: NDP expenditure increased by 73%, Liberal expenditure by 98%, and the Conservatives by a staggering 210%. The second point of comparison is not unrelated to the first and that is the difference between the parties in operating expenses. It is evident from the figures that in 1977–80 the expenses of the parties were much closer together than they are now. In fact, in the four-year period 1977–80, the figures reveal that Liberal operating expenses were 85% of the Conservatives; NDP operating expenses were 89% of the Conservatives; and Liberal operating expenses were 96% of the NDP. The third issue of interest is the fact that in the first period the NDP actually spent more on operating costs than did the Liberals (more in 1977 and 1979, and less in 1978 and 1980). As we have seen this feature of party spending was not maintained overall in 1981–4, though the NDP did outspend the Liberals on operating expenditure in all but the election year when Liberal costs rose by 143% on the previous year. It is to be borne in mind, however, that reported NDP expenditures are for the federal and provincial wings of the party, unlike the Liberals and the Conservatives which report only federal expenditures.

2. TRANSFERS OF FUNDS

A second major area of expenditure by the parties relates to the transfer of money from the centre to help local organizations. Potentially this is a very important item of expenditure which could have a general equalizing impact. It may be, for example, that a party (in the case of Canada the Conservatives) is so much better financed than its rivals simply because it raises all of its money centrally. Whereas the other parties raise money for local needs at local level, the centrally well-financed party must give out substantial sums to support local associations. That is perhaps one explanation for the fact that the Tories are so well funded relative to the other parties. Indeed it was an explanation offered by a senior Liberal Party official in an interview with the author. The claim can be checked in one of two ways. The first and most accurate but most difficult is to examine the accounts of each constituency association. The second and admittedly less satisfactory is to examine how much the central organization is spending to support grass-roots activity. Although this does not tell us how much the local parties are raising, it does give us some idea of whether the money is coming in centrally at the expense of constituency associations and if it is coming in centrally in order to be distributed where there is need. Looking at this evidence, there is nothing to suggest that Conservative associations are any less effective in fund-raising than the Liberals, and there is nothing to suggest that in contributing large amounts to the federal party donors and supporters are neglecting the needs of the local associations. It is to be pointed out in any event that local needs are met to a large extent (in all parties) by the public subsidy for election expenses, at least in those constituencies where the candidate secures enough votes to qualify for a rebate. Indeed, rather than having insuffient funds, officials of both of the main parties complain of the squirrel instincts of the local parties: they hoard money and are often reluctant to give any to the central organizations.

Tables 16, 17, and 18 are interesting because they demonstrate that there is in fact little difference between the parties in so far as the amount of intra-party transfers is concerned. It is true that the Liberals are spending more of their central income on this item than the Conservatives but the difference between the Liberals and the Conservatives is only $18,052. In this respect there is in fact some difference between the period 1981 to 1984, and the earlier period 1977 to 1980 in which the Liberals spent $4.1 million on intra-party transfers in contrast with the $5.7 million spent by the Tories. In other words, the Tories spent $1.6 million more than the Liberals, which amounted to 39% more than the total Liberal expenditure on

TABLE 16. *Intra-party transfers by the Progressive Conservative Party, 1981–1984* ($)

	1981	1982	1983	1984	Total
Transfers to candidates for general election purposes	0	0	0	912,246	912,246
By-election expenses reported by polling day	81,865	31,746	44,712	0	158,323
Allocation of contributions to constituency and other party organizations	659,334	1,181,686	2,177,281	1,708,692	5,726,993
Total expenditure on intra-party transfers	741,199	1,213,432	2,221,993	2,620,938	6,797,562

Source: Chief Electoral Officer of Canada, 1985*b*.

TABLE 17. *Intra-party transfers by the Liberal Party, 1981–1984* ($)

	1981	1982	1983	1984	Total
Transfers to candidates for general election purposes	11,054	0	0	474,212	485,266
By-election expenses	62,195	39,537	27,679	0	129,411
Transfers to provincial sections and riding associations	1,614,871	2,633,578	1,633,213	319,275	6,200,937
Total expenditure on intra-party transfers	1,688,120	2,673,115	1,660,892	793,487	6,815,614

Source: Chief Electoral Officer of Canada, 1985*b*.

TABLE 18. *Intra-party transfers by the New Democratic Party, 1981–1984 ($)*

	1981	1982	1983	1984	Total
Transfers to candidates for general election purposes	0	0	0	0	0
By-election expenses	17,648	21,458	25,214	0	64,320
Transfers to provincial sections and riding associations	2,017,891	1,075,483	2,344,807	908,425	6,346,606
Total expenditure on intra-party transfers	2,035,539	1,096,941	2,370,021	908,425	6,410,926

Source: Chief Electoral Officer of Canada, 1985*b*.

this item. Yet although the Liberals and the Tories are now spending roughly the same on such transfers, it is to be noted that this expenditure is a much smaller proportion of central expenditure for the Tories than the Liberals. This hardly supports the view that the former are assiduous fund-raisers at the centre in order to feed their undernourished constituency associations (the difficulties, if any, of which have in any event been met to some extent by the rebate of election expenses). Indeed, if we take the period 1981–4, we find that intra-party transfers accounted for 20% of NDP central expenditure, 19% of Liberal central expenditure, but only 12% of Tory expenditure.

3. ELECTION EXPENSES

The third major area of expenditure is election expenses. Because of the limits, however, these are not as high as they might be otherwise, nor do they form as large a proportion

TABLE 19. *Party expenditures at the federal election, 1979 ($)*

	Progressive Conservative	Liberal	NDP
Advertising	267,209	576,168	314,613
Broadcasting			
Radio	939,272	563,029	247,616
Television	1,539,020	1,295,208	770,851
Hire of premises	12,644	53,996	21,153
Salaries and wages	116,897	145,942	413,065
Professional services	231,409	231,146	0
Travelling expenses	632,321	691,019	233,073
Administrative expenses	106,445	356,318	187,262
Miscellaneous expenses	0	0	2,460
Total election expenses	3,845,217	3,912,826	2,190,093
Limits of election expenses	4,459,249	4,459,249	4,459,249
Reimbursement	793,967	718,020	496,350

Source: Chief Electoral Officer of Canada, 1979*b*.

TABLE 20. *Party expenditures at the federal election, 1980 ($)*

	Progressive Conservative	Liberal	NDP
Advertising	578,246	402,504	425,943
Broadcasting			
Radio	651,541	578,597	233,105
Television	1,876,284	1,612,532	1,167,232
Hire of premises	27,532	15,514	24,547
Salaries and wages	57,543	155,254	591,743
Professional services	100,827	373,928	63,722
Travelling expenses	639,448	420,914	378,122
Administrative expenses	470,928	284,377	197,474
Miscellaneous expenses	4,858	2,603	4,288
Total election expenses	4,407,207	3,846,223	3,086,176
Limits of election expenses	4,546,192	4,546,192	4,531,562
Reimbursement	977,835	909,923	677,481

Source: Chief Electoral Officer of Canada, 1980*b*.

of total party expenses as they would otherwise. Details of expenditures by the parties in the elections of 1979, 1980, and 1984 are presented in Tables 19, 20, and 21. The first issue which arises is to determine what proportion of the maximum permitted expenditure the parties actually spent. Tables 19, 20, and 21 show that since 1979 there has been a tendency for the parties to spend closer to the maximum, despite the obvious drain on resources caused by the 1980 election, and despite the increase in the level of permitted expenditure (by some 40%) in 1984. So in 1979 the Liberals spent 88% of the permitted maximum, the Tories 86%, and the NDP 49%. In 1980 the Tories and the NDP had risen to 97% and 68% of the permitted maximum, whereas the Liberals had fallen back slightly to 85%. In 1984, however, the Tories spent 99.9% of the maximum permitted, the Liberals 98% of the maximum permitted, and the NDP 74%. In the campaigns of 1979 and 1980 Liberal election expenditure was 94% that of the Conservatives; NDP

TABLE 21. *Party expenditures at the federal election, 1984 ($)*

	Progressive Conservative	Liberal	NDP
Advertising	206,651	763,482	153,846
Broadcasting			
Radio	1,236,075	1,069,248	494,466
Television	1,757,944	1,695,186	1,158,150
Hire of premises	9,372	41,092	107,505
Salaries and wages	137,283	202,760	702,275
Professional services	1,032,716	128,640	28,021
Travelling expenses	1,129,512	880,817	145,784
Administrative expenses	253,946	431,321	367,582
National Office expenses	619,160	1,080,437	1,179,442
Miscellaneous expenses	6,282	—	393,652
Total election expenses	6,388,941	6,292,983	4,730,723
Limits of election expenses	6,391,497	6,391,497	6,391,497
Reimbursement	1,437,512	1,415,921	1,064,413

Source: Chief Electoral Officer of Canada, 1985*b*.

TABLE 22. *Election expenses as a proportion of party expenditures, 1977–1980* ($)

Party	(1) Total expenditure	(2) Total election expenses	(2) as % of (1)
Progressive Conservative	27,961,568	8,252,424	30
Liberal	23,701,211	7,759,049	33
NDP	22,564,742	5,276,269	23

Source: Chief Electoral Officer of Canada, 1979*b*, 1980*b*, 1985*b*.

election expenditure was 64% that of the Conservatives; and NDP election expenditure was 68% that of the Liberals. In contrast, in the 1984 campaign Liberal election expenditure was 98% that of the Conservatives; NDP election expenditure was 74% that of the Conservatives; and NDP election expenditure was 75% that of the Liberals. So as the NDP has become better financed, it has caught up with the other two parties and is now able to compete in terms closer to the maximum permitted level.

A second issue which arises is the amount of the parties' four-yearly expenditure which is consumed by election campaign costs. The details for the first period, 1977–80, are shown in Table 22. It is to be pointed out, however, that election expenses in this period would be abnormally high in view of the incidence of two general election campaigns in 1979 and 1980. The difficulty in raising the money to fight two campaigns in such quick succession may help to explain why the NDP spent such a noticeably smaller proportion of its expenditures on elections than the other two parties. So far as the second period is concerned, 1981–4, the details of election expenses as a proportion of total expenditure are provided in Table 23. Given that only one election was fought in this period, the information presented in Table 23 is likely to be more realistic and typical. We ought to expect, however, that the Conservatives would account for a smaller portion of their expenditures on elections than the other parties, given the

TABLE 23. *Election expenses as a proportion of party expenditures, 1981–1984 ($)*

Party	(1) Total expenditure	(2) Total election expenses	(2) as % of (1)
Progressive Conservative	56,427,252	6,388,941	11
Liberal	36,466,476	6,292,983	17
NDP	31,509,819	4,730,723	15

Source: Chief Electoral Officer of Canada, 1985*b*.

great advantage which they enjoyed over the others in terms of income and expenditure.

A third issue which arises flows naturally from the second. Given that the parties spend such a small proportion of their expenditures officially on 'election expenses', are they spending a large proportion on this item 'unofficially'? In other words, is there a tendency towards the avoidance of the spending limits by the large amounts of funds available to the parties, and by the Tories in particular, thereby undermining the equalizing impact which the spending limits have had? As might be expected, there is no hint of this in the annual returns of the parties. The parties generally report election expenditures less than, and in some cases considerably less than, the statutory maximum which is permitted. It is possible that not all expenditures are reported, but there is no evidence of this and the fact remains that party accounts are audited annually. There is, however, one indication of possible avoidance of the limits within the law. Thus annual returns reveal on the one hand a coincidence between a large increase in the operating expenses of the Conservatives and the Liberals in 1984, and the fact that an election was held in the year in question on the other.[6] Tory operating expenses increased by 65% on their 1983 total (and 148% on their 1982 total) while Liberal operating

[6] See also Stanbury, 1986: 801, 819.

expenses increased by 143% on their 1983 level. Indeed 42% of Tory operating expenses for the four-year period were incurred in the election year while no less than 48% of Liberal operating expenses were incurred in the election year. These figures contrast with the 30% of NDP operating expenses for the four-year period which were incurred in the election year. Looking at individual items of expenditure, it is interesting to note that in the case of the Conservatives wages, travelling expenses, and rent, heat, light, and power all increased sharply on the 1983 level. And so too did advertising (up an astonishing $1,084,048 on its 1983 level of $64,049), printing and stationery (up $2,679,023 on the 1983 level of $2,566,045), and telephone (up $652,435 on the 1983 level of $471,135). Important items of Liberal expenditure also increased by a large amount in areas which might be associated with an election. For example, 'surveys' increased from $166,970 in 1983 to $1,435,124 in 1984. There is no comparable item of expenditure in the Conservatives' accounts.

VI. Conclusion

What, then, have been the implications of the 1974 Act? On the one hand there have clearly been advantages. The requirement of disclosure has permitted studies such as this one to be conducted. In the past there was no public accountability, the system being protected by a veil of secrecy. It also appears that the tax relief has encouraged the parties to seek contributions from individuals and it is now the case that almost half or more of party funds come from individual contributors.[7] This is not to deny that there is also still a considerable dependence on corporations, though it is to recognize that they are no longer the only sources of funding, nor indeed the principal sources of funding. Thirdly, and importantly, the limit on election expenses prevents the Conservative Party from using its enormous income advantage during the campaign period by dominating the market-place of ideas with its own message. On the other hand, however, the quest for political equality

[7] See also Stanbury, 1986: 817.

has not been fully realized by the Act. In the 1980s in particular there existed wide differences in the levels of income of the parties, with the NDP, which is well supported in terms of *numbers* of individual contributors, faring badly in terms of the amount of contributions. It is also the case that the limit on election expenses does not create genuine equality in view of the (quite lawful) extent to which party operating expenses increase in an election year, with some of these expenses likely to impact to some extent on the election campaign. If the vision of equality of electoral opportunity is to be realized, this is something which will have to be addressed.

6

Campaign Financing and the Charter of Rights and Freedoms

HAVING looked at the origins, content, and operation of the federal law on campaign financing, it is now time to assess the impact of the Charter on the legislation. In Chapter 2 we identified two goals of such legislation. The first was to promote equal access to power in the sense that persons and corporations should not have influence merely by reason of financial contributions to a political party. The second was to promote equality of opportunity in the sense that candidates and political parties should be able to compete on more or less equal terms with one another. In particular, no one party should enjoy advantages in an election merely because it is better financed than its rivals. As we saw in Chapters 3 and 4, legislation was introduced to promote these goals. First, the legislation sought to encourage and stimulate small donations by individual donors by the use of the tax incentive. If successful this would thereby reduce the dependence of the parties on corporate and trade union money to the extent that such contributions would constitute a smaller portion of the income of the parties in question. Secondly, the legislation went a long way towards promoting equality of opportunity in a campaign. Thus, free time was provided to the parties for broadcasting, limits were imposed on the amount of permitted expenditure by candidates and parties in a campaign, and rebates were provided for qualifying candidates and parties to help offset the cost of election expenses. And in order to ensure laboratory conditions so far as possible, tight controls were eventually imposed on third-party expenditures incurred in the course of a campaign, though as we shall see these restrictions failed to survive constitutional challenge.

It is clear from the evidence provided in Chapter 5 that the legislation has been only partially successful. In the first place, considerable amounts of corporate money have been pumped into the political process, and these are apparently increasing in volume. In the period 1977 to 1980, corporations donated $26,123,620 to the Liberal and Progressive Conservative parties, which accounted for 60% and 55% of the total income of these parties respectively. Although it is true that in the period 1981 to 1984 corporate contributions made up only 49% and 42% of party funds, total company donations to the two parties in this period was a staggering $35,428,947. Union contributions were in contrast much smaller, with only $3,783,919 being donated to the NDP in the period in 1981–4, amounting to only 19% of party contribution income. In the earlier period 1977–80 union contributions had amounted to 28% of party income. A second point to note is that only an imperfect equality is being secured in an election. Ultimately this is a feature of the unequal funding of the parties. The only parties between which the differences have been fairly static are the Liberals and the NDP, with NDP income being 70% that of the Liberals between 1981 and 1984, as opposed to 74% in the period 1977–80. But Liberal income in 1981–4 was only 58% that of the Conservatives, as opposed to 83% in 1977 to 1980, while NDP income was a mere 40% of that of the Tories, as opposed to 62% between 1977 and 1980. These differences in income cannot be reflected in differences in election expenditure because such expenditure is subject to limits and restriction. Both Liberals and Conservatives spent at or close to the maximum permitted in 1984. Although it is true that the NDP was still some way behind (by about 25%) the major problem related to non-election expenses.

The experience of the first ten years in the life of the Act suggests that there is a need to consider both the continued dependence on corporate money, and the growing financial inequalities between the parties (which are unlikely to be electorally insignificant). There is, however, a new factor which must be considered before addressing any reform proposals. This is the Charter of Rights and Freedoms introduced in 1982 and already having an impact on the election expenses legislation. Indeed, the Charter is not simply a factor to be considered in the shaping future reform, it has in fact created the need for further reform. Yet, rather than help resolve or respond to the operational problems already discussed, decisions under the Charter have made it more likely that corporations and other special interests will become engaged in the political process. Thus in one of the major decisions, to which we now turn, a court has held the independent expenditure restrictions in an election to be unconstitutional, thereby facilitating high-profile and high-level election expenditures by wealthy groups.[1] It has also been held that unions may use the funds of dissenting agency fee payers to support political causes unrelated to collective bargaining.[2] The court has thereby failed to take another opportunity to restrict special interests and in the process, as Corcoran (1991) has pointed out, may have made it more difficult to introduce further legislation to confine the electoral activities of the special interests. But before we deal with these issues we must first deal with the decision upholding public funding for candidates and parties.[3]

I. Endorsing Public Funding

Re Mackay and Government of Manitoba[4] is the only one of three major cases under the Charter which did not at some stage in some way disturb or disrupt existing arrangements, though even then the issue was finely balanced in the Manitoba Court of Appeal, the Court dividing 2:1 with only two judgments being written. Although it is true that the Supreme Court of Canada upheld the majority, it did so on technical rather than substantive grounds, so the matter may not yet be closed. At issue was whether the provisions in the Manitoba Election Finances Act[5] were consistent with the Charter. Although dealing with provincial legislation, the case is nevertheless significant from the perspective of the federal Act, a point not lost by Huband J. A. (dissenting), who remarked that

---

[1] *National Citizens' Coalition Inc.* v. *Attorney-General for Canada* (1985) 11 DLR (4th) 481.
[2] *Lavigne* v. *Ontario Public Service Employees' Union.* Judgment rendered on 27 June 1991. Unreported at the time of writing.
[3] *Re Mackay and Government of Manitoba* (1986) 24 DLR (4th) 587 (Manitoba Court of Appeal); (1990) 61 DLR (4th) 385 (Supreme Court of Canada).
[4] Ibid.
[5] Election Finances Act 1982–1983–1984 (Man.), c.45.

the legislation under attack was 'not unique. There is federal legislation dealing with federal elections of a similar character.'[6] The aspects of the Act under challenge were to be found in sections 71 and 72. Under section 71 a political party is entitled to reimbursement of election expenses subject to a limit which is the lesser of 50% of the total permitted expenses of the party and 50% of the actual election expenses incurred by the party. The payments are drawn from the Consolidated Fund. Section 72 provides similarly that candidates are entitled to a reimbursement from the same fund of the lesser of 50% of the total permitted expenses of the candidate and 50% of the actual election expenses incurred by the candidate. As suggested, in the case of both candidates and parties the Act set a limit on the amount of total permitted expenditures.[7]

The attack on the reimbursement was wide-ranging. As we saw in Chapter 1, section 2 of the Charter provides:

Everyone has the following fundamental freedoms:
(a) freedom of conscience and religion;
(b) freedom of thought, belief, opinion and expression, including freedom of the press and other media of communication.

It was argued that the public-funding provisions of the Act violated freedom of conscience, religion, thought, belief, opinion, and expression. But writing for the majority in the Manitoba Court of Appeal, Twaddle J. A. held first that there was no violation of section 2(b) of the Charter. Thus the impugned parts of the legislation 'do not impede the freedom of the applicants, or anyone else, to think what thoughts they will as to the good or evil of the policies the subsidized minority espouses; nor do they restrict the applicants from expressing their own views and incurring whatever expenditure they think appropriate for the purpose'.[8] In so holding, Twaddle J. A. found support in the landmark decision of the US Supreme Court in *Buckley* v. *Valeo*,[9] a decision which as we shall see has had considerable impact on the development of Canadian campaign finance law. In that case the American

[6] (1986) 24 DLR (4th) 587, at p. 590.
[7] Election Finances Act 1982–1983–1984 (Man.), c.45, s.50.
[8] (1986) 24 DLR (4th) 587, at p. 594.
[9] 424 US 1 (1976).

court rejected the view that government financial aid to political candidates violated the right to freedom of expression as protected by the First Amendment of the US Constitution. On the contrary, in a passage quoted by the Manitoba court, the US Supreme Court said that financial aid was '. . . a congressional effort, not to abridge, restrict, or censor speech, but rather to use public money to facilitate and enlarge public discussion and participation in the electoral process, goals vital to a self-governing people'.[10]

So far as section 2(a) of the Charter is concerned, Twaddle J. A. concluded that the protection of conscience was of 'more relevance to the present case'.[11] Here it was argued for the plaintiff that the relevant provisions of the legislation were constitutionally objectionable on two grounds:

(i) they require citizens '. . . to make compulsory contributions . . .';
(ii) they involve support of political parties which may '. . . espouse Communism, Fascism, or other forms of totalitarianism which are inimicable [*sic*] to citizens . . .'.[12]

The majority of the Court responded to this argument in the following terms:

Citizens are not, however, required to make contributions. The Act obligates the government to reimburse certain candidates and political parties out of the Consolidated Fund a portion of their expenses. The Consolidated Fund receives revenue from many sources and out of it many expenditures for different public purposes are made. It would be impossible and inappropriate to say which item of expenditure was supported by which item of revenue. The financial support given to a political candidate or his party cannot be attributed to any particular tax or to a payment by any particular individual or group. No citizen, by payment of tax or otherwise, is required to contribute to or support a political cause. The citizen pays a tax: the State uses it not as the citizen's money, but as part of a general public fund.[13]

Again support was found in the majority opinion in *Buckley* v. *Valeo* where it was said that '. . . every appropriation made by Congress uses public money in a manner to which some tax-

---

[10] 424 US 1 (1976), at p. 92.
[11] (1986) 24 DLR (4th) 587, at p. 594.
[12] Ibid., at p. 595.
[13] Ibid.

payers object'.[14] The Manitoba Court of Appeal continued by holding that

Monetary support by the State for the expression of minority views, however distasteful to the majority or to another minority group, cannot offend the conscience of those opposed to the viewpoint. No one is compelled to agree with the minority view nor forbidden to espouse a contrary one. To borrow the words of Dickson C. J. C. in *R*. v. *Big M Drug Mart* 'No one is . . . forced [by the impugned sections of the *Elections Finance Act* (*sic*)] to act in a way contrary to his beliefs or his conscience'. The Constitution does not guarantee that the State will not act inimically to a citizen's standards of proper conduct: it merely guarantees that a citizen will not be required to do, or refrain from doing, something contrary to those standards (subject always, of course, to the reasonable limitations recognised by s.1 of the Charter). The support given by the government to political causes hostile to the general, or a minority, viewpoint cannot induce in anyone a pang of conscience for the moral quality of their own conduct or lack of it.[15]

In the dissenting judgment (which was longer than the combined efforts of the majority, though much less persuasive) Huband J. A. was as forceful in his condemnation of public funding as Twaddle J. A. had been in its defence. First, Huband J. A. set the scene by stating that

The simple issue raised in this case is whether there is interference with freedom of conscience, and of thought, belief and opinion, when the State provides funding from general revenues to assist certain parties to attain elective office—parties who espouse views which are inimical to the opinions of the complaining citizen.[16]

He then proceeded to enquire rhetorically and tendentially:

Putting the applicants argument in stark terms, can a taxpayer be required to contribute to pay part of the election expenses of a neo-Nazi or a Maoist . . . ? Indeed, why should the taxpayer be required to pay part of the election expenses of a Liberal or a Conservative candidate with whose views there may be strenuous disagreement on matters of conscience, thought, belief and opinion?[17]

---

[14] 424 US 1 (1976), at p. 92.
[15] (1986) 24 DLR (4th) 587, at p. 596.
[16] Ibid., at p. 590.
[17] Ibid., at p. 591.

Finally, he referred to the argument of the plaintiffs that they should not be compelled to contribute to the funds of a party which may be elected to government and proceed with what the plaintiffs conceive to be repressive or immoral legislation. To all of this Huband J. A. replied and concluded simply that 'the State cannot become involved in the financing of political propaganda'.[18] But a decision that legislation violates section 2 does not of course conclude the matter, for the impugned measure can still be retrieved by section 1 which permits such 'reasonable limits prescribed by law as can be demonstrably justified in a free and democratic society'. The majority had no need to consider this, having concluded that there was no violation of s.2. But it became crucial for Huband J. Nevertheless he gave it fairly short shrift. While accepting that 'there are various schemes [of this kind] utilized in different democratic states', he noted also (without citing any authority) that 'there are . . . continuing disputes as to whether such schemes are consonant with democratic principles, and whether it is a proper function of the State to use tax dollars to support the propaganda of certain political parties or candidates'.[19] And in an unsustainable passage he concluded that 'It can hardly be said that the particular scheme embodied in the Manitoba legislation is "a reasonable limitation" once it is found to be in conflict with the fundamental freedoms declared in s.2 of the Charter'.[20] If correct this would render s.1 redundant, for the logic of his position is that a breach of s.2 can never be justified under s.1.

II. Releasing the Special Interests . . .

A second case concerning the application of the Charter dealt exclusively with freedom of expression, protected by section 2(b). The case in question, *National Citizens' Coalition Inc.* v. *Attorney-General of Canada*,[21] was a challenge to the restrictions on third-party advertising contained in s.70 of the federal Act.

[18] (1986) 24 DLR (4th) 587, at p. 592.
[19] Ibid.
[20] Ibid., at p. 592.
[21] (1985) 11 DLR (4th) 481.

It will be recalled that s.70.1 made it an offence for a person (other than a candidate, party, or agent) to incur an election expense. Until the passing of Bill C-169 in 1983 this was subject to the defence in s.70.1(4) which it will be recalled from Chapter 4 protected a person who incurred election expenses

(a) for the purpose of gaining support for views held by him on an issue of public policy, or for the purpose of advancing the aims of any organization or association, other than a political party or an organization or association of a partisan political character, of which he was a member and on whose behalf the expenses were incurred; and

(b) in good faith and not for any purpose related to the provisions of this Act limiting the amount of election expenses that may be incurred by any other person on account of or in respect of the conduct or management of an election.

In 1983 this defence was removed with the result that only the blanket prohibition remained. The question which arose in the *NCC* case was whether the blanket prohibition on election expenses by those other than parties and candidates violated the right to freedom of expression.

1. CAMPAIGN FINANCING AND THE BILL OF RIGHTS

Respect for freedom of expression has a long tradition in Canada. In one famous dictum from a decision of the Supreme Court of Canada in 1938, the Chief Justice of Canada, Sir Lyman Duff, said:

Under the constitution established by the *B.N.A. Act*, legislative power for Canada is vested in one Parliament consisting of the Sovereign, an upper house styled the Senate, and the House of Commons. Without entering in detail upon an examination of the enactments of the Act relating to the House of Commons, it can be said that these provisions manifestly contemplate a House of Commons which is to be, as the name itself implies, a representative body; constituted, that is to say, by members elected by such of the population of the united Provinces as may be qualified to vote. The preamble of the statute, moreover, shows plainly enough that the constitution of the Dominion is to be similar in principle to that of the United Kingdom. The statute contemplates a Parliament working under the influence of public opinion and public discussion. There can be no controversy that such institutions derive their efficacy from the free public discussion of affairs, from criticism and answer and counter-criticism, from attack upon policy and administration and defence and counter-attack; from the freest and fullest analysis and examination from every point of view of political proposals. This is signally true in respect of the discharge by Ministers of the Crown of their responsibility to Parliament, by members of Parliament of their duty to the electors, and by the electors themselves of their responsibilities in the election of their representatives.[22]

The right of public discussion was of course 'subject to legal restrictions; those based upon considerations of decency and public order, and others conceived for the protection of various private and public interests with which, for example, the laws of defamation and sedition are concerned'.[23] In the same case it was also said, however, that:

Under the British system, which is ours, no political party can erect a prohibitory barrier to prevent the electors from getting information concerning the policy of the Government. Freedom of discussion is essential to enlighten public opinion in a democratic State; it cannot be curtailed without affecting the right of the people to be informed through sources independent of the Government concerning matters of public interest. There must be an untrammelled publication of the news and political opinions of the political parties contending for ascendancy. As stated in the preamble of the British North America Act, our constitution is and will remain, unless radically changed, 'similar in principle to that of the United Kingdom'. At the time of Confederation, the United Kingdom was a democracy. Democracy cannot be maintained without its foundation: free public opinion and free discussion throughout the nation of all matters affecting the State within the limits set by the Criminal Code and the common law.[24]

More recently, the Bill of Rights of 1960 introduced a more limited form of judicial review of legislation than that now permitted under the Charter. The 1960 document set out a series of fundamental freedoms,[25] and provided that Acts of the federal Parliament (whether passed before or after the

[22] *Re Alberta Legislation* (1938) 2 DLR 81, at p. 107.
[23] Ibid., at p. 107.
[24] Ibid., at p. 119 (Cannon J.).
[25] Canadian Bill of Rights, SC 1960, 8 & 9 Eliz. II, c.44. See Tarnopolsky, 1978.

introduction of the Bill of Rights)[26] should not be regarded as abrogating its terms unless there was an express provision to this effect in the legislation in question.[27] It is to be noted that the Election Expenses Act 1974 did not contain a clause of this kind, and the question did arise as to whether even the un-reformed s.70.1(4) was consistent with the Bill of Rights. In *Roach*, more fully discussed in Chapter 4, it was said by a Provincial Court judge that the Bill of Rights did not need to be considered in view of the fact that the accused's conduct was not in any event unlawful under the Election Expenses Act.[28] He did say, however, that in his opinion 'the Parliament of Canada has the power, within the legislative fields over which it has jurisdiction under the British North America Act, to pass legislation which may limit the freedoms of public discussion where the common good requires such a limitation'.[29] For its part, the appeal court in *Roach* did not expressly address the Bill of Rights point, although it does appear to have been argued before it. Perhaps there was no need to make such reference in view of the interpretation placed by the Court on s.70.1(4), though it is to be noted that the generous interpre-tation in favour of the accused was influenced strongly, if not by the Bill of Rights, then clearly by the passage from the 1938 decision referred to above.[30] So *Roach* was rather inconclusive on the impact of the Bill of Rights and the 1974 Act. To the extent that it was considered, the view appears to have been that there was no violation, though it is far from clear what the position would have been had the expenditure not been permitted by the defence.

The Bill of Rights was also considered in the rather different circumstances of *R. v. Risdon*,[31] which related to events at a by-election in 1978 held in a riding in Toronto. Risdon was not a candidate for the election, unlike Mr David Crombie. The prosecution related to allegations that Risdon had arranged for the distribution of leaflets with the words 'Crombie Lied',

---

[26] s.5(2).
[27] s.2.
[28] Unreported, 24 Oct. 1977 (Judge H. E. Zimmerman).
[29] Ibid., at pp. 8–9.
[30] *R. v. Roach* (1980) 101 DLR (3d) 736, esp. at p. 742.
[31] Unreported, n.d. (Judge J. Murphy).

which were designed to prevent the election of the candidate in question. Unlike in *Roach*, the prosecution here succeeded, the Court taking the view that 'this is the type of material and action that is envisaged in Section 70.1',[32] which was unprotected by s.70.1(4), the material being a personal and political attack unrelated to any question of public policy. In such circumstances the Bill of Rights clearly assumed a significance which it did not have in *Roach*. The Provincial Court took the view again, however, that there was no violation on the simple ground that there was no limitation of Risdon's right of free speech; 'He could have attended every election meeting Mr Crombie attended and given his views that Mr Crombie was a liar. He could have knocked on every door and obtained volunteers to knock on every door to express his views.'[33] On appeal the conviction was upheld, the Court again taking the view that s.70.1(4) did not apply here on the ground that the personal views of a private individual concerning the honesty of a candidate for election is not a matter of public policy.[34] The Bill of Rights points also failed here too, though it is not clear why. According to the judgment the reasons on this point were delivered orally and had no particular relevance to the merits of the appeal.[35] It would thus appear (perhaps paradoxically) that the legislation had met the challenge of judicial review (at least at this level), despite the willingness of the Court in *Risdon* (as in *Roach*) to interpret the defence in s.70.1(4) as widely as possible in favour of the accused. This interpretative approach was a reflection of the belief that 'the history and foundation of [the] nation's concept of the proper conduct of the electoral process involves the philosophy that elections are the proper time and place to raise issues of every kind, which affect the public or a significant number of them, so that the electorate can cast informed ballots'.[36]

---

[32] *R.* v. *Risdon*, unreported, n.d., at p. 6.
[33] Ibid., at p. 7.
[34] Unreported, 24 Oct. 1980 (Judge A. C. Whealy).
[35] Ibid., at p. 2.
[36] Ibid., at p. 12.

2. The Charter and Third-Party Expenditures

Although the repeal of s.70.1(4) by Bill C-169 in 1983 tightened the law on third-party expenditures, it did not prohibit such expenditures altogether. As the Chief Electoral Officer pointed out in 1984, 'the act as it was amended still allowed the debate or the discussion of issues during an election. The only thing that was not allowed was to promote directly or to oppose directly a candidate or a political party. Any single-issue group or pressure group could still promote its own platform. It could still promote pro-life or abortion or capital punishment or free enterprise or anything, as long as in so doing it was not promoting or opposing directly, by naming him, the candidate or a political party.'[37] A number of groups did intervene in electoral politics, the most notable being the National Citizens' Coalition, which had been campaigning to reverse the repeal of s.70.1(4).[38]

The Coalition is a non-profit-making organization with a track record of funding political causes normally identified with the Right. It is an incorporated body with a constitution, its members 'participating' by letter and telephone. At the head of the organization is a board of directors and a board of advisers. Neither is elected, both existing on a 'permanent basis'.[39] These boards are appointed in turn by an 'inner circle'[40] of three or four people, of whom Mr Colin Brown appeared to be one. According to Brown, in evidence to the House of Commons Standing Committee on Privileges and Elections, the NCC had 30,000 members, who in 1984 had contributed more than $1 million in total. Some members give more than others and some forget in some years. But he denied that the Coalition had any donations in excess of $10,000 and admitted to only one or two that were between $3,000 and $5,000. Indeed, if the Coalition does have 30,000 members, then a donation from each of less than $35 would yield an income in excess of $1

---

[37] Minutes of Proceedings and Evidence of the Standing Committee on Privileges and Elections, 12 Dec. 1984, p. 13.

[38] See Minutes of Proceedings and Evidence of the Standing Committee on Privileges and Elections, 18 Dec. 1984, pp. 24–5.

[39] Ibid. 25–7.

[40] Ibid. 27.

million. Mr Brown did not state (and in fairness he was not asked) how much of this money was used in the 1984 federal election campaign, and to what effect. Nevertheless, it does indicate that considerable sums of money are available for election campaigning by organizations other than the parties themselves. As we shall see, however, although the NCC is willing to provide this limited amount of information about its organization and expenditures, it is not willing to provide details about the identity of its donors.[41]

Anyone whose Charter rights are infringed may apply to a court of competent jurisdiction to obtain such remedy as the court considers just and appropriate in the circumstances.[42] The challenge to the statutory provisions was heard by the Alberta Court of Queen's Bench. It may or may not be a coincidence that the Alberta courts are reputedly conservative and that the Calgary court is particularly so regarded. Be that as it may, a number of preliminary points arose: the law being challenged had not yet come into force; the plaintiff had no standing, having no special interest in the impugned law; and the plaintiff was a corporation. All were rejected, it having been already held in *Big M Drug Mart* that the Charter protects corporations as well as individuals,[43] on the ground that it is the nature of the law and not the character of the accused which is in issue. Having thus dismissed the preliminary objections, the attention of the Court was turned to the questions of substance. First, did the legislation restrict freedom of expression (the section 2 question) and if so, secondly, could that restriction be permitted as being demonstrably justified in a free and democratic society (the section 1 question)? The Alberta Court of Queens Bench had little difficulty in answering the section 2 question in the affirmative: the legislation on its face limited the action of anyone other than registered parties or candidates from incurring election expenses during the prescribed time.[44]

[41] See Minutes of Proceedings and Evidence of the Standing Committee on Privileges and Elections, 18 Dec. 1984, pp. 10–21.

[42] Canadian Charter of Rights and Freedoms, s.24(1).

[43] *R. v. Big M Drug Mart Ltd.* (1984) 5 DLR (4th) 121, affirmed by the Supreme Court of Canada (1985) 18 DLR (4th) 321.

[44] *National Citizens' Coalition Inc.* v. *Attorney-General of Canada* (1985) 11 DLR (4th) 481, at p. 487.

The principal question, then, was whether the 1983 amendments could be protected under section 1, a question said the judge (Medhurst J.) which 'involves a weighing of the individual right of freedom of expression in relation to the said benefits to society of an effective system for the election of Members of Parliament'.[45] The onus of establishing a section 1 defence lay on the government, which argued mainly that the spending limits on candidates and political parties were necessary 'to ensure a level of equality amongst all participants in federal elections'[46] and that the controls under challenge were in turn necessary to protect the spending limits from being undermined by third parties. Apart from the *Roach* case, other examples were provided of the possible mischief of uncontrolled third-party activities. One was an advertisement published by the Jewish Joint Public Relations Committee just before the 1980 election in opposition to the candidate Frank Epp in Kitchener–Waterloo. Evidence was also given by Douglas Fisher, a Liberal MP who alleged that threats had been made by the anti-seal-hunting organization to the effect that large sums of money would be spent in opposition to Liberal candidates unless their policy on seal-hunting was changed. And further evidence was led about expenditures by the NCC during the 1979 and 1980 general elections in opposition to unnamed candidates.[47] The legislation was also supported as being a reasonable limit in evidence given by Professor Courtney, who wrote:

Were special interest groups or individuals free to participate in the electoral process totally without constraints, they would enjoy advantages not otherwise available to the political parties. The fact is that the respective roles and responsibilities of political parties and special interest groups are different. Political parties are electorally accountable for their acts, which is one of the ways in which the term 'responsible government' is given meaning in a parliamentary system. Generally every three or four years political parties are held to account by the electorate. By definition, special interest groups are necessarily different. They have more narrowly-defined interests, goals and

---

[45] Ibid.
[46] Ibid., at p. 495.
[47] Ibid., at p. 491.

memberships than political parties and, in the final analysis, they are not electorally responsible for their activities.[48]

The Court, however, rejected the defence, noting that freedom of expression is said by many to be one of the most significant of freedoms in a democratic society since the political structure depends on free debate of ideas and opinions, something of particular importance at election time. The attention of the Court was drawn to the decision of the US Supreme Court in *Buckley* v. *Valeo*,[49] which dealt with the constitutionality of federal legislation setting limits on campaign contributions and expenditures. The Court concluded that the contribution limits were lawful, but that the spending limits were not, being a violation of the First Amendment, holding that:

A restriction on the amount of money a person or group can spend on political communication during a campaign necessarily reduces the quantity of expression by restricting the number of issues discussed, the depth of their exploration and the size of the audience reached. This is because virtually every means of communicating ideas in today's mass society requires the expenditure of money.[50]

The attention of the Alberta Court was also drawn to the fact that there were less intrusive means of dealing with the problem with which Bill C-169 (the 1983 amendments to s.70.1) was concerned. Mr Hamel, the Chief Electoral Officer, in giving evidence said that there were two ways of dealing with the problem. One was to repeal subsection 4 (as was done by the 1983 Act). The other would be to rewrite subsection 4 'to make it more specific in line with preserving the right of third parties to express themselves while maintaining the intent of the legislation'.[51] In the circumstances, it is perhaps unsurprising that Medhurst J. should reject the section 1 defence, and conclude that:

Care must be taken to ensure that the freedom of expression, as guaranteed by s.2 of the Charter, is not arbitrarily or unjustifiably

[48] (1985) 11 DLR (4th) 481, at p. 492.
[49] 424 US 1 (1976).
[50] Ibid., at p. 19.
[51] (1985) 11 DLR (4th) 481, at p. 491.

limited. Fears or concerns of mischief that may occur are not adequate reasons for imposing a limitation. There should be actual demonstration of harm or a real likelihood of harm to a society value before a limitation can be said to be justified.[52]

3. The Response to the *NCC* Case

The effect of the *NCC* decision has been to leave federal law on this matter in a very unhappy state. Technically the decision is binding in Alberta only. However, in order to have consistency throughout Canada, the Chief Electoral Officer and the Commissioner have decided not to apply the law anywhere else. So there is the remarkable situation of a law on the books which the law enforcement agencies refuse to enforce. Clearly the matter begs for resolution by the Supreme Court. One solution would have been to appeal the decision, but surprisingly the government failed to do so, despite the advice from the Chief Electoral Officer that an appeal should be taken. The Chief Electoral Officer was favourable to an appeal because the matter was 'sufficiently important to have a superior court, including the Supreme Court of Canada, rule on the matter'.[53] Nevertheless, it is clear that the Liberal government was opposed to the decision, with Mr Trudeau strongly defending s.70.1 in the House of Commons.[54] In the absence of an appeal, another possibility is that an interested party in a province other than Alberta will seek judicial review to compel the CEO to enforce his statutory duties. In that way the matter could be reviewed by another court, and ultimately perhaps by the Supreme Court itself.

In the meantime the decision has given rise to concern from a range of quarters, its effect being to remove any constraints from electioneering by potentially well-financed special-interest groups. Parliamentarians have been particularly anxious, with some members being concerned about the lack of public accountability by those special interests which participate in

[52] Ibid., at p. 496.
[53] Minutes of Proceedings and Evidence of the Standing Committee on Privileges and Elections, 11 Dec. 1984, p. 31.
[54] House of Commons Debates, 2nd session, 32nd Parliament, vol. i, 19 Jan. 1984, p. 556.

the electoral process. Thus when the NCC appeared before the Commons Standing Committee on Privileges and Elections, some members of the Committee expressed concern that the membership lists of the Coalition were not publicly available. This had been sought by one member of the Committee on the ground that 'in a free and democratic society', the public has 'a right to know who the people are that run full-page ads in major newspapers across the country'.[55] The same member continued by claiming that the 'public should be aware of who is paying the piper'.[56] Another member claimed that if there is disclosure of donations to political parties 'perhaps the same rules should apply to those who try to influence the politics of Canada'.[57] For its part, the NCC responded to these concerns in three ways. First, it argued that there is a confidence between the Coalition and the people who support it, and to reveal identities of supporters without their consent would break that confidence. And in this context it was asserted that 'Many people do prefer anonymity, and that is something that should be respected unless there is some compelling reason to overcome that'.[58] Secondly, the NCC argued that the public already has access to sufficient information about the organization and its activities. Thus, Mr Colin Brown replied that the members of the Committee could have the NCC's annual statement; they could know who were its advisers and its board; and they could have access to the names of those members who published letters in the organization's newspaper. And thirdly, it was claimed that there was no compelling reason to disclose any further information. In the words of Mr Alan Hunter, the Coalition's counsel:

I am not sure whether it is necessary to know. What is the vice? What are you afraid of? Is there some collusion? Is there some illegal activity here that must be brought out? The National Citizens' Coalition has indicated what its values are. People presumably agree with those sufficiently to give the money. Are we not entitled to use the product of our labours in such a way? I should think so. Should that be chilled

[55] Minutes of Proceedings and Evidence of the Standing Committee on Privileges and Elections, 18 Dec. 1984, p. 10.
[56] Ibid. 11.
[57] Ibid. 14.
[58] Ibid.

by saying, if you do this, then you lose your anonymity? Is there some compelling reason to do that?[59]

Expressions of concern have also come from the CEO who had originally proposed the tightening up of s.70.1 by removing the s.70.1(4) defence. The *NCC* case led the CEO to produce new proposals. Now unable to propose a complete ban on third-party advertising, he made the following recommendation in his Annual Report for 1984:

Recommendation: That the question of third party advertising be looked at with a view to striking a proper balance between the adequate control of election expenses and the freedom of expression of Canadians. In my opinion, the solution should probably lie in the imposition of certain restrictions on third parties not amounting to a total prohibition. In this way, third parties would be free to participate fully in the election campaign in a manner that would strive to ensure fairness in the system. However, news items and regular editorials should be specifically excluded from the application of any new provision. (Chief Electoral Officer of Canada, 1984: 24)

One possible way of implementing this idea would be to ban the expensive media campaigns, but to permit other forms of third-party advertising (such as bumper-stickers). But although this is an important compromise of the legislation which was struck down by Medhurst J., it is unclear whether even this would survive Charter challenge. It is to be recalled that in the *NCC* case, the US Supreme Court decision in *Buckley* v. *Valeo*[60] proved to be very influential and perhaps even decisive. It is to be pointed out that in that case what the Court struck down was not a ban on third-party expenditures, but a $1,000 ceiling on expenditures to promote a clearly identified candidate. A restriction on the amount of money a person or group can spend on political communication during a campaign, the Court said, necessarily reduces the quantity of expression by restricting the number of issues discussed, the depth of their exploration, and the size of the audience reached.[61] The Court continued by pointing out that

---

[59] Ibid.
[60] 424 US 1 (1976).
[61] Ibid., at p. 19.

The expenditure limitations contained in the Act represent substantial rather than merely theoretical restraints on the quantity and diversity of political speech. The $1,000 ceiling on spending 'relative to a clearly identified candidate . . .' would appear to exclude all citizens and groups except candidates, political parties, and the institutional press from any significant use of the most effective modes of communication.[62]

It would, for example, be 'a federal criminal offence for a person or association to place a single one-quarter page advertisement "relative to a clearly identified candidate" in a major metropolitan newspaper'.[63]

If the Canadian courts continue slavishly to follow *Buckley* v. *Valeo* then it is highly likely that the more modest proposals of the CEO would also be struck down. They are in fact indirect limits on the amount which may be spent and could indeed reduce the quantity of expression, particularly by restricting the size of the audience reached. And it does seem likely that a further challenge will be mounted if this particular proposal is implemented, the NCC having made clear that it objects to the suggestion. In evidence to the House of Commons Standing Committee on Privileges and Elections, the organization's counsel, Mr Alan Hunter, referred to the 1984 Report of the CEO and to the recommendation on third-party advertising in particular. He continued by observing that

the reasons for the recommendation are the same reasons for the recommendations that led to Bill C-169. Those reasons were advanced before the court. They were found to be wanting. There are no further reasons that are placed before Parliament in this report for the consideration of the imposition of restrictions. Given that, I would observe that it is not likely that a restriction based on evidence that had already been before the court and subject to examination and cross examination, would survive a further constitutional attack.[64]

So far as Mr Hunter was concerned, 'there would have to be egregious mischief to warrant restrictions on freedom of expression and the right to an informed vote', and he could find 'no evidence of that in the Chief Electoral Officer's re-

---

[62] 424 US 1 (1976), at p. 19.

[63] Ibid., at p. 40.

[64] Minutes of Proceedings and Evidence of the Standing Committee on Privileges and Elections, 18 Dec. 1984, p. 7.

port'.[65] In the absence of any such mischief the NCC was opposed to spending limits on independent advertising, as they appeared also to be against spending limits for candidates and political parties. Thus, Mr Hunter again:

The limit on expenditure necessarily limits the amount of political speech. That affects the people who want to speak, but it also affects the people who are entitled to listen. It cuts down the amount of information available to the body politic. So freedom of expression is not just freedom to speak but also the freedom of others to hear what you have to say, and if you would limit expenditure on political speech you will necessarily limit and amount of information available to be considered by the elector.[66]

Yet, perhaps inconsistently, the Coalition did not declare itself against all controls on third-party election expenditure. In response to a question from Mr Patrick Boyer, Hunter suggested that the Coalition lived happily under the law as it existed before 1983—that is to say before the subsection 4 defence was removed from the operation of s.70.1.[67]

III. . . . But New Problems for the Unions

A third major issue which has arisen relates to trade union political activity and affects both donations to political parties by unions and also their independent expenditures in the course of a campaign. This is a problem which has been encountered in many jurisdictions, including the United States and the United Kingdom. The problem essentially is whether a dissenting minority within a trade union should be empowered and permitted to restrain the political activity of the union which may have the tacit support of the majority. The problem had been raised in Canada before the introduction of the Charter. In 1961 for example, legislation in British Columbia provided that a union could not use for political purposes any money deducted from an employee's wages or paid as a condition of membership of a union.[68] This did not prohibit union

---

[65] Ibid.
[66] Ibid. 17.
[67] Ibid. 20.
[68] Labour Relations Amendment Act, SBC 1961, c.31, s.5.

145

political donations,[69] but it made it very difficult for them to collect money for this purpose. The only money which could be used would be that collected specifically for political activities. Nevertheless the legislation was unsuccessfully challenged on constitutional grounds in the famous *Oil Workers'* case,[70] the Supreme Court of Canada taking the view that the legislation fell within provincial jurisdiction as it dealt with 'property and civil rights'. The restriction was not removed until the enactment of the British Columbia Labour Code in 1973[71] introduced by the NDP government which had been elected in 1972.

1. THE ISSUE IN *LAVIGNE*

The issue in Charter litigation has been not whether legislation limiting trade union political expenditure is unconstitutional. Rather, it has been whether the omission of such legislation is a violation of the constitutional rights of individuals who object to this form of trade union activity. Although the issue has been raised in several cases now,[72] the leading case is clearly *Lavigne* v. *Ontario Public Service Employees' Union.*[73] The plaintiff, a college teacher, was concerned ultimately with the use by the union and his employer of powers conferred by the Colleges Collective Bargaining Act 1980[74] which provided for the conferring of exclusive bargaining status on the appropriate representative trade union,[75] which in this case was OPSEU.[76] The Act also provided by s.53:

[69] *Oil, Chemical and Atomic Workers' International Union, Local 16-601* v. *Imperial Oil Ltd.* [1963] SCR 584, at p. 594 where Martland J. said that the legislation did not 'prevent a trade union from engaging in political activities. It does not prevent it from soliciting funds from its members for political purposes, or limit, in any way, the expenditure of funds so raised. It does prevent the use of funds, which are obtained in particular ways, from being used for political purposes.'
[70] [1963] SCR 584.
[71] Labour Code of British Columbia, SBC 1973 (2nd session), c.122.
[72] See *Baldwin* v. *B.C. Government Employees' Union* (1986) 28 DLR (4th) 301.
[73] (1986) 55 OR (2d) 449.
[74] RSO 1980, c.74.
[75] Ibid., s.52.
[76] OPSEU represents approximately 87,000 workers in Ontario. They include 63,000 direct employees of the government of Ontario—the largest single bargaining unit in Canada. They also include 12,000 academic and support staff

53(1) The parties to an agreement may provide for the payment by the employees of dues or contributions to the employee organization.

(2) Where the Ontario Labour Relations Board is satisfied that an employee because of his religious convictions or belief objects to paying dues or contributions to an employee organization, the Ontario Labour Relations Board shall order that the provisions of the agreement pertaining thereto do not apply to such employee and that the employee is not required to pay dues or contributions to the employee organization, provided that amounts equivalent thereto are remitted by the employer to a charitable organization mutually agreed upon by the employee and the employee organization and failing such agreement then to such charitable organization registered as such under Part I of the Income Tax Act (Canada) as may be designated by the Ontario Labour Relations Board.

(3) No agreement shall contain a provision which would require, as a condition of employment, membership in the employee organization.

It is important to note what section 53 actually provides. First, it authorized an agreement between the parties whereby employees in the unit could be required to pay either dues or fees to the union (s.53(1)), but no one could be required to join the union (s.53(3)). It thus authorized an agency shop agreement (or Rand formula, as it is known in Canada) rather than a union shop agreement, whereby everyone could be required to join the union as a condition of employment. Secondly, it provided expressly that not everyone was required to pay an agency fee. Those with religious objections were excused, provided that they were not free-riders (s.53(2)). In 1982 a collective agreement was concluded, the agreement containing a union security clause which provided that 'There shall be an automatic deduction of an amount equivalent to the regular monthly membership dues from the salaries of all employees in the bargaining unit covered hereby'.[77] Mr Lavigne did not in fact join the union, but he was required, nevertheless, under the terms of the agreement to pay $338 to OPSEU, the money

of the Colleges of Applied Arts and Technology, and 23,000 other employees in over 200 separate bargaining units—including hospitals, laboratories, ambulance services, welfare agencies, and legal aid services.

[77] (1986) 55 OR (2d) 449, at p. 458.

being paid into the general revenues of the union and used for any purpose permitted under its constitution. The aims and objects of the union are set out in Article 4 of its Constitution, as follows:

(a) to regulate labour relations between the members and their employers and managers, said labour relations to include the scope of negotiation, collective bargaining, and the enforcement of collective agreements and health and safety standards;

(b) to organize, sign to membership, and represent employees in Ontario;

(c) to advance the common interests, economic, social and political, of the members and of all public employees, wherever possible, by all appropriate means;

(d) to bring about improvements in the wages and working conditions of the membership, including the right of equal pay for work of equal value;

(e) to defend the right to strike;

(f) to promote full employment and equitable distribution of wealth within Canadian society;

(g) to co-operate with labour unions and other organizations with similar objectives in strengthening the Canadian labour union movement as a means towards advancing the interests and improving the well being of workers generally in Canada;

(h) to promote justice, equality, and efficiency in services to the public;

(i) to strengthen, by precept and example, democratic principles and practices both in the Canadian labour union movement and in all manner of institutions, organizations and government in Canada.[78]

The union used this power under its Constitution to contribute to a number of causes, unrelated to immediate questions of collective bargaining. These were, first, financial contributions to the NDP; secondly, financial contributions to disarmament campaigns including the Campaign against Cruise Missile Testing; thirdly, financial contributions to a campaign opposing the expenditure of municipal funds for a domed stadium in Toronto; fourthly, financial contributions to Arthur Scargill and the striking British coalminers; and fifthly, financial

---

[78] (1986) 55 OR (2d) 449, at pp. 458–9.

contributions to Nicaragua. In each case the amount of money involved was very small, and in each case the amount of Mr Lavigne's contribution would have been infinitesimal. For example, the disputed donations to the NDP included a donation of $100 to the Oshawa NDP, $500 to the Ontario NDP, and $3,500 to the Ontario NDP for a commemoration dinner. In addition to these disputed payments, Lavigne drew attention to the fact that OPSEU is affiliated to both the Ontario Federation of Labour (OFL) and to the National Union of Provincial Government Employees (NUPGE) which is in turn affiliated to the Canadian Labour Congress (CLC). As an affiliated member of these organizations OPSEU pays to NUPGE 83 cents per month per employee (of which 43 cents is passed on to the CLC), and to the OFL 24 cents per month per employee. All three of these organizations were involved in supporting a number of social and political causes to which Lavigne objected. These included the extensive support by the CLC in particular for the NDP. In 1979 Congress had given $389,000 for the general election campaign in that year; in 1980 this rose to $433,000 for the general election in that year; and in 1984 it amounted to at least $353,000. In addition, money had been donated to the party on other occasions to help with by-elections, and roughly $200,000 had been spent in 1983 and 1984 to mobilize union support for the party.

It has to be said that for many years much of this expenditure by OPSEU would have been unlawful. Until 1969 a voluntary dues check-off regime operated in the public sector in Ontario. In that year a provincial regulation passed under the Public Service Act[79] introduced a new regime whereby a voluntary check-off arrangement would operate in the public service for existing employees but that the check-off would be mandatory for all future employees.[80] The regulation provided, however, a limitation on the uses to which mandatory dues could be applied:

the deductions referred to in this section shall be remitted to the [union] and shall be used only for purposes directly applicable to

---

[79] RSO 1960, c.202.
[80] O.Reg. 403/69.

the representation of Crown employees, and shall not be used for activities carried on by or on behalf of any political party.[81]

So it was unlawful for unions governed by the regulation to spend check-off income on party political purposes.[82] And it is to be noted that the regulations applied to collective agreements concluded by the colleges.[83] But it is also to be noted that the regulations were repealed in 1977 and that the ban on political action was never reintroduced.[84] So given the mandatory check-off arrangement and no restriction as to how the money so deducted might be used, the question is whether offended members of the bargaining unit could claim that their rights under the Charter had been violated. As already suggested, the question has been raised in other provinces,[85] but none of the other cases quite captured the same attention as *Lavigne*. Nor were they as well argued. So although the Supreme Court of British Columbia discussed a similar challenge, it did so on the basis of arguments which were neither as subtle nor as sophisticated as those advanced in *Lavigne*.

2. The Response of the High Court

Having established that the Charter applied in this case, the question was whether there was a violation. This essentially embraced two issues: did the agreement violate the right to freedom of association as protected by section 2(d); and, if so,

---

[81] O.Reg. 403/69, reg. 24a(b).

[82] Though this restriction would not have prohibited expenditures other than partisan political ones.

[83] The Ministry of Colleges and Universities Act, SO 1971, c.66 expressly made the Crown Employees Collective Bargaining Act, SO 1972, c.67 applicable to the community colleges. The 1972 Act had replaced the Public Service Act.

[84] O.Reg 870/77, reg. 15. The Colleges Collective Bargaining Act, SO 1975, c.74 subsequently governed collective bargaining. In 1975 a new collective agreement was signed with a dues check-off clause subject to the Ontario regulations. Although the regulations were repealed in 1977, the clause appeared in successive agreements until 1981 when the clause under dispute was introduced.

[85] See *Baldwin* v. *B.C. Government Employees' Union* (1986) 28 DLR (4th) 301. See also *Re Bhindi et al and British Columbia Projectionists Local 348 of International Alliance of Picture Machine Operators of the United States and Canada* (1985) 20 DLR (4th) 386.

could the breach be justified wholly or partially under section 1 which, as also already pointed out, provides that the rights guaranteed by the Charter are subject to 'such reasonable limits prescribed by law as can be demonstrably justified in a free and democratic society'? As to the section 2 question, the difficulty facing the Court was that in protecting the freedom to associate the Charter said nothing of the freedom not to associate. But in constructing such a right, White J. began by analysing the function of freedom of association. This, he said, was essentially twofold. First it is necessary if pluralism is to survive:

> The combining of the efforts of individuals to achieve a common end is essential to the dynamics of a democratic political system. Indeed, a democracy is government by association, and social and political change within a democracy is brought about largely through association. Individuals express their views and disseminate information through associations; when acting in concert with others an individual gains the capacity required to effect a political or social result. Although the maintenance of a 'free market place of ideas' is really a freedom of expression theme, in view of the fact that associations have great impact on that market, freedom of association is a necessary precondition to its existence.[86]

And, secondly, he held that associations are the means by which individual citizens may actively participate in the political process. Thus, within 'a democratic political system, voluntary private associations can serve to increase opportunities for self-realization, counterbalancing the strength of centralised power'.[87] In promoting this argument, White J. was strongly influenced by the writings of Emerson (1964: 4), who wrote that 'Association is an extension of individual freedom. It is a method of making more effective, of giving greater depth and scope to, the individual's needs, aspirations and liberties.'

How then can the negative right be extracted from this? As to the first rationale of the freedom (the need to promote pluralism), it was held that 'Forced association can restrict the free flow of ideas and thus distort the market place'.[88] The meaning of this is not explained. But it could presumably be

---

[86] (1986) 55 OR (2d) 449, at p. 494.
[87] Ibid.
[88] (1986) 55 OR (2d) 449, at p. 495.

argued that forced association distorts the market-place first by giving some associations a louder voice than they should have, and secondly by impairing greater competition by preventing new associations from becoming established. It would, however, be a mistake to exaggerate this argument. For it is equally true that in reality people who do not join will not go off and form rival associations and that pluralism may depend on a measure of compulsory association. Labour is already the weaker party in the struggle with capital. The more convincing basis of the negative right, then, is derived from freedom of association as a means of self-expression and self-realization. Of some importance here are the following remarks of Chief Justice Dickson in the Supreme Court of Canada in an earlier Charter case. There, he said:

Freedom can primarily be characterized by the absence of coercion or constraint. If a person is compelled by the state or the will of another to a course of action or inaction which he would not otherwise have chosen, he is not acting of his own volition and he cannot be said to be truly free. One of the major purposes of the Charter is to protect, within reason, from compulsion or restraint. Coercion includes not only such blatant forms of compulsion as direct commands to act or refrain from acting on pain of sanction; coercion includes indirect forms of control which determine or limit alternative courses of conduct available to others. Freedom in a broad sense embraces both the absence of coercion and constraint, and the right to manifest beliefs and practices. Freedom means that, subject to such limitations as are necessary to protect public safety, order, health, or morals or the fundamental rights and freedoms of others, no one is to be forced to act in a way contrary to his beliefs or his conscience.[89]

White J. concluded from this that 'a right to freedom of association which did not include a right not to associate would not really ensure "freedom"'.[90] It is true that here Lavigne was not required by the agreement to join the union. But that was not conclusive, for the 'question which arises under s.2 . . . is whether or not Mr. Lavigne is being forced to combine with others to achieve a common end'.[91] White J. had little difficulty

---

[89] *R.* v. *Big M Drug Mart Ltd.* (1985) 11 DLR (4th) 321, at p. 354.
[90] (1986) 55 OR (2d) 449, at p. 495.
[91] Ibid., at p. 496.

dealing with this question, thereby concluding that there had been a prima-facie breach of the Charter.[92]

As a result, the focus of attention switched to section 1. In addressing this question the Court followed the guidelines expounded by Chief Justice Dickson in *R. v. Oakes*[93] where he said that section 1 requires the defendant to establish two points as a condition precedent to success. The first is that there is a need to protect 'collective goals of fundamental importance',[94] or in the words of White J. that there is 'an important governmental objective which is acceptable in a free and democratic society'.[95] Secondly, the requirement that the restriction should be reasonable and demonstrably justified involves a form of proportionality test which has three important components:

First, the measures adopted must be carefully designed to achieve the objective in question. They must not be arbitrary, unfair or based on irrational considerations. In short, they must be rationally connected to the objective. Second, the means, even if rationally connected to the objective in this first sense, should impair as little as possible the right or freedom in question. Third, there must be a proportionality between the effects of the measures which are responsible for limiting the Charter right or freedom, and the objective which has been identified as of sufficient importance.[96]

In this case White J. was prepared to accept that there was an important governmental objective, namely, the elimination of free riders in collective bargaining, the defendant thereby overcoming the first of the s.1 hurdles.

The difficulty, however, related to the proportionality test. True, it was held that there was a rational connection between the governmental objective sought to be achieved and the governmental action that was challenged: 'there is a rational connection between the fostering of collective bargaining and the prevention of "free riders" and the forced payment of dues'.[97] But the second aspect of the proportionality test

---

[92] Ibid., at p. 498.
[93] (1986) 26 DLR (4th) 200.
[94] Ibid., at p. 225.
[95] (1986) 55 OR (2d) 449, at p. 513.
[96] (1986) 26 DLR (4th) 200, at p. 227.
[97] (1986) 55 OR (2d) 449, at p. 514.

presented rather more difficulty, with White J. concluding that
the government had not promoted its interests by employing
means which were least restrictive of the individual's freedom.
Thus, it was held, after a review of comparative material,[98] that
the 'collective bargaining process can be both advanced and
financed by those who benefit without the use of compulsory
dues for purposes beyond the immediate concerns of collective
bargaining and settlement of disputes arising out of the collective agreements'.[99] White J. continued by pointing out that
in other countries where 'a less obtrusive means has been
employed than that challenged in the instant application,
unions have not been paralysed and continue to be effective in
advancing the interests of their members, and society at large,
both through collective bargaining and political activism'.[100] He
concluded therefore, that

it is not necessary in order to finance collective bargaining to require
non-members to pay full union dues to the union which may be
applied to any purpose that its constitution permits including contributions to ideological and political causes. It would be possible to
draft a clause in a collective agreement providing for compulsory dues
check off that restricts the use of such dues to finance activities that
are directly related to the objective sought to be achieved, that is, to
collective bargaining and the administration of the collective agreement. Although it may be difficult to segregate spending related to
collective bargaining and collective agreement administration and
spending for other purposes, it has been done in other free and
democratic societies and, therefore, such a distinction could be implemented in collective agreements in Ontario affecting public sector unions. . . . perceived administrative hardship imposed on the
union in earmarking compulsory dues used for permissible and non-
permissible purposes, and in following a pattern least obtrusive to the
applicant's Charter rights, is no answer to the applicant's case.[101]

In a subsequent hearing[102] White J. ordered that Lavigne was
entitled to a declaration which would require the union to set

[98] This was legislation in force in several industrialized nations such as the
United Kingdom, Australia, France, Ireland, Italy, Switzerland, and West
Germany. White J. referred also to the constitutional law of the United States.
[99] (1986) 55 OR (2d) 449, at p. 514.
[100] Ibid.
[101] Ibid., at pp. 514–15.
[102] (1987) 60 OR (2d) 486.

up an administrative arrangement giving people such as himself the right to opt out of any obligation financially to support political purposes.[103]

[103] The order read as follows:

(1) A declaration that to the extent that ss.51, 52 and 53 of the *Colleges Collective Bargaining Act* R.S.O. 1980, c.74, and any collective agreement enabled thereby, compel the payment of dues to the Ontario Public Service Employees Union ('the Union') and such dues are used for any of the purposes set out in appendix 'A', when a non-member of the union objects to the use of such dues for such purposes, ss.51, 52 and 53 aforesaid, are in violation of s.2(d) of the *Constitution Act, 1982*, and are of no force or effect.

(2) A declaration that the entering into of a collective agreement by the Ontario Council of Regents for Colleges of Applied Arts and Technology, (the Council of Regents) with the Union, which collective agreement provides for the compulsory payment of dues to the Union, by an employee affected by the *Colleges Collective Bargaining Act*, R.S.O. 1980, c.74, who is a non-member of the Union, is in violation of s.2(d) of the *Constitition [sic] Act, 1982* to the extent that such agreement permits the use of such dues for any of the purposes set out in Appendix 'A' hereto, when the non-member of the Union objects to such use of dues.

(3) A declaration that in the event that a non-member of the Union, who has notified the Union of an objection to dues paid by him or her to the Union, being used for purposes not related to collective bargaining or the administration of the collective agreement, including those set out in Appendix 'A' hereto, and the Union are unable to agree on the percentage of dues related to collective bargaining and the administration of the collective agreement, then the amount of dues in dispute shall be placed in an interest bearing escrow account until such time as the procedure mentioned in paragraph 4 hereof has been set in place and is functioning and such amount and accrued interest shall be disposed of pursuant to paragraph 4 hereof.

(4) A declaration that the union shall within six months from the date of this order, or any period of extension granted by a judge of this court, propose a procedural scheme to the non-members, who object to the use of dues for purposes not related to collective bargaining or the administration of the collective agreement, including those set out in Appendix 'A' hereto, whereby such non-members shall be given an opportunity to challenge the union's decision on the perecentage purporting to relate to collective bargaining and the administration of the collective agreement; such procedure shall include advance written notice of the opportunity to challenge the decision, the provision of copies of, and access to any relevant financial records, and books of account as are mentioned in paragraph 5, hereof, and a hearing before an impartial decision-maker having the discretion to make a prompt decision on the percentage in issue; and providing further that pending such decision, the amount of any dues of the non-member in dispute shall be held in an interest bearing escrow account and the funds held in such account and interest accrued shall be apportioned forthwith after such decision in accordance therewith.

(5) A declaration that the Union shall maintain financial records and books of account in sufficient detail to enable a non-member who has objected to the use of dues for purposes not related to collective bargaining and the

3. THE RESPONSE OF THE SUPREME
COURT OF CANADA

The *Lavigne* case, which had been billed as 'the labour trial of the century', was received by the unions as a great threat to their political freedoms. Indeed, at the heart of the case were fundamental questions. Thus, what are the proper purposes of trade unions? Who is to determine these purposes? Is it to be the members or the courts? But apart from being import-ant from these and other perspectives, as already suggested *Lavigne* had important implications for political financing generally and for the NDP and the unions in particular. The decision was all the more troubling in this sense for the fact that other developments in Charter jurisprudence tended to suggest that a similar action could be brought by workers employed in the private sector, as well as by those engaged in government service or in government-related service.[104] The Ontario Labour Relations Act, for example, empowers a union to require an employer to accept an agency shop arrangement or Rand formula in a collective agreement.[105] Under the Act the parties may also agree on more far-reaching security arrange-

administration of the collective agreement including those set out in Appendix 'A' hereto, at any time on reasonable notice to the Union to determine the percentage of dues related to collective bargaining and the administration of the collective agreement; such financial records shall be kept in sufficient detail to enable such non-member to trace the expenditure of all funds derived from the non-member's dues, either as expended directly by the union or indirectly through any affiliated organization financially supported by the Union.

(6) A declaration that the procedural scheme mentioned in paragraph (4) hereof, shall permit the impartial decision maker to take into account all relevant accounting and financial data, including the historical use of the union's funds and those of any relevant affiliated organization financially supported by the union for the previous two fiscal periods of the union.

(7) A declaration that at the end of each fiscal period of the Union, the Union shall reconcile the percentage of Union dues collected from the non-member with its actual expenditures for collective bargaining and collective agreement administration and shall forthwith refund any overpayment to the objecting non-member. Similarly, if reconciliation indicates an underpayment by the non-member for collective bargaining and collective agreement administration the non-member shall forthwith pay over the amount of any underpayment to the union. . . .

[104] Appendix 'A' is not reproduced. See esp. *Re Blainey and Ontario Hockey Association* (1986) 26 DLR (4th) 728, approved by the Supreme Court of Canada in *RWSDU* v. *Dolphin Delivery* [1986] 2 SCR 573.
[105] RSO 1980, c.228, s.43.

ments, such as a union shop or preference for union members.[106] Suppose that a union elected to insist on the Rand formula or that the parties agreed to a union shop. An employee member of the bargaining unit might then seek a declaration that the employer cannot lawfully deduct money from his or her wages to hand over to the union if the money is then to be used for political purposes. Even though the employer is not a government actor, the action might well succeed in the case of an agency shop (or mandatory Rand formula) on the ground that the employer had been required by legislation to violate the plaintiff's Charter right to freedom of association, and in the case of the union shop that the employer had been authorized (though not required) to violate the rights of the plaintiff.[107]

A series of court orders of this kind could clearly have led to a reduction in the amount of money which unions had available for political purposes. A growing number of unions could gradually have been required to introduce arrangements permitting agency fee payers to opt out of payment of that part of their dues which were to be used for political purposes. Indeed in practice unions might have been required to extend the facility to members as well as fee payers to stop the former from defecting to avoid payment of the political contribution. This is not to deny that there are arguments in favour of reducing the level of union support for the NDP as well as the amount of trade union money which is spent as independent expenditures during election campaigns. One difficulty, however, is that indirect restrictions of this kind would be curiously one-sided. Thus, while trade union support of the NDP might be hit, there would be no corresponding regulation of company support for the other parties, even though the dependence of these parties on corporate money is greater than NDP

---

[106] RSO 1980, c.228, s.46.

[107] In *Blainey* a girl had been prevented by the Ontario Hockey Association from competing in hockey competitions because of her sex. Under the Ontario Human Rights Code, sporting activity was expressly excluded from the Act. It was held by a majority (2:1) that the Code violated s.15 of the Charter. So although the action was a suit between private parties, the Charter was of crucial importance to challenge the Human Rights Code (government action) which permitted (but did not require) the discriminatory practices of the Association.

dependence on the unions. By the same token, while independent campaign expenditures by trade unions might be reduced, there would be no corresponding regulation of independent expenditures from the business community, even though its electoral spending is thought greatly to exceed that incurred by the unions. In other words, labour is already engaged in an unequal struggle in the political arena, particularly after the free-for-all encouraged by the *National Citizens' Coalition* case[108] which makes it difficult to justify any direct or indirect restriction on labour's political spending, at least for the time being. This is a matter to which we return in Chapter 8. But for the meantime it may be enough to suggest that if controls on trade union political spending are to be introduced, they should be met by balanced and even-handed restrictions on the business community. For that reason the decision of the Supreme Court of Canada to uphold the Ontario Court of Appeal's reversal of White J.[109] is to be welcomed, even if by effectively reinforcing the approach taken in the *NCC* case it does little to help the overall spirit of the legislation.

In dismissing Lavigne's appeal the Supreme Court of Canada split as to the reasons for its decision.[110] One view given in the judgment of La Forest J. (with the concurrence of Sopinka and Gonthier JJ.) was that although the challenged practice did amount to a breach of the appellant's constitutional right to freedom of association under section 2(d) of the Charter, this could be justified under section 1 as a reasonable limit which is justified in a free and democratic society. As to the former issue it was held first that the guarantee of freedom of association did not simply guarantee the positive right to join an association without penalty, but embraced also the 'freedom from compelled association', on the ground that 'forced association will stifle the individual's potential for self-fulfilment and realization as surely as voluntary association will develop it'. Having so concluded, La Forest J. held secondly that even though Lavigne was not required by the terms of the legislation or the agreement made thereunder to join the union or to

---

[108] *National Citizen's Coalition Inc.* v. *Attorney-General for Canada* (1984) 11 DLR (4th) 481.
[109] (1989) 56 DLR (4th) 474.
[110] Judgment rendered on 27 June 1991. Unreported at the time of writing.

participate in its affairs, nevertheless 'financial contribution to an organisation alone may constitute association within the meaning of the Charter'. But having gone this far, La Forest J. was reluctant to hold that all compulsory financial contributions to a union were unconstitutional. A distinction was drawn between contributions used for collective bargaining purposes and those used for political purposes. According to La Forest J. there was no violation of freedom of association by compelling a worker to associate with a union to 'the extent that it addresses itself to the matters, the terms and conditions of employment for members of his bargaining unit, with respect to which he is naturally associated with his fellow employees'. On these matters 'the union is simply viewed as a reasonable vehicle by which the necessary interconnectedness of Lavigne and his fellow workers is expressed'. But different considerations applied when employees were being asked financially to support political causes, relating to their membership of the wider community rather than the narrow bargaining unit. On these 'broader' matters, an individual was entitled to claim the right 'to be free to make his own choices, unfettered by the opinion of those he works with, as to what associations, if any, he will be associated with outside the workplace'.

So unlike White J. at first instance, La Forest J. was unwilling to hold that the Rand formula was *per se* a violation of the constitutional right to freedom of association or that an unqualified freedom not to associate was the direct corollary of the freedom to associate. But although he did hold that compulsory contributions violated constitutional rights when used for political purposes, also unlike White J., La Forest J. held that this could be justified under section 1 of the Charter. As in the High Court, the section 1 analysis was centred on the test which had been expounded in the earlier decision in *R.* v. *Oakes*.[111] Once again there was little difficulty in establishing that the restrictions on constitutional rights were in the interests of collective goals of fundamental importance, one of which was 'to ensure that unions have both the resources and the mandate necessary to enable them to play a role in shaping the

---

[111] (1986) 26 DLR (4th) 200.

political, economic and social context within which particular collective agreements and labour relations disputes will be negotiated or resolved'. But in contrast to the proceedings before White J., on this occasion the union was able to satisfy the Court that the restrictions met the proportionality limb of the test. Much discussion centred on the claim that 'the state objectives of fostering a politically active union movement guided by democratic decision-making could be achieved while more fully respecting the rights of those in the position of the appellant'. In particular it was suggested that such people could be given the right to opt out of the obligation to support political causes of which they disapprove. But unlike the decision at first instance, this solution was rejected by La Forest J. on the ground that opting out 'could seriously undermine unionism's financial base' with the result that the ability of unions by their support for the NDP and pressure groups favourably to 'affect the political, social and economic environment in which collective bargaining and dispute resolution take place will be correspondingly reduced'. Significantly, it was noted that 'if individuals can opt out of supporting the NDP, the unions will simply have much fewer dollars to support it'.

A rather different approach to this question was adopted by the other members of the Court, who also took the view that there had been no violation of Lavigne's freedom of association. In giving the leading judgment for this group, Wilson J. (with whom L'Heureux-Dubé J. and Cory J. concurred on this issue) held that the purpose which section 2(d) of the Charter is meant to advance 'is the collective action of individuals in pursuit of their common goals' and she could not find any sufficiently compelling reason to justify extending freedom of association, having regard to its purpose, to include a freedom not to associate. In taking this position, Wilson J. argued that a right not to associate would lead to absurd results and referred in particular to the compelling analogy of the mandatory payment of taxes. She continued,

Following the line of logic which the negative freedom analysis commands, our system of taxation arguably brings all taxpayers into forced association with the political party in power, its policies and the uses to which our tax money is put. If it were the case that s.2(d) protected such compelled associations, all taxpayers with a grievance to air would theoretically be able to come before the courts and insist that each tax expenditure be subjected to analysis under s.1.

Despite attempts by counsel to establish otherwise, Wilson J. was unable to identify any difference in principle between the compulsory association with others through the mandatory payment of an agency fee to a trade union. In so holding she noted that under the 'labour relations regime all members of the bargaining unit have an equal opportunity to participate in choosing who is to represent them and to join the ranks of the union or not as they see fit'. Moreover, 'as in our system of representative democracy, members of a bargaining unit may also decide to oust their bargaining agent if dissatisfied with its performance'. It may be noted in passing that the unwillingness of at least three members of the Court to scrutinize individual items of government as well as trade union expenditure tends to provide further evidence that the public funding of candidates and political parties would survive constitutional scrutiny under section 2(d).

Although there was strictly no need to do so in view of the holding that there was no breach of the right to freedom of association in this case, Wilson J. nevertheless addressed the section 1 question. Here she held that even if there had been a violation of section 2 this would have been justifiable, but for apparently different reasons from those advanced by the group who clustered around La Forest J. Wilson J. accepted that any possible restriction on freedom of association was for the purpose of promoting industrial peace through the encouragement of free collective bargaining, which axiomatically was a social goal sufficiently pressing and substantial as to warrant overriding a constitutional right. The real question following *R. v. Oakes*,[112] however, was whether the means chosen, that is to say the compulsory payment of dues, were appropriate or proportionate to meet this particular goal. It was argued for Lavigne that compelling non-members to pay the equivalent of union dues was rationally connected to the objective of industrial peace but only to the extent that the money is used for collective bargaining purposes. But, the argument continued, there is no rational connection with the government

---

[112] (1986) 26 DLR (4th) 200.

objective of promoting industrial peace through the encouragement of free collective bargaining when the money com-
pulsorily levied is allowed to be used for political purposes and
causes. This, however, was rejected by Wilson J., who contended that union involvement outside the realm of strict contract negotiation and administration helps to advance the
interests of the union at the bargaining table but that in any
event neither trade unions nor collective bargaining should be
viewed from an exclusively economic perspective: 'Unions'
decisions to involve themselves in politics by supporting particular causes, candidates or parties, stems from a recognition
of the expansive character of the interests of labour and a
perception of collective bargaining as a process which is meant
to foster more than mere economic gain for workers.' Consequently she too was unwilling to support Lavigne's case for
an opt-out formula, which in her view would weaken unions
first by constant litigation about what would and would not be
regarded as being related to collective bargaining and secondly
by reducing the amount of money available for political purposes. On this last point, it was naïve to suggest that 'an
obligation to refund dues will not work an unfair burden on
unions'.

IV. Conclusion

In the introduction to this chapter we identified the two principal weaknesses of the 1974 Act, as it has operated in practice.
In the first place it has failed to eliminate the substantial
dependence of the parties on corporate money, and it has also
failed to fulfil its goal of equality of electoral opportunity,
though this latter goal was met to a very large extent in the
period 1975 to 1980. This chapter has demonstrated that the
Charter of Rights has tended to exacerbate rather than help
resolve these problems. Although public funding was upheld,
limits on interest groups were not, the financial free-for-all
which this permits being only encouraged by the admittedly
justifiable decision of the Supreme Court of Canada in *Lavigne*.
Equality of electoral opportunity would clearly have been
further undermined by a regime in which interest groups

generally are unrestrained but in which restrictions are imposed albeit indirectly on the sources of funding of one party but not the other, particularly where the party so restricted is already at a financial disadvantage. Perhaps the most significant feature in these judicial developments has been the influence of the US Supreme Court. We have already seen how the much-criticized landmark decision in *Buckley* v. *Valeo* influenced both the Manitoba and the Alberta courts. It is to be noted also that the Ontario court in *Lavigne* was strongly influenced by the US Supreme Court jurisprudence, including *Abood* v. *Detroit Board of Education*[113] (and its progeny[114]) which led to a similar result being reached in the United States in the resolution of a similar problem.[115] There are encouraging signs, however, that the Supreme Court of Canada is willing to break free from this dependence on US decisions. If it does not then the campaign finance law and practice of Canada may be subject to more successful constitutional challenges. For the fact is that *Buckley* v. *Valeo*[116] did not strike down only the limits on independent expenditures. It is true that the Court upheld contribution limits and reporting and disclosure requirements as well as public funding for presidential candidates. But is also struck down as violating the First Amendment limits on the amount of permitted expenditure by candidates. If a similar decision was reached in Canada (and if it applies also to the limits on the permitted expenditures of political parties) the heart would be torn out of the 1974 Act. Democracy in Canada would be set back considerably in the interests of political liberty. The harsh reality, as already suggested in Chapter 2, is that democracy and unrestrained political liberty are not necessarily synonymous.

---

[113] 431 US 209 (1977).
[114] See especially *Ellis* v. *Brotherhood of Railway, Airline and Steamship Clerks* 466 US 435 (1984).
[115] See Ewing, 1987*b*: 443–7.
[116] 424 US 1 (1976).

7

Lessons from the United States

As we saw in Chapter 6, the Canadian arrangements for the funding of political parties are threatened by the Charter of Rights and Freedoms. Equality (the goal of the legislation) and liberty (the goal of the Charter) are in conflict. The danger is that the latter will win simply because those who operate the Charter have the last word on political questions. The previous chapter has shown how the Charter has already become the basis for a direct assault on the legislation by loosening up the constraints on political liberty which are evident, particularly in the spending limits. This is a process which has been developed much further by the US courts where campaign finance legislation has had an unbroken run since 1907, despite encountering hostile judicial attention.

I. The Origins of the Legislation

The first federal regulation of election campaigns in the United States was the Tillman Act of 1907.[1] Concern about the role of corporations in both federal and state politics had been a live issue since the Civil War, with 'wealth gravitating rapidly into the hands of a small portion of the population' (Morison and Commager, 1950: 355), and the power of wealth threatening 'to undermine the political integrity of the Republic' (ibid.). Indeed 'Concern over the size and source of campaign funds so actively entered the presidential campaign of 1904 that it crystallized popular sentiment for federal action to purge national politics of what was conceived to be the pernicious influence of "big money" campaign contributions'.[2] This sentiment was captured by President Roosevelt, who in his annual message to Congress recommended that

---

[1] Act of 26 Jan. 1907.
[2] *US* v. *International Union, UAW*, 352 US 567 (1957), per Justice Frankfurter, at pp. 571–2, a seminal historical review of the legislation.

All contributions by corporations to any political committee or for any political purpose should be forbidden by law; directors should not be permitted to use stockholders' money for such purposes; and, moreover, a prohibition of this kind would be, as far as it went, an effective method of stopping the evils aimed at in corrupt practices acts.[3]

This recommendation was implemented in 1907, when Congress enacted that 'it shall be unlawful for any national bank, or any corporation organized by authority of any laws of Congress, to make a money contribution in connection with any election to any political office'.[4] The penalty for violation was a fine on the corporation of up to $5,000, and any officer or director of the corporation who consented to the payment could be fined (up to $1,000) or imprisoned (for up to one year), or both.[5]

It has been pointed out this was 'merely the first concrete manifestation of a continuing congressional concern for elections free from the power of money'.[6] In 1910 further legislation provided for 'publicity of contributions made for the purpose of influencing elections at which Representatives in Congress are elected',[7] thereby translating into law 'popular demand for further curbs upon the political power of wealth'.[8] The 1910 Act in fact introduced a number of important duties and restrictions on political committees, a term defined to include

the national committees of all political parties and the national congressional campaign committees of all political parties and all committees, associations, or organizations which shall in two or more States influence the result or attempt to influence the result of an election at which Representatives in Congress are to be elected.[9]

Every committee was required to have a chairman and treasurer,[10] with the treasurer being under a duty to maintain a detailed and exact account of the income and expenditure of

[3] Ibid., at p. 572.
[4] Act of 26 Jan. 1907.
[5] Ibid.
[6] *US* v. *International Union, UAW*, 352 US 567 (1957), at p. 575.
[7] Act of 25 June 1910.
[8] *US* v. *International Union, UAW*, 352 US 567 (1957), at p. 575.
[9] Act of 25 June 1910, s.1.
[10] Ibid., s.2.

the committee.[11] Treasurers were also required 'within thirty days after the election at which Representatives in Congress were chosen in two or more States' to file with the Clerk of the House of Representatives an itemized, detailed statement of accounts, the statement to be preserved by the Clerk for fifteen months and to be open to public inspection.[12] The information to be disclosed included the name and address of each contributor of $100 or more, the total amount of all contributions, and the total expenditure by the committee.[13] But the Act did not require disclosure only by political committees. Also important was section 7, which sought to control independent expenditures, that is to say advertising expenses by groups on behalf of parties or candidates but incurred directly by the group rather than the party. Thus every person, firm, association, or committee (other than a political committee) that spent $50 or more at a federal election was required to report and disclose the expenditure to the Clerk of the House.

The process of reform was thus moving fast. Yet the pace was to quicken when in the following year further major initiatives were taken. An amending Act of 1911 required pre-election as well as post-election reporting and disclosure[14] and more importantly, perhaps, extended the reporting and disclosure requirements to include candidates as well as committees.[15] Moreover, the Act introduced for the first time a limit on the permitted expenditure of candidates.[16] War saw a brief respite from this flurry of legislative activity though the trail was being blazed again in 1918 with further legislation making it unlawful either to offer or to solicit anything of value to influence voting.[17] The major development after 1907–11, however, was to take place in 1925, when in the Corrupt Practices Act[18] of that year Congress overhauled the legislation

[11] Act of 25 June 1910, s.2.
[12] Ibid., s.5.
[13] Ibid., s.6.
[14] Act of 19 Aug. 1911.
[15] Ibid., s.2.
[16] Ibid.
[17] Act of 16 Oct. 1918.
[18] Federal Corrupt Practices Act of 1925.

with a measure which was to survive (albeit itself subjected to major surgery and amendment) until the overhauls of 1971 and 1974. The first change introduced in 1925 was paradoxically to limit the scope of the Act. In *Newberry* v. *US*[19] the Supreme Court had struck down the federal regulation of Senate primary elections. The campaign finance legislation was thus amended to exclude primary elections and party conventions from its scope. Otherwise, however, the Act was expansive in the obligations it imposed, thereby responding again to 'one of the great political evils of the time', namely 'the apparent hold on political parties which business interests and certain organizations seek and sometimes obtain by reason of liberal campaign contributions'.[20] Thus, the meaning of political committee was extended, as also was the meaning of a contribution. The former was defined to include

any committee, association, or organization which accepts contributions or makes expenditures for the purpose of influencing or attempting to influence the election of candidates or presidential and vice presidential electors (1) in two or more States, or (2) whether or not in more than one State if such committee, association, or organization (other than a duly organized State or local committee of a political party) is a branch or subsidiary of a national committee, association, or organization.

The latter was defined to include financial donations, as well as anything of value, thereby bringing into the regulatory framework donations in kind. The Act was broadened still further by making it an offence to receive as well as to make a forbidden contribution.

Otherwise the 1925 Act was similar and in many respects identical to the obligations which had been imposed since 1907. The ban on corporate contributions survived, without any amendments to the size of the penalty, while the duty to report and disclose remained substantially the same. This was subject to an important additional obligation as to timing. As well as mandatory reporting in both the pre-election and the post-

[19] 256 US 232 (1921).
[20] Senator Robinson, as quoted by Justice Frankfurter in *US* v. *International Union, UAW*, 352 US 567 (1957).

167

election period, the treasurers of political committees were required to file with the Clerk of the House of Representatives in January, March, June, and September of each year a statement of income and expenditure, containing the information which was required in the reports submitted at the time of an election. The statement submitted in January would cover the previous financial year, whereas the others would cover only the reporting period. Candidates for office were also required to report and disclose income and expenditure. And apart from the restrictions on contributions and the requirement to report and disclose, also important were the limits on the permitted expenditure of candidates. Spending limits had been contained initially in the 1911 Act which provided that no candidate for Representative in Congress could spend more than $5,000 in any campaign for his nomination and election, with a limit of $10,000 being imposed on candidates for the Senate. These limits did not include personal expenses of the candidates, and they could be reduced by state law for individual states. This was replaced by the 1925 Act which provided:

(a) Unless the laws of his State prescribe a less amount as the maximum limit of campaign expenditures, a candidate may make expenditures up to—
   (1) The sum of $10,000 if a candidate for Senator, or the sum of $2,500 if a candidate for Representative, Delegate, or Resident Commissioner; or
   (2) An amount equal to the amount obtained by multiplying three cents by the total number of votes cast at the last general election for all candidates for the office which the candidate seeks, but in no event exceeding $25,000 if a candidate for Senator or $5,000 if a candidate for Representative, Delegate, or Resident Commissioner.

Although the 1925 Act remained the major statute until 1971, it was subject to amendment and modification on several occasions in the intervening years. An Act of 1940 introduced further contribution and expenditure restrictions.[21] Thus it was

---

[21] Act of 19 July 1940. This was an amendment to the well-known Hatch Act, which was concerned mainly to limit the political activities of civil servants. The Act of 1940, though also dealing with civil service political activity, dealt with a wide range of other issues as well.

declared to be 'a pernicious political activity' and to be unlawful for any person 'directly or indirectly, to make contributions in an aggregate amount in excess of $5,000, during any
calendar year, or in connection with any campaign for nomination or election, to or on behalf of any candidate for an elective
federal office . . . or to or on behalf of any committee or other
organization engaged in furthering, advancing, or advocating
the nomination of election of any candidate for any such office
or the success of any national political party'. For the purposes
of the Act the term person was defined to mean an individual,
partnership, committee, association, corporation, or any other
organization or group of persons. This, however, was not the
only change introduced in 1940:

- government contractors were prohibited from making
  political contributions, as were those tendering for such
  contracts;
- it was unlawful to buy goods, commodities, advertising,
  or articles of any kind where the proceeds of the purchase
  would directly or indirectly inure to the benefit of any
  candidate for federal office;
- a ceiling of $3 million was imposed on the amount of
  money which political committees could receive and
  spend in the course of a calendar year, with the chairman and treasurer of the committee being liable for any
  violation.

The other important initiative between 1925 and 1971 related
to a surprising omission from the legislation, namely the failure
to apply the regulatory framework to the unions. This was no
doubt because for much of the time the American unions,
imbued with voluntarism, did not actively participate in the
political process. All that changed dramatically in the 1936
presidential campaign, however, when 'interstate labor organizations mounted a major (and controversial) effort, spending
over three quarters of a million dollars' (Sabato, 1985: 5). Wartime resentment against the unions gave an opportunity to
extend the 1925 Act to labour,[22] the Smith–Connally Act of

---

[22] See *US* v. *International Union, UAW*, 352 US 567 (1957) per Justice Frankfurter at p. 578.

1943[23] providing that it was unlawful for any labour organization 'to make any contribution in connection with any election at which Presedential and Vice Presidential electors or a
Senator or Representative in . . . Congress are to be voted
for'.[24] For this purpose a labour organization was defined
as having the same meaning as under the National Labor
Relations Act of 1935. It is to be noted, however, that the
Smith–Connally Act was a wartime measure only, but that
the extension of the campaign finance legislation to labour
unions was re-enacted in the so-called Taft-Hartley Act of
1947.[25] This was important also for extending the ban on
corporate and union political activity to include both election
contributions and expenditures, and also for extending the
relevant elections to include 'any primary election or political
convention or caucus held to select candidates'[26] for any of the
offices to which the Act applied. The definition of a labour
organization remained unchanged, applying to 'any organization of any kind, or any agency or employee representation
committee or plan, in which employees participate and which
exists for the purpose, in whole or in part, of dealing with
employers concernings grievances, labor disputes, wages, rates
of pay, hours of employment, or conditions of work'.[27]

II. The Impact of the Constitution

1. A FAVOURABLE RESPONSE

As suggested in Chapter 2, a major problem facing campaign
finance legislation may be the constitution in those jurisdictions where there is some legal protection of fundamental
rights. In the United States the issue was engaged as early as

[23] War Labor Disputes Act of 1943.
[24] Ibid., s.9.
[25] Labor Management Relations Act of 1947.
[26] The bringing in of the primaries after the exclusion in 1925 was facilitated
by the decision of the Supreme Court in *US* v. *Classic*, 313 US 299 (1941).
[27] Labor Management Relations Act of 1947, amending Federal Corrupt
Practices Act of 1925.

1916, though not by the Supreme Court. In *US* v. *United States Brewers' Association*[28] a corporation was charged with violating the provisions of the campaign finance legislation, a prosecution which succeeded, with various constitutional defences being resisted. These included a claim that the Act violated the First Amendment guarantees of free speech, which was rejected by the Court on the ground that the ban on corporate contributions 'neither prevents, nor purports to prohibit, the freedom of speech or of the press. Its purpose is to guard elections from corruption, and the electorate from corrupting influences in arriving at their choice.'[29] So far as the Supreme Court is concerned, an opportunity to consider this aspect of the legislation did not arise until after the Second World War. It is true that the legislation was considered by the Court in several cases before the war. But these dealt with the division of powers between federal and state governments rather than the extent to which the power of Congress in this area is constrained by the Bill of Rights, the more interesting question for present purposes. In these cases the Court held that although Congress had authority to regulate election financing, this did not extend to the primary elections,[30] a decision which (as we have seen) led to the revision of the legislation in 1925. It is to be noted that in one of these cases the Court stated that 'The power of Congress to protect the election of President and Vice President from corruption being clear, the choice of means to that end presents a question primarily addressed to the judgment of Congress. If it can be seen that the means adopted are really calculated to attain the end, the degree of their necessity, the extent to which they conduce to the end, the closeness of the relationship between the means adopted and the end to be attained, are matters for congressional determination alone.'[31]

2. Evasion by the Supreme Court

The ensnaring of the unions brought into sharp relief the potential conflict between the legislative and judicial branches.

---

[28] 239 Fed. Rep. 163 (1916).
[29] Ibid., at p. 169.
[30] *Newberry* v. *United States*, 256 US 232 (1921).
[31] *Burroughs and Cannon* v. *United States*, 290 US 534 (1934), at pp. 547–8.

The first Supreme Court case to raise First Amendment issues was *US* v. *CIO*.[32] The Congress of Industrial Organizations (CIO) and its president, Mr Philip Murray, were charged with violating the Federal Corrupt Practices Act of 1925 (as amended by the Taft–Hartley Act). The indictment related to a publication of *CIO News*, a weekly journal published by the CIO, the issue in question carrying a front-page statement by Mr Murray urging all members of the Organization to vote for Judge Ed Garmatz, then a candidate for Congress in Maryland. The statement said that the message was being issued despite the campaign finance legislation in the belief that the legislation was un-constitutional, as abridging First Amendment guarantees of free speech. The constitutional challenge was accepted by the District Court, which ruled against the Act, but only to the extent that it applied to unions. On appeal, the Supreme Court upheld the decision of the District Court, though for different reasons. The Court preferred not to decide on the constitutional question, but held for the union as a matter of construction of the statutory provisions. In his judgment Mr Justice Reed for the Court distinguished between 'a trade journal, a house organ or a newspaper, published by a corporation, . . . expressing views on candidates or political proposals in the regular course of its publication'[33] and a 'periodical financed by a corporation or labor union for the purpose of advocating legislation advantageous to the sponsor or supporting candidates whose views are believed to coincide generally with these deemed advantageous to such organization'.[34] In the view of the Court 'explicit words'[35] would be required to convince it that Congress intended to prohibit the former activity. And in that case, if the legislation were to be so construed 'to prohibit the publication, by corporations and unions in the regular course of conducting their affairs, of periodicals advising their members, stockholders or customers of danger or advantage to their interests from the adoption of measures or the election to office of men, espousing such

---

[32] *United States* v. *CIO*, 335 US 106 (1948).
[33] Ibid., at p. 123.
[34] Ibid., at p. 122.
[35] Ibid., at p. 123.

measures, the gravest doubt would arise in our minds as to its constitutionality'.[36]

The victory of the unions in *CIO* was a rather hollow one. Although they were vindicated on the facts, they had failed to obtain a ruling on the constitutionality of the legislative provision, the Court saying clearly that it did not wish to 'express [an] opinion as to the scope of this section where different circumstances exist and none upon the constitutionality of the section'.[37] The Court was equally reluctant in *US* v. *International Union, UAW*[38] where the indictment charged that the union had violated the Act by incurring expenditures during the 1954 elections. It was alleged that the defendant union had used general treasury funds to pay for television broadcasts promoting the election of candidates for political office. It was further alleged that the money used came from union dues and was not obtained by voluntary political contributions or subscriptions from members of the union. Unsurprisingly perhaps, it was accepted that if proved this conduct could be an offence, thus reversing a lower court holding that the statute did not reach the conduct alleged in this case. Nevertheless the Court declined to rule on the constitutional question on the ground that such adjudication was unnecessary to decide the matter. For although the lower court was reversed, it did not follow that a conviction would result, the matter being sent back to the lower court 'for further proceedings not inconsistent with [the] opinion'[39] of the Supreme Court. But although the Court suggested that the events as charged could sustain a conviction, it also recognized that 'prosecutions under the Act may present difficult questions of fact'.[40] Thus, the lower court was effectively instructed to inquire whether the facts were as per the indictment. If not, it was strongly suggested that the defendant should be acquitted if circumstances such as the following prevailed:

For example, was the broadcast paid for out of the general dues of the union membership or may the funds be fairly said to have been

[36] Ibid., at p. 121.
[37] Ibid., at p. 124.
[38] 352 US 567 (1957).
[39] Ibid., at p. 593.
[40] Ibid., at p. 592.

obtained on a voluntary basis? Did the broadcast reach the public at large or only those affiliated with appellee? Did it constitute active electioneering or simply state the record of particular candidates on economic issues? Did the union sponsor the broadcast with the intent to affect the results of the election?[41]

But although the majority in both cases managed to avoid constitutional questions by confining their discussions to questions of construction, ominous and powerful judgements were delivered in both cases, in addition to those of the majority. In *CIO*, four justices clustered around Mr Justice Rutledge to concur in the result but to argue on constitutional grounds that the restriction on union spending violated the First Amendment. In the view of the minority (views later to be trumpeted by a majority of the Court[42]), restricting expenditures for the publicizing of political views 'necessarily deprives the electorate, the persons entitled to hear, as well as the author of the utterance, whether an individual or a group, of the advantage of free and full discussion and of the right to free assembly for that purpose'.[43] 'The most complete exercise of these rights', said the minority, 'is essential to the full, fair and untrammeled operation of the electoral process',[44] which can be sustained only if the authors of the legislation discharge the burden of justifying 'the contraction by demonstrating indubitable public advantage arising from the restriction outweighing all disadvantages'.[45] The argument that the legislation could be justified to eliminate corruption and undue influence was presented as a possible basis for the legislation. But there was 'no showing, legislative or otherwise, of corruption so widespread or of 'undue influence' so dominating as could possibly justify so absolute a denial of these basis rights'.[46] The minority concluded by contending that

A statute which, in the claimed interest of free and honest elections, curtails the very freedoms that make possible exercise of the franchise by an informed and thinking electorate, and does this by indiscriminate

---

[41] *US* v. *International Union, UAW*, 352 US 567 (1957), at p. 592.
[42] *Buckley* v. *Valeo*, 424 US 1 (1976).
[43] 335 US 106 (1948), at p. 144.
[44] Ibid.
[45] Ibid., at p. 145.
[46] Ibid., at p. 146.

blanketing of every expenditure made in connection with an election, serving as a prior restraint upon expression not in fact forbidden as well as what is, cannot be squared with the First Amendment.[47]

Many of these sentiments were adopted by the minority[48] in the *UAW* case.[49] There the rhetoric was just as strong, it being said, for example, that 'Under our Constitution it is We the People who are Sovereign. The people have the final say. The legislators are their spokesmen. The people determine through their votes the destiny of the nation. It is therefore important—vitally important—that all channels of communication be open to them during every election, that no point of view be restrained or barred, and that the people have access to the views of every group in the community.'[50] The minority would have dismissed the indictment as 'a broadside assault on the freedom of political expression guaranteed by the First Amendment'.[51]

3. The Constitution and Statutory Interpretation

Although the *CIO* and *UAW* cases failed to settle the constitutional status of the legislation, they did nevertheless indicate that despite the statutory controls there was some considerable scope for manœuvre in the sense that unions and corporations could still take an active part in federal elections. This scope for manœuvre was highlighted still further by a range of lower court decisions which exposed even more loopholes in the Act, the courts in some cases showing astonishing restraint in light of the clear language of the statute. Although the courts refused to decide on constitutional grounds, the constitution was nevertheless very important in restricting the scope of the legislation and in justifying narrow constructions.

(i) *The Use of Union Labour*

One tactic which was accepted by the courts as legitimate was the use of union employees to campaign and work for political

---

[47] Ibid., at p. 155.
[48] Mr Justice Douglas, the Chief Justice, and Mr Justice Black.
[49] 352 US 567 (1957).
[50] Ibid., at p. 593.
[51] Ibid., at p. 598.

candidates. The issue arose for consideration in *US* v. *Construction and General Laborers' Local Union No. 264*[52] where employees of the union devoted a considerable portion of their time to political activities, some of which—the registration of voters—benefited all candidates, and some of which—campaigning on behalf of a specific candidate for Congress—benefited only individual candidates. As to the former types of expenditure, the Court refused to believe that it could have been 'the intention of the Congress to deprive any group, labor organization or corporation from making expenditures, if necessary, in connection with the registration of voters, for such registration is beneficial to all candidates for office, local, state or federal, and to all political parties'.[53] And as to the latter type of expenditure—partisan campaigning by people on the payroll—the Court held that if such activity was to be caught by the Act,

then any political activity of any person on the payroll of a labor organization from its president to its janitor, would render that Union and its principal officers liable, if such persons devoted any appreciable time in support of, or in opposition to any candidate for President, Vice President, Senator or Representative in Congress. If . . . any . . . president of a labor organization should draw a salary while making a speech in support of or in opposition to any candidate for Federal office, or if any of the expenses during that time were paid by a labor organization, such an activity would raise a serious question as to whether or not the labor organization and its officers might not be prosecuted under this Act.[54]

Such a prospect clearly made the Court feel rather uneasy, as did the possibility that the same would be true of 'any corporation which permitted one of its employees while on its payroll to spend a few hours hauling voters to a place of registering, to vote, or to engage in any other type of political activity'.[55]

(ii) *Voting Record Advertisements*

A second tactic accepted by the courts was in issue in *US* v. *Lewis Food Company, Inc.*[56] which concerned publications in

---

[52] 101 F. Supp. 869 (1951).
[53] Ibid., at p. 875.
[54] Ibid., at p. 876.
[55] Ibid.
[56] 236 F. Supp. 849 (1964).

general circulation newspapers paid for by the company. The sum spent amounted to $5,509.62 in total and was designed to influence primary elections held in California in which candidates for the House and the Senate were to be selected. The offending advertisement purported to show the voting record of candidates in favour of 'constitutional principles', employing a rating system the basis of which did not appear. Yet although this must presumably have been intended to influence voters, the Court held that no violation had take place. Two reasons were given, the first being that the expenditure did not compromise the statutory purpose of preventing corporations and unions 'with their power and wealth from controlling elections'. Thus,

The Court is of the view that the voting record of said candidates 'in favour of constitutional principles' is in the same category as the records of candidates on economic issues. The advertisement does not constitute active electioneering. It merely states the voting record of said candidates 'in favour of constitutional principles'. Obviously it was not an attempt to control the election.[57]

The Court then addressed a second question: did the expenditure compromise the other statutory purpose of protecting the individual stockholder from having corporate officials endorse candidates or attempt to influence voters in a manner which may be contrary to the wishes of the individual stockholder? On this the Court was unable to decide for want of evidence, and so on this ground was compelled to decide for the accused. In other words, there was no evidence that the funds used were from the general funds of the corporation rather than funds voluntarily provided by the stockholders.

(iii) *Radio and Television Broadcasts*

A third device permitted by the courts relates to the decision in the *CIO* case, and concerned expenditure on general broadcasting and newspaper advertisements which reached the community as a whole and not only union members. The matter arose for the first time after *CIO* in *US* v. *Painters' Local Union No. 481*,[58] where a small union used general treasury

[57] Ibid., at p. 853.
[58] 172 F 2d 854 (1949).

177

funds (less than $150) to pay the costs of an advertisement in the *Hartford Times*, a daily newspaper of general circulation, and to pay the costs of a political broadcast on a local radio station. Both the advertisement and the radio broadcast advocated the rejection of Senator Robert A. Taft as a candidate for the Republican nomination for President and his defeat in the 1948 presidential election, if nominated. In reversing the conviction for what appeared to be a clear breach of the language of the Act, the Circuit Judge (A. N. Hand) drew parallels with the *CIO* case, holding that it was impossible to distinguish that case from the facts of the instant case. Thus, 'It is hard to imagine that a greater number of people would be affected by the advertisement and broadcasting in the present case than by publication in the union periodical dealt with in the *CIO* litigation. In a practical sense the situations are very similar, for in the case at bar this small union owned no newspaper and a publication in the daily press or by radio was as natural a way of communicating its views to its members as by a newspaper of its own.'[59] A similar result was reached some twelve years later in *US* v. *Anchorage Central Labor Council*[60] where a television broadcast was held not to violate the legislation even though it constituted 'political advocacy' which 'reached the public at large' on the ground that 'the media used in this broadcast was maintained by the union in its regular course as the only means the union had . . . to communicate with the members'.[61] The courts were influenced in both cases by the fact that the payments had been voted by the members.

III. New Approaches to Control

1. BACKGROUND

It was perhaps inevitable that this spirit of laxity in the courts should be reflected in practice. Much has been written of the

---

[59] 172 F 2d 854 (1949), at p. 856.
[60] 193 F. Supp. 504 (1961).
[61] Ibid., at p. 507.

lamentable failure of the 1925 Act. Thus, Sabato (1985: 4) has synthesized the data as follows:

Some corporate executives merely gave themselves or their employees 'raises' which were then contributed by these individuals to favored candidates. Corporations often extended to candidates free use of company goods, office equipment, or travel in company automobiles and airplanes. Some employees were loaned full time to a campaign while remaining on the company payroll.

As we have seen, these are just the type of practices endorsed by the lower courts, just as an additional problem was endorsed by the Supreme Court, that is to say 'the invention and proliferation of political committees that purported to be independent and outside the knowledge and control of the candidates and designated campaign committees'.[62] Not endorsed, however, was the outright evasion of the law, though this lack of endorsement did not appear to make much difference to the corporate willingness to contribute.[63] Thus, 'throughout the twentieth century millions in corporate funds continued to flow directly to candidates despite any legal prohibition' (Sabato, 1985: 4). The reforms of 1971 which these weaknesses demanded were overhauled and dramatically extended and improved following the 'escalation of the 1972 elections and the shock of the aftermath'. Sabato (ibid. 5) has written that

The 1972 reelection effort for President Richard Nixon included practices bordering on extortion, in which corporations and their executives were, in essence, 'shaken down' for cash donations. Up to $30 million was legally and illegally contributed by the business sector to Nixon in 1972.

Of these different problems, the outright illegality is clearly the most alarming. Yet in the long term, the emergence of the independent political committees has proved the most troublesome. The first political action committee (PAC) had been set up by the CIO in 1943, financed by $1 contributions knowingly and freely made by individual CIO members, the

---

[62] *Buckley* v. *Valeo*, 519 F 2d 821 (1975), at p. 837.
[63] For details of corporate involvement, see Heard, 1960, and Alexander, 1972.

money being used for political education activities. A second labour PAC was formed by the American Federation of Labor in 1947, and the two PACs merged with the merger of the AF of L and the CIO in 1955, the new body becoming the Committee on Political Education (COPE).[64] A number of corporate interests and individual unions followed this example, and inevitably the legal status of this activity was eventually challenged. In *Pipefitters Local Union No. 562* v. *US*[65] the indictment charged that the union had from 1963 to 1968 established and maintained a fund that would receive regular and systematic payments from union members, the fund being separate from the union, though administered by union personnel, and contributions to the fund being voluntary. Although some evidence cast doubt on the voluntary nature of the fund, the evidence also indicated that donations to the fund were not in fact necessary for employment or union membership. Contributors were generally required to sign authorization cards which contained a statement that donations were voluntary and formed no part of the dues of the union. By this method the union appeared to raise substantial sums of money, with as much as $1 million being mentioned in the reports, though it is not clear for what period this figure relates. There were, however, disbursements of about $150,000 to candidates in federal elections. The question arose whether these facts revealed a conspiracy to violate the prohibition in the Federal Corrupt Practices Act against corporate and union political donations? The Supreme Court answered in the negative (and as we shall see Congress had, before the decision of the Court, legislated to permit practices of the kind at issue in *Pipefitters*).

The first holding of the Court was that the Act 'does not prohibit a labor organization from making, through the medium of a political fund organized by it, contributions or expenditures in connection with federal elections, so long as the monies expended are in some sense volunteered by those asked to contribute'.[66] This point was in fact conceded by the

[64] See again for a review of the background, *US* v. *International Union, UAW*, 352 US 567 (1957).
[65] 407 US 385 (1973).
[66] Ibid., at p. 401.

government; it was supported by the Congressional Record; and as already suggested, it was developed by the courts in some of the earlier cases. Where the government challenged the union, however, was on the nature of the fund, taking the view that it is not enough that the contributions are voluntary if in fact the fund is simply a subterfuge through which the union itself made proscribed political contributions. The fund must be separate from the sponsoring union, and 'may not be the alter ego of the sponsoring union in the sense of being dominated by it and serving its purposes'.[67] The Court rejected this, holding that 'a fund must be separate from the sponsoring union only in the sense that there must be a strict segregation of its monies from union dues and assessments'.[68] There was no requirement that 'the political organization be formally or functionally independent of union control or that union officials be barred from soliciting contributions or even precluded from determining how the monies raised will be spent'.[69] The only condition imposed by the Court was that any solicitation should be 'conducted under circumstances plainly indicating that donations are for a political purpose and that those solicited may decline to contribute without loss of job, union membership or any other reprisal within the union's institutional power'.[70]

This decision clearly met one of the apparent goals of the legislation, namely the protection of individuals who do not wish their money to be used to support candidates they oppose. But what about the other, and ultimately perhaps the more important, purpose—the protection of the political process from the influence of wealth and power? On this the Court was not at its best, holding:

When Congress prohibited labor organizations from making contributions or expenditures in connection with federal elections, it was, of course, concerned not only to protect minority interests within the union but to eliminate the effect of aggregated wealth on federal elections. But the aggregated wealth it plainly had in mind was the

[67] Ibid., at p. 413.
[68] Ibid., at p. 414.
[69] Ibid., at p. 415.
[70] Ibid., at p. 414.

general union treasury—not the funds donated by union members of their own free and knowing choice.[71]

Unconvincing though this seems, support was drawn from the Congressional Record and from Senator Taft in particular, one of the sponsors of the 1947 amendments. In one of many relevant passages, he said expressly that 'If the labor people should desire to set up a political organization and obtain direct contributions for it, there would be nothing unlawful in that . . . just so long as members of the union know what they are contributing to, and the dues which they pay into the union treasury are not used for such purpose'.[72] In expressing these views Senator Taft referred expressly to the CIO's Political Action Committee as an example of an organizational form which could continue to operate once the amendment was implemented, a form which he suggested could be used also by corporations.

The Supreme Court drew further support for its decision from the fact that before the decision had been reached, Congress had acted to permit arrangements similar to those in issue in *Pipefitters*,[73] the Court being influenced by the fact that the legislation was intended to be declaratory of the existing law. So far as relevant the new legislation provided that the prohibition on campaign contributions and expenditures did not apply to

[T]he establishment, administration, and solicitation of contributions to a separate segregated fund to be utilized for political purposes by a corporation or labor organization: *Provided*, That it shall be unlawful for such a fund to make a contribution or expenditure by utilizing money or anything of value secured by physical force, job discrimination, financial reprisals, or the threat of force, job discrimination, or financial reprisal; or by dues, fees, or other monies required as a condition of membership in a labor organization or as a condition of employment, or by monies obtained in any commercial transaction.

This was a profoundly important development, for reasons which we shall discuss. For the present it is sufficient to note

---

[71] *Pipefittes Local Union No. 562* v. *US*, 407 US 385 (1973), at pp. 415–16.

[72] Ibid., at pp. 416–17. Emphasis deleted.

[73] Federal Election Campaign Act of 1971.

that what it did was not only to authorize retrospectively a particular form of labour and corporate political activity which effectively sidestepped the requirements of the 1925 Act (as amended in 1940 and later in 1947). It also authorized prospectively, and encouraged, corporate political involvement in the campaign and election processes provided that it was done by the creation of a separate segregated fund financed by the voluntary contributions of stockholders.[74] Although perhaps not an unreasonable compromise on paper, this device (intended to rescue the unions) was to give rise to great difficulty for it encouraged the explosion of special-interest political action committees, the flames being fanned by the Supreme Court's subsequent writing out of other safeguards of the legislation.[75] So in 1971 the US federal law moved from a situation of formal prohibition of corporate and union campaign contributions and expenditures to one where the formal prohibitions continued to apply, but were qualified substantially by the power to create what were effectively front organizations. As we shall see, the intended safeguards introduced in 1974 against undue influence proved illusory. But for the present, it is to be noted that the PACs could not donate more than $5,000 to any one candidate (though they could donate to as many as they liked), and they could not spend more than $1,000 independently of a candidate to influence an election.[76]

2. THE FEDERAL ELECTION CAMPAIGN ACT

Legitimizing the political action committee was only one of several reforms introduced by the Federal Election Campaign Act of 1971. In addition, the reporting and disclosure requirements were tightened up again, limits were imposed on the ability of candidates to use personal wealth in campaigns, and restrictions were imposed on the amount of permitted broadcasting expenditure by candidates. These measures were soon complemented by far-reaching and wide-ranging reforms to

---

[74] On permitted methods of raising funds, see *FEC* v. *National Education Association*, 457 F. Supp. 1102 (1978).
[75] See esp. *Buckley* v. *Valeo*, 424 US 1 (1976).
[76] Federal Election Campaign Act Amendments Act of 1974.

the 1971 Act. Two factors were responsible for the 'comprehensive corrective measures'[77] of 1974. The first was the alarming increase in the cost of federal elections. Thus, an estimated $400 million was spent in 1972 for nomination and election campaigns—almost a 300% increase since 1952, in a period when the consumer price index rose by 57.6%.[78] Presidential campaign spending alone totalled $94.4 million in 1972, compared with $56.4 million in 1968, $38.1 million in 1964, and $27.2 million in 1960.[79] Increasing expenditure led in turn to an increasing dependence on large contributions from 'monied and special interests', with 1% of the people accounting for 90% of the dollars contributed to federal candidates, political parties, and committees.[80] Indeed, it was a matter of judicial notice that 'Contributions to both parties were made in 1972 by Gulf Oil (illegal contributions—to President Nixon, Senator Jackson, Congressman Mills), and by American Milk Producers Inc., a large dairy cooperative whose legal and illegal contributions were made to Nixon, Mills and Humphrey'.[81] Political scientists were less restrained. As already mentioned above, Sabato (1985: 5) has claimed that practices bordering on extortion formed part of Nixon's 1972 re-election effort. It is thus not surprising that reforms should be introduced with alacrity. The reforms covered a number of issues.

(i) The first area of concern was with contribution and expenditure limits: a person[82] could contribute up to $1,000 to a candidate for federal office in the primary election, and another $1,000 in the general election.[83] So far as expenditures are concerned, an individual was limited to $1,000 for an expenditure 'relative to a clearly identified candidate' and advocating

---

[77] *Buckley* v. *Valeo*, 519 F 2d 821 (1975), at p. 837.
[78] Ibid.
[79] Ibid.
[80] Ibid.
[81] Ibid., at p. 838.
[82] A person is defined broadly to include an individual, partnership, committee, association, corporation, or any other organization or group of persons.
[83] Persons were free to support any number of candidates by $1,000 expenditures, though contributions could not exceed $25,000 in total.

the election or defeat of such candidate, the purpose of this being to prevent 'would-be contributors from avoiding the contribution limitations by the simple expedient of paying directly by media advertisements or for other portions of the candidate's campaign activities'.[84] So far as political committees are concerned, the limit was set higher in the sense that a committee could donate up to $5,000 to a candidate, provided that the committee had been registered with the Federal Election Commission (FEC) for not less than six months. So far as expenditure by candidates and political parties is concerned, a number of different restrictions applied. First, a ceiling was imposed on the amount of permitted expenditure by candidates for President, the Senate, and the House of Representatives; in the case of the presidency this was $10 million for the primaries and $20 million for the general election. House candidates, in contrast, could spend $70,000 on the primary and the same on the general election. Secondly, limits were imposed on the spending of national committees of political parties. For the presidency this was 2 cents multiplied by the voting-age population of the United States. So far as the Senate is concerned, the parties were permitted to spend in connection with a candidate's campaign no more than 2 cents per elector in the state or $20,000, whichever was the greater. So far as House elections are concerned, the limit on party expenditures per candidate depended upon the number of Representatives returned by the state, together with the population of the state.

(ii) The second area of congressional concern was reporting and disclosure which, as we have seen, had its origins in the legislation of 1910. The new legislation required political committees to keep detailed records of individuals contributing more than $10. This information need not be disclosed, but would be subject to audit by the Federal Election Commission. In the case of donations of more than $100, political committees were to disclose the names, occupations, and principal places of business of such donors. Reports were to be filed quarterly by candidates and political committees; and pre- and post-

[84] *Buckley* v. *Valeo*, 424 US 1 (1976), at p. 46.

election reports were to be filed in an election year. As to the content of reports, this was extremely detailed, and included the following in addition to those matters already identified:

- cash in hand at the beginning of the reporting period;
- the total sum of contributions in the reporting period of $100 or less;
- the name and address of any political committee from which the reporting committee or the candidate received funds;
- details of loans to or from any person in the calendar year in excess of $100 in aggregate amounts;
- the total amount of money raised from fund-raising events such as dinners and rallies, and from the sale of items such as hats, banners, and literature;
- details of expenditures, including the total sum of expenditures made during the calendar year as well as the identity of each person to whom an expenditure in excess of $100 (in aggregate) was made.

(iii) The third major reform of the 1970s was the creation of the Presidential Election Campaign Fund by the Presidential Election Campaign Fund Act.[85] Unlike the contribution and expenditure limits and the reporting and disclosure provisions, which apply to congressional as well as presidential campaigns, the campaign fund applies only to the latter. The Fund is financed by the voluntary contributions of taxpayers who check off one or two dollars on their income tax returns. Taxpayers do not specify which candidate is to receive their money, the fund being disbursed in accordance with more objective criteria. Under the Act three different types of party are recognized: major parties, being ones whose candidates received more than 25% of the vote at the previous presidential election; minor parties, being those whose candidates received 5% or more (but less than 25%) of the vote at the previous election; and new parties, which covers all the others. All the major party candidates were entitled to a subvention from the

---

[85] On the background to the Fund, see *Buckley* v. *Valeo*, ibid., at p. 85 n. 114.

fund of $20 million, subject to a number of conditions being met. First, a candidate must agree to furnish to the FEC, upon request, books, records, and evidence of expenses, together with an audit of campaign expenses. Secondly, a candidate may not incur election expenses in excess of the public funding entitlement. And, thirdly, each major party candidate accepting public money must undertake not to accept private funding, except to the extent that the Fund is incapable of meeting the full entitlement. Minor parties were entitled to less than $20 million, the amount being based upon their share of the vote in previous presidential general elections. They are, however, entitled to accept private funding provided that they will not incur expenses in excess of the major party entitlement. Retrospective payments may be made to these parties if they 'garner more votes than their track record would have indicated'[86] as they are made also to new parties with no track record, provided that they win 5% or more or the vote.

(iv) In addition to these three major substantive measures (contribution and expenditure limits, reporting and dis-closure requirements, and public funding of presidential campaigns) important administrative and enforcement initiatives were taken, most notably by the creation in 1974 of the Federal Election Commission of eight members. The Secretary of the Senate and the Clerk of the House of Representatives are ex officio non-voting members of the Commission, with the remaining six members being appointed by the Senate (two), the House (two), and the President (two). The two appointees of each of these three bodies must not be members of the same political party, and all appointees (including those nominated by the President) are subject to confirmation by both Houses of Congress. Appointment is generally for six years, but the initial appointments were made to ensure that one vacancy arose every year. As already suggested, the function of the Commission is to administer and to ensure compliance with the Act, for the fulfilment of which it has been given considerable powers by Congress. Included among its major powers were 'rulemaking, subpoena, a power to require submission of

---

[86] *Buckley* v. *Valeo*, 519 F 2d 821 (1975), at p. 849.

written reports, a power to conduct investigations and hear-
ings, a power to initiate civil actions to enforce FECA [Federal
Election Campaign Act], a power to request the Attorney-
General to institute civil actions to obtain compliance with
FECA and certain election law criminal provisions, and a
power to issue advisory opinions'.[87] It is to be noted also that
the powers of the FEC do not relate only to FECA. Thus, the
Commission has supervisory powers under the Presidential
Election Campaign Fund Act and may institute civil actions for
declaratory or injunctive relief concerning any matter covered
by that Act.

3. SUBVERTING THE ACT

This comprehensive legislation was comprehensively challenged in *Buckley* v. *Valeo*, which clustered together an extraordinary range of plaintiffs, including Senator James L. Buckley,
Eugene J. McCarthy, the Conservative Party of the State of
New York, the Libertarian Party, and the New York Civil
Liberties Union. Many aspects of the legislation were challenged, though these failed in the Court of Appeals where
the majority wrote a strong and uncompromising defence of
the legislation.[88] This endorsement applied equally to the
measures dealing with expenditure limits—the major area of
disagreement between the Court of Appeals and the Supreme
Court[89]—as it did to the other provisions, which generally
proved less controversial. Tracing the congressional history of
the legislation, the Court of Appeals suggested that the spending limits had a strategic role to play, and highlighted the
presence of both 'ever-increasing campaign expenditures,
and reliance on large contributions from monied and special
interests'.[90] According to the Court, 'The sheer volume of
special interest group money is enormous. The findings identify for the 1972 and 1974 elections not only the millions of total

[87] *Buckley* v. *Valeo*, 519 F 2d 821 (1975), at pp. 888–9.
[88] 519 F 2d 821 (1975). See also J. Skelly Wright, 1976 and 1982.
[89] 424 US 1 (1976).
[90] 519 F 2d 821 (1975), at p. 837.

contributions by labor groups, business groups, health groups and agricultural groups, but also how large they loom to individual candidates'.[91] Congress found that 'such contributions were often made for the purpose of furthering business or private interests by facilitating access to government officials or influencing governmental decisions, and that, conversely, elected officials have tended to afford special treatment to large contributors'.[92] Although the obvious method for controlling influence by special interests would be to limit the source or size of contributions, rather than expenditures, 'After extensive investigation, Congress concluded that such corrupt and pernicious practices are more likely to occur when there are no effective limits on amount of campaign expenditure. In short, big spending campaigns pull like a magnetic field.'[93]

The Supreme Court took a rather different position, upholding the contribution limits,[94] the reporting and disclosure requirements,[95] and the public financing of presidential campaigns.[96] But so far as spending limits were concerned, questions were raised about the impact of the legislation on freedom of expression, protected by the First Amendment. As pointed out in the Chapter 6, the Court said that a restriction on the amount of money a person or group can spend on political communication during a campaign necessarily reduces the number of issues discussed, the depth of their exploration, and the size of the audience reached.[97] The Court continued by pointing out that

The expenditure limitations contained in the Act represent substantial rather than merely theoretical restraints on the quantity and diversity of political speech. The $1,000 ceiling on spending 'relative to a clearly identified candidate' would appear to exclude all citizens and groups

---

[91] Ibid.
[92] Ibid., at p. 383 n. 32.
[93] Ibid., at p. 840.
[94] 424 US 1 (1976), at p. 58.
[95] Ibid., at p. 84.
[96] Ibid., at p. 108. The Court did, however, hold that the method of appointment of the members of the FEC was unconstitutional, as violating the separation of powers clause in the constitution.
[97] Ibid., at p. 19.

except candidates, political parties, and the institutional press from any significant use of the most effective modes of communication.[98]

It would, for example, be 'a federal criminal offense for a person or association to place a single one-quarter page advertisement "relative to a clearly identified candidate" in a major metropolitan newspaper'.[99] Clearly concerned about this particular limit, the Court struck it down on First Amendment grounds. In contrast, the contribution limits entail only a 'marginal restriction upon the contributor's ability to engage in free communication'.[100] Thus 'A limitation on the amount of money a person may give to a candidate or campaign organization . . . involves little direct restraint on his political communication, for it permits the symbolic expression of support evidenced by a contribution but does not in any way infringe the contributor's freedom to discuss candidates and issues'.[101]

The Court also upheld a challenge to restrictions on candidates' personal expenditures, and more importantly, the limits on candidates' permitted campaign expenditures. In justifying the latter decision the Court concluded that the 'major evil associated with rapidly increasing campaign expenditures is the danger of candidate dependence on large contributions',[102] but that the 'interest in alleviating the corrupting influence of large contributions is served by the Act's contribution limitations and disclosure provisions',[103] which were upheld. It is interesting to note, however, that the Court did not strike down the limits on the general election expenditures by national and state committees of political parties. These had not been challenged on First Amendment grounds, but were raised under the Fifth Amendment on the ground that they discriminated against independent candidates and regional political parties without national committees. Although the reasons were not specified, this is presumably because the candidate of national political parties could (i) spend up to his

[98] 424 US 1 (1976), at pp. 19–20.
[99] Ibid., at p. 40.
[100] Ibid., at p. 20.
[101] Ibid., at p. 21.
[102] Ibid., at p. 55.
[103] Ibid.

or her own personal limit, and (ii) enjoy the benefit of the party's spending. The independent in contrast would be permitted to spend only up to his or her personal limit, while any group spending money in his or her support would be limited by the $1,000 ceiling on expenditure relative to a specified candidate. In view of the decision of the Court on other spending limits the basis for this challenge evaporated. Thus, the decision that independent expenditure limitations and campaign expenditure ceilings were unconstitutional 'remove[d] the predicate for appellants' discrimination claim by eliminating any alleged advantage to political parties with national committees'.[104] So we are left with the paradoxical result that while there are still spending ceilings on national party expenditure in a general election, there are no limits on candidate expenditure. It is hard not to believe, however, that if the national party limits were challenged on First Amendment grounds, these too would be struck down as unconstitutional.

The invalidation of the spending limits could potentially have been of quite limited significance. In an ideal world the Act could still have worked well, and this it seems is how the Supreme Court calculated. Thus, the major evil, in view of the Court, arising from high expenditure, is 'the danger of candidate dependence on large contributions'.[105] But this was dealt with by the Act's contribution limits and its reporting and disclosure requirements. These were likely to help keep down campaign costs by requiring 'candidates and political committees to raise funds from a greater number of persons'.[106] It would also help to reduce the dependence on special interests and consequently reduce in turn their influence on politicians by removing the vulnerability of politicians from any withdrawal of financial support. But the ideal was not translated into practice. Since 1976 three major developments have taken place. The first is that congressional election spending has increased dramatically. Thus, it has been claimed that 'In 1974 the average cost of campaigning for the House was $50,000;

---

[104] Ibid., at p. 58 n. 66.
[105] Ibid., at p. 55.
[106] Ibid., at p. 22.

in 1980 the average was $150,000 and [in 1982] races costing $500,000 [were] not uncommon' (*Time*, 1982). The *New York Times* was to point out that 'Political campaign spending soared across the nation in 1982 as candidates spent 69% more to win a seat in the Senate than in 1980 and 48% more to win a seat in the House'.[107] The *New York Times* also confirmed that 'the median expenditure by winning campaigns increased far faster than the 14.6% increase in the Consumer Price Index from November 1980 to November 1982'.[108] Another indication of increased spending is the fact that in 1980, 32 campaigns by Senate candidates topped $1 million whereas in 1982, 39 did so. Similarly in 1980, 28 House candidates spent $500,000 or more, while 55 did in 1982.[109] More recently, it has been claimed that average campaigns for the House would be $500,000 in 1986 and average campaigns for the Senate would be at least $2 million, with candidates for 34 Senate seats and 435 House seats expected to spend a minimum of $450 million in total. In addition, the two principal parties were hoping to raise $500 million between them for expenditure in the same elections (*The Economist*, 1986).

The second major development since 1976 has been the pro-liferation of the political action committees (PACs), which have been largely responsible for the vast increase in campaign costs. With the ceiling removed, pressure existed to push costs continually upwards, and that role has been filled by the PACs. In 1974 there were 608 such committees, and the number rose to 1,146 in 1976, the year of *Buckley* v. *Valeo*. By 1980, however, this had more than doubled to 2,551, a figure which almost doubled again between 1980 and 1987 when there were no fewer than 4,567 registered committees.[110] Although the first committees were created by labour unions, the corporations now have many more, as do trade associations, such as the National Association of Realtors, the American Medical Association, and the National Automobile Dealers' Association (*Time*, 1982). Also important are those PACs which are re-

---

[107] *New York Times*, 3 Apr. 1982.
[108] Ibid.
[109] Ibid.
[110] The figures for 1987 are drawn from *New York Times*, 7 June 1987. The other figures are provided in Sabato, 1985.

lated to 'ideological' rather than 'economic interests', including National Conservative Political Action Committee (NCPAC), and which are formed to support a particular political party or a particular candidate for the presidency (Sabato, 1985). This increase in PACs is related to the third major development, which is the enormous dependence of many candidates on PAC money. Although there are limits on the amount of single PAC contributions to individual candidates, 'PACs tend to run in packs' (*Time*, 1982), so that a popular candidate may be well supported by and heavily dependent upon special interests for money. Again valuable evidence is provided by the *New York Times*, which demonstrates both an increase in PAC spending and also the scale of candidate dependence. In 1979 and 1980 the PACs gave congressional candidates $51,789,155, this rising by 53% to $79,119,402 in 1981 and 1982.[111] In the 1982 elections the PACs provided one-third of the money raised, and for the winners the committees provided 35% of all money raised, up from 31% in 1980, 28% in 1978, and 26% in 1976.[112] High though this is, the trend has continued, and it has been estimated that in 1986 nearly half the Representatives got 50% or more of their money from PACs.[113] But although there is thus a great dependence on special interests, it does not follow that special interests have a proportionately greater role than they had before the 1971–4 reforms. Nevertheless it can hardly be suggested that the current state of affairs is one which Congress had intended in 1974. For this encouragement of special interests, the Supreme Court must accept some of the responsibility.

4. SUBSEQUENT DEVELOPMENTS

Although *Buckley* v. *Valeo*[114] is clearly the most important decision of the campaign finance legislation, there have been several others. In some of these cases the Supreme Court resisted the challenge, while in others it whittled away more of the structure, though these later attacks were not quite as

---

[111] *New York Times*, 3 Apr. 1983.
[112] Ibid., 19 Jan. 1983.
[113] Ibid., 7 June 1987.
[114] 424 US 1 (1976).

dramatic or devastating as the blow to the legislation which had been struck in *Buckley*.

(i) *Qualifying the Obligation to Disclose*

The Supreme Court in *Buckley* had, in principle, upheld the reporting and disclosure requirements of FECA, even though 'compelled disclosure, in itself, can seriously infringe on privacy of association and belief guaranteed by the First Amendment'.[115] This is because there were 'government interests sufficiently important to outweigh the possibility of infringement, particularly when the "free functioning of our national institutions" is involved'.[116] In this case there were three such governmental interests. First, 'disclosure provides the electorate with information as to where political campaign money comes from and how it is spent by the candidate in order to aid the voters in evaluating those who seek federal office. It allows the voters to place each candidate in the political spectrum more precisely than is often possible solely on the basis of party labels and campaign speeches. The sources of a candidate's financial support also alert the voter to the interests to which a candidate is more likely to be responsive and thus facilitate predictions of future performance in office.'[117] Secondly, it was accepted that disclosure deters 'actual corruption' and avoids the appearance of corruption by exposing large contributions and expenditures to the light of publicity.[118] And, thirdly, it was accepted that record-keeping, reporting, and disclosure requirements are an essential means of gathering the data necessary to detect violations of the contribution limitations.[119] It was accepted, however, that the state's interest was less strong in the case of small parties with no chance of election, but that the threat to the First Amendment rights to these parties was great if publicity would cause harassment leading to a fall-off in contributions. But the Court refused to give an exemption on this ground, and

[115] 424 US 1 (1976), at p. 64.
[116] *Communist Party* v. *Subversive Activities Control Board*, 367 US 1 (1961), quoted in *Buckley* at p. 66.
[117] *Buckley* v. *Valeo*, 424 US 1 (1976), at p. 67.
[118] Ibid.
[119] Ibid., at p. 68.

required evidence that compelled disclosure of a party's contributors' names would lead to harassment. Such evidence was
provided in *Brown* v. *Socialist Workers '74 Campaign Committee
(Ohio)*[120] with the result that Ohio disclosure laws were held
unconstitutional to the extent that they applied to the Socialist
Workers Party. It is possible that a similar challenge to FECA
with similar evidence would lead to a similar result.

(ii) *Releasing the PACs*

A second development since *Buckley* is perhaps more controversial. The decision of the Supreme Court in *Federal Election
Commission* v. *National Conservative PAC*[121] related to the
Presidential Election Campaign Fund Act which, as we have
seen, offers presidential candidates of the major parties public
financing for their campaigns. In so doing the Act makes
it an offence for any independent political committees to
spend more than $1,000. Two PACs, NCPAC and Fund for a
Conservative Majority (FCM) announced an intention to spend
large sums of money to secure the re-election of President
Reagan in 1984, following which the Democratic Party and the
Federal Election Commission sought declaratory relief that the
$1,000 limitation was constitutional, and therefore effective to
restrain the anticipated expenditure. The action failed, with a
majority of the Court holding that the PACs were entitled to
full First Amendment protection. In the view of the Court, 'The
First Amendment freedom of association is squarely implicated
in this case. NCPAC and FCM are mechanisms by which large
numbers of individuals of modest means can join together
in organizations which serve to amplify the voice of their
adherents.'[122] And having concluded that the PACs were entitled to full First Amendment protection (and that a financial
restriction is a restriction on the quantity of expression—'like
allowing a speaker in a public hall to express his views while
denying him the use of an amplifying system')[123] the question
for the Court was whether there was a sufficiently strong

---

[120] 459 US 87 (1982).
[121] 470 US 480 (1985).
[122] Ibid., at p. 494.
[123] Ibid., at p. 493.

governmental interest served by the restriction. Applying *Buckley*, the Court held that 'preventing corruption or the appearance of corruption are the only legitimate and compelling government interests thus far identified for restricting campaign finances'.[124] But as in *Buckley*, it was held that independent expenditures do not present that danger, as there is in the case of contributions. Thus, quoting from the landmark decision, the Court in *NCPAC* said:

Unlike contributions, such independent expenditures may well provide little assistance to the candidate's campaign and indeed may prove counterproductive. The absence of prearrangement and co-ordination of an expenditure with the candidate or his agent not only undermines the value of the expenditure to the candidate, but also alleviates the danger that expenditures will be given as a quid pro quo for improper commitments from the candidate.[125]

It was in any event difficult to see how NCPAC or its members (who generally donated less than $1,000) were likely to be rewarded by the successful candidates.

(iii) *Releasing Other Special Interests*

A third development since *Buckley* concerned the prohibition on contributions and expenditures by corporations. It will be recalled that under the Act corporations are prohibited from using treasury funds to make any such payments which must be financed, if at all, by voluntary contributions to a separate segregated fund. In *Federal Election Commission* v. *Massachusetts Citizens For Life, Inc.*[126] the appellant was incorporated as a non-profit, non-stock corporation under Massachusetts law, its purpose being to 'foster respect for human life and to defend the right to life of all human beings, born and unborn, through educational, political and other forms of activities'.[127] The association did not have a separate segregated fund and raised money in a variety of ways, including garage sales, raffles, and dances. The money was used to promote a wide range of educational and legislative activities which in 1978 included the

---

[124] 470 US 480 (1985), at p. 496.
[125] *Buckley* v. *Valeo*, 424 US 1 (1976), at p. 47.
[126] 93 L Ed 2d 539 (1986).
[127] Ibid., at p. 546.

publication of a special edition of a newsletter promoting pro-
life issues with a view to influencing the 1978 elections. This
led to a complaint being filed with the FEC alleging that the
special edition was unlawful, being an expenditure of funds
from a corporate treasury to distribute to the general public a
campaign flyer on behalf of certain political candidates. The
Commission took the view that a violation had occurred and
brought legal proceedings for a civil remedy.[128] In the Supreme
Court it was held that the special edition did amount to an
expenditure within the meaning of the Act, but that so far
as the Act constrained the Massachusetts Citizens For Life
(MCFL) it was unconstitutional. In other words, not all corporations may be forbidden from incurring contributions or
expenditures for political purposes. It is true that the MCFL
was free, like other corporations, to set up a separate segregated fund through which members could voluntarily contribute for political purposes. This would mean, however, that
the organization would be subject to more onerous administrative obligations than if it were an unincorporated organization
whose main purpose was not campaign advocacy.[129] This in

[128] See text accompanying n. 87 *supra*.
[129] Thus, the Court said, at 552–3:

> If it were not incorporated , MCFL's obligations under the Act would be
> those specified by s.434(c), the section that prescribes the duties of
> '[e]very person (other than a political committee)'. Section 434(c)
> provides that any such person that during a year makes independent
> expenditures exceeding $250 must: (1) identify all contributors who
> contribute in a given year over $200 in the aggregate in funds to influence
> elections; (2) disclose the name and address of recipients of independent
> expenditures exceeding $200 in the aggregate, along with an indication of
> whether the money was used to support or oppose a particular
> candidate; and (3) identify any persons who make contributions over
> $200 that are earmarked for the purpose of furthering independent
> expenditures. All unincorporated organizations whose major purpose is
> not campaign advocacy, but who occasionally make independent
> expenditures on behalf of candidates, are subject only to these
> regulations.
> Because it is incorporated, however, MCFL must establish a 'separate
> segregated fund' if it wishes to engage in any independent spending
> whatsoever. Since such a fund is considered a 'political committee' under
> the Act, all MCFL independent expenditure activity is, as a result,
> regulated as though the organization's major purpose is to further the
> election of candidates. This means that MCFL must comply with several
> requirements in addition to those mentioned. Under s.432, it must
> appoint a treasurer; ensure that contributions are forwarded to the

itself was a violation of First Amendment freedoms, making political activity more burdensome. Indeed, 'Faced with the need to assume a more sophisticated organizational form, to adopt specific accounting procedures, [and] to file periodic detailed reports . . . it would not be surprising if at least some groups decided that the contemplated political activity was simply not worth it'.[130]

The question before the Court was whether this burdening of First Amendment rights could be justified by a compelling state interest. Interestingly, the Court endorsed the concern of its predecessors over the corrosive influence of concentrated corporate wealth. Thus:

Direct corporate spending on political activity raises the prospect that resources amassed in the economic marketplace may be used to provide an unfair advantage in the political marketplace. Political 'free trade' does not necessarily require that all who participate in the political marketplace do so with exactly equal resources . . . Relative availability of funds is after all a rough barometer of public support. The resources in the treasury of a business corporation, however, are not an indication of popular support for the corporation's political ideas. They reflect instead the economically motivated decisions of investors and customers. The availability of these resources may make a corporation a formidable political presence, even though the power of the corporation may be no reflection of the power of its ideas.[131]

But this concern for corporate power was limited. In the first place it did not extend to the corporate PACs, the resources

treasurer within 10 or 30 days of receipt, depending on the amount of contribution; see that its treasurer keeps an account of: every contribution regardless of amount, the name and address of any person who makes a contribution in excess of $50, all contributions received from political committees, and the name and address of any person to whom a disbursement is made regardless of amount; and preserve receipts for all disbursements over $200 and all records for three years. Under s.433, MCFL must file a statement of organization containing its name, address, the name of its custodian of records, and its banks, safety deposit boxes, or other depositories; report any change in the above information within 10 days; and may dissolve only upon filing a written statement that it will no longer receive any contributions nor make disbursements, and that it has no outstanding debts or obligations.

[130] 93 L Ed 2d 539 (1986), at p. 554.
[131] Ibid., at p. 556.

of which reflect their level of popular support.[132] Secondly, and more importantly for present purposes, it did not justify prohibitions on the political activity of non-economic corporations, the Court explaining:

Regulation of corporate political activity . . . has reflected concern not about use of the corporate form per se, but about the potential for unfair deployment of wealth for political purposes. Groups such as MCFL, however, do not pose that danger of corruption. MCFL was formed to disseminate political ideas, not to amass capital. The resources it has available are not a function of its success in the economic marketplace, but its popularity in the political marketplace. While MCFL may derive some advantages from its corporate form, those are advantages that redound to its benefit as a political organization, not as a profit-making enterprise. In short, MCFL is not the type of traditional corporation organized for economic gain . . . that has been the focus of regulation of corporate political activity.[133]

So corporate organizations of this kind are as free to campaign electorally as they are to engage in other political activity. There is no need to fund election expenditure from a separate segregated fund in the way that is required of economic corporations.

IV. Conclusion

The experience of American legislation from 1907 until 1971 suggests that campaign financing legislation is likely to meet major problems, even if it is aggressively promoted by legislators. The Canadian restrictions of 1908 failed largely because there was insufficient interest in enforcing them and insufficient administrative support to encourage enforcement. But even if these problems are overcome, and the law is not simply a collection of meaningless platitudes, the American experience suggests three additional problems. The first is that there is a need for persistent and continuous assessment and amendment to deal with fresh problems as they erupt. The American federal legislation was amended several times between 1907

---

[132] Ibid.
[133] Ibid., at p. 557.

and 1947 and even then it did not prove effective. The second problem is that legislation of this kind will almost certainly lead to a conflict between the legislative and judicial branches. The impact of constitutionalism is that even if all or part of the legislation is not invalidated, the effect of the constitutional protection of freedom of expression will be very restrictive interpretations of the statutory language in order to accommodate constitutional guarantees. The courts are thus, in effect, validating and encouraging the exploitation of loopholes and the development of additional evasive devices. The third problem is that in order to deal with possible threats from the courts, important compromises may have to be made, which although appearing reasonable, nevertheless may be far removed from the original intentions of the legislators. Not only will such compromises eventually destroy the legislation, they may also lead to abuses as great as the abuses which the legislation was designed initially to address.

A good example of this is provided by the validation by the Supreme Court and Congress of the political action committee. Although the PACs have not won all of their cases in the Supreme Court,[134] they won the major ones, the impact of which has been greatly to encourage their development and increase their power. The effect of judicial intervention has in fact been to undermine seriously the goals of the legislation. First, the courts have helped to ensure the high cost of campaigns, thereby making it more rather than less likely that there will be an unequal competition for office. Secondly, by wiping out the spending limits the courts have raised the profile of and increased the power of special interests. The result is that many politicians, political scientists, and lawyers are engaged in another round of law reform in an attempt to regulate a new manifestation of an old problem of American government.[135] One proposal is first to prohibit political action committees from contributing to congressional candidates; and

---

[134] See e.g. *California Medical Association* v. *Federal Election Commission*, 453 US 182 (1981); *Bread Political Action Committee* v. *Federal Election Commission*, 455 US 577 (1982); *Federal Election Commission* v. *National Right to Work Committee*, 459 US 197 (1982).

[135] *New York Times*, 23 May 1991. Other proposals are discussed ibid., 3 Feb. 1983, and 7 June 1987.

secondly to offer incentives like discounted television time for candidates who agree to voluntary spending limits. It remains to be seen whether these or competing proposals (including total public funding for congressional elections) will ever bear fruit. In the meantime we may reflect that the problems of campaign finance which have arisen in the United States are perhaps inevitable in a legal system which gives the last word on political questions to judges, given the bias of constitutional law towards political liberty rather than political equality. Nevertheless, those responsible for the operation of the Charter (the people, the politicians, and the judges) bear a heavy responsibility to ensure that the jungle of special-interest politics in the United States is not imported into Canada in the name of constitutional liberalism.

8

Conclusion

THE Election Expenses Act 1974 can be said to have made at
least three important contributions to the Canadian electoral
system. It has promoted greater openness in party finances; it
has stimulated greater participation by citizens in the funding
of the political parties; and it has encouraged greater equality
of opportunity between parties fighting campaigns. This is
not to say, however, that the legislation has been an unqualified success or that there are no important questions
which have been left unanswered. The Conservative and
Liberal parties still rely to a very large extent on corporate
donations in particular; the election expenses limits have been
seriously undermined by the inflated party budgets on non-
election expenditures; and the integrity of the whole system
has been called into question by the Charter-inspired decision
in the *National Citizens' Coalition* case.[1] Concern about the
failure of the 1974 Act to realize its full potential has led to
many calls for reform, which culminated in the appointment of
a Royal Commission in 1989 'to inquire into and to report on
the appropriate principles and process that should govern the
election of members of the House of Commons and the financing of political parties and of candidates' campaigns'. Without
limiting the generality of these wide terms, the Commission
was also directed to consider 'the practices, procedures and
legislation in Canada', as well as 'the means by which political
parties should be funded, the provision of funds to political
parties from any source, the limits on such funding and the
uses to which such funds ought, or ought not, to be put'.[2] The
Commission was chaired by Mr Pierre Lortie, a Quebec businessman, and consisted of four other members. At the time of
writing, it is not known what the Commission is likely to
recommend by way of change, but in a sense this is not essen-

---

[1] *National Citizens' Coalition Inc.* v. *Attorney-General for Canada* (1985) 11 DLR
(4th) 481.
[2] Press Release, Prime Minister's Office, 15 Nov. 1989.

tial, it being sufficient simply to identify the problems and the range of options available. For it does not follow that the Commission's recommendations will win political approval; nor does it follow that the recommendations would be appropriate for adoption by other jurisdictions which were otherwise minded to embrace the principles of 1974.

I. Individual Contributions

One of the great benefits of the 1974 Act was to encourage the political parties to extend their contribution base. As we saw in Chapter 5 the parties actively engaged in raising funds from a large number of individuals with a great deal of success. The Progressive Conservatives' direct-mail fund-raising programme continues to thrive, though it now has a smaller bank of donors (some 60,000–80,000) than in 1982, these donors being pursued even more assiduously than in the past. Details of Conservative Party income from individual donors are provided in Table 24. Conservative Party contribution income from individual donors thus continued to increase, with the 1985–8 total representing an increase of 11% on 1981–4 (compared with 170% between 1977–80 and 1981–4). It is also to be noted, however, that the individual donations as a proportion of Conservative Party funds actually declined in the period 1985–8. So while in 1981–4 the Conservatives raised 57% of their contribution income from individuals, this, as Table 24 shows, was to fall to 48%.

The Liberals are also active with direct-mail fund-raising, though their programme has taken some time to develop. In 1988, for example, the *Globe and Mail* reported that 'Through direct-mail fund-raising in 1986, the Liberals collected nearly $1 million. But they spent $750,000 of it on administration and a steady stream of consultants whose ideas, themes and lists were uniformly outdated.'[3] Since then matters appear to have improved, and although direct-mail solicitations are still not as successful as the party had hoped, with a bank of some 30,000 donors in 1988 the party 'netted' more than $1 million

---

[3] *Globe and Mail*, 2 Jan. 1988.

TABLE 24. *Contribution income of the Progressive Conservative Party from individual donors, 1985–1988* ($)

	(1) Total contribution income	(2) Total contribution income from individuals	(2) as % of (1)
1985	14,565,652	7,872,289	54
1986	15,177,750	7,874,533	52
1987	12,761,155	6,065,219	48
1988	24,542,036	10,181,404	41
TOTAL	67,046,593	31,993,445	48

Note: Column 1 includes contributions from individuals, businesses and commercial organizations, governments, trade unions, and other organizations. However, the last three categories involve the payment of very small total amounts ($4,142 in 4 years).

Source: Chief Electoral Officer of Canada, 1989*b*.

in this way. Details of Liberal Party income from individual donors are provided in Table 25. Liberal contribution income from individual donors thus also continued to grow, with the 1985–8 total representing an increase of 24% on 1981–4 (compared with 82% between 1977–80 and 1981–4). It is also to be noted, as with the Conservatives, that individual donations as a proportion of Liberal Party funds showed a small decline in 1985–8. So while in 1981–4 the party raised 47% of its total contribution income in this way, as Table 25 shows, this was to fall to 45%.

The NDP has also developed a direct-mail operation, thereby confounding to some extent the scepticism of party officials in the early 1980s that direct mail depends for its success on the target audience being mainly middle-class people accustomed to sending money through the post. As the NDP has a considerable working-class support, it was thought that this would present more of a problem for the New Democrats than for the other parties. But the party may well have underestimated its support and its supporters, as a bank of some

TABLE 25. *Contribution income of the Liberal Party from individual donors, 1985–1988 ($)*

	(1) Total contribution income	(2) Total contribution income from individuals	(2) as % of (1)
1985	5,570,822	3,129,232	56
1986	10,619,007	5,752,902	54
1987	8,832,377	3,471,932	39
1988	13,211,364	4,748,305	36
TOTAL	38,233,570	17,102,371	45

Note: Column 1 includes contributions from individuals, businesses and commercial organizations, governments, trade unions, and other organizations. However, the last three categories involve the payment of very small total amounts ($59,492 in 4 years).

Source: Chief Electoral Officer of Canada, 1989*b*.

25,000 names brings in $1.6 million gross annually, this being worth some $900,000 net. Details of NDP income from individual donors are shown in Table 26. As with the Conservatives and the Liberals, NDP contribution income from individuals has continued to grow, with the 1985–8 total representing a 41% increase on 1981–4 (compared with 53% between 1977–80 and 1981–4). Like both the other parties, however, individual contributions as a proportion of NDP income decreased in 1985–8 (albeit slightly), from 78% to 76%. All this is subject to the qualification made in Chapter 5 concerning the fact that much of this money may have been raised on federal tax receipts by provincial sections of the party, by no means all of which may come to Ottawa to be used for federal purposes.

II. Corporate and Trade Union Funding

The Canadian political parties now raise a smaller proportion of their income from corporations and trade unions than do at

TABLE 26. *Contribution income of the New Democratic Party from individual donors, 1985–1988* ($)

	(1) Total contribution income	(2) Total contribution income from individuals	(2) as % of (1)
1985	5,609,412	4,611,704	82
1986	6,461,460	5,036,131	78
1987	6,174,903	4,782,200	77
1988	10,914,220	7,844,753	72
TOTAL	29,159,995	22,274,788	76

Note: Column 1 includes contributions from individuals, businesses and commercial organizations, governments, and trade unions. But unlike Table 24 and 25 it does not include contributions from 'other organizations'. In the cases of the NDP this is a substantial entry, as it now includes contributions to provincial sections of the party.

Source: Chief Electoral Officer of Canada, 1989*b*.

least the Conservative and Labour Parties in Britain. For this the legislation, with its disclosure and reporting requirements and with its income tax credit to stimulate donations, appears to be at least partially responsible. It remains the case, however, that dependence on institutional support is still high. As we saw in Chapter 5, the dependence of both the Conservatives and the Liberals on corporate funds declined in the period 1981–4. So while the parties relied on this source for 55% and 60% respectively of their contribution income between 1977 and 1980, this had fallen to 42% and 49% in the following period. This is a development which has, however, been arrested, with income from corporations in the period 1985–8 showing an increase. As is shown in Table 27, corporate donations accounted for 52% of the contribution income of the Conservatives and 55% of the contribution income of the Liberals. And this was at a time when corporations were spending heavily in the political process independently of the parties, a point to which we return later in this chapter. The

TABLE 27. *Contribution income of the Progressive Conservative Party and the Liberal Party from corporations, 1985–1988* ($)

	Progressive Conservative Party			Liberal Party		
	(1) Total contribution income	(2) Total contribution income from corporations	(2) as % of (1)	(3) Total contribution income	(4) Total contribution income from corporations	(4) as % of (3)
1985	14,565,652	6,693,363	46	5,570,822	2,432,398	44
1986	15,177,750	7,301,230	48	10,619,007	4,845,901	46
1987	12,761,155	6,695,571	52	8,832,377	5,343,968	61
1988	24,542,036	14,358,842	59	13,211,364	8,449,440	64
TOTAL	67,046,593	35,049,006	52	38,233,570	21,071,707	55

Note: Columns 1 and 3 include contributions from individuals, businesses and commercial organizations, governments, trade unions, and other organizations. However, the last three categories involve the payment of very small total amounts.

Source: Chief Electoral Officer of Canada, 1989b.

TABLE 28. *Contribution income of the New Democratic Party from trade union affiliation fees and donations, 1985–1988* ($)

	(1) Total contribution income	(2) Total trade union affiliation fees and donations	(2) as % of (1)
1985	5,609,412	869,401	15
1986	6,461,460	1,172,784	18
1987	6,174,903	1,345,227	22
1988	10,914,220	2,718,009	25
TOTAL	29,159,995	6,105,421	21

Note: Column 1 includes contributions from individuals, businesses and commercial organizations, governments, and trade unions. But unlike Tables 24, 25, and 27 it does not include contributions from 'other organizations'. In the case of the NDP this is a substantial entry, as it includes contributions to provincial sections of the party.

Source: Chief Electoral Officer of Canada, 1989*b*.

NDP also saw its reliance on institutional funding increase as a proportion of total funds. In 1981–4 the party relied on trade union contributions and affiliation fees for 19% of its income. As Table 28 shows, in the period 1985–8 this rose to 21%, perhaps failing fully to reflect the sharp rise in the amount of money actually paid by the unions, from $3.7 million in 1981–4 to $6.1 million in 1985–8.

The currently high level of corporate support for the parties has generated some comment and controversy. Indeed, in recent years concern has been expressed by both business-men and politicians alike. In a speech delivered in 1991 the Chairman of the Royal Bank of Canada argued that close atten-tion should be paid to the Quebec system with its complete ban on contributions other than from individuals (Taylor, 1991). A few years earlier the parliamentary secretary to the Minister of Justice in the Mulroney government resigned his post ostensibly to campaign for just such a reform. Apart from questions of principle, allegations have also been made of

Conclusion

doubtful practices, including 'kickbacks' or 'toll-gating' whereby companies which are awarded federal government contracts are expected to make a contribution to the funds of the governing party in return.[4] If these allegations are proved to be true, then clearly the case for some form of intervention will be irresistible. One possibility would be completely to prohibit corporate political donations to eliminate this and other dangers of corruption. Another possibility would be to deal specifically with this particular problem. It has been shown in Chapter 7 that in the United States legislation in force since 1907 and 1940 respectively prohibits both corporations and government contractors from making political contributions. In each case, however, the prohibition is rendered largely ineffective by the provision which permits corporations (including those which tender for and hold government contracts) to create political action committees, funded by the voluntary subscription of stockholders and employees. These committees are free, subject to contribution limits, to make donations to candidates and parties. But the transplantation of the prohibition on contributions from corporations and contractors need not be accompanied by a provision which permits the creation of corporate political action committees to promote the political goals of the enterprise.

Yet although a strong case in principle, supported by (admittedly largely unsubstantiated) allegations of unethical practices, can be made to sustain an argument for the banning of corporate contributions, the case is not one-sided. Clearly those with economic power should not be able to buy political favours, and political parties should not be accountable to corporate paymasters. On the other hand, however, in a society which respects the right to freedom of association, it must be open to groups to present candidates for election to Parliament and indeed to form a political party for this purpose, the party being funded if necessary primarily by the group. A leading example of this phenomenon in Canadian politics is the NDP which clearly had sectional goals when first established.[5] If a

[4] *Globe and Mail*, 12 Nov. 1987.
[5] It was pointed out in the *Oil Workers'* case that 'The plaintiff local further alleges that the Co-operative Commonwealth Federation, a political party in Canada, and the Canadian Labour Congress, at their respective conventions

ban on corporate and trade union funding had been in force in 1960 it would have been impossible for the NDP to have been born in the shape initially conceived or, without union money, to have grown to its present strength. Institutional money (in this case trade union money) was an important means of ensuring the political representation of a significant group of Canadians who otherwise would effectively have been disenfranchised. Historically, then, there is at least an argument against restricting corporate and trade union support of political parties in Canada. Although the case is perhaps not now as powerful, with the institutional and financial links between the NDP and the unions being weaker than those between the Labour Party and the unions in Britain, the argument nevertheless remains valid. Given that the federal office of the NDP depends on trade unions for (at least) 21% of its funds, it is not surprising that in its evidence to the Lortie Royal Commission it expressed itself against any prohibition or restriction on corporate or trade union donations (NDP, 1990*b*).

III. Unequal Funding

Party income continued to increase in 1985–8, though at a much slower pace than in the period 1981–4. It is also the case that political money continued to fall unevenly upon the parties, as demonstrated in Table 29. If we look at this period as we looked at the earlier periods in Chapter 5, we find that Liberal income was 57% that of the Conservatives; NDP income was 43% that of the Conservatives; and NDP income was 76% that of the Liberals. The difference between the three parties is

held in 1960, decided to form a new political party in Canada, to be known as the "New Party", to be comprised of individuals and affiliated trade unions; that a national committee has been set up, composed of members chosen by the Canadian Labour Congress and the Co-operative Commonwealth Federation; that said committee has arranged for a founding convention for the New Party to be held in Ottawa in August 1961; and that the said committee has proposed that the per capita membership dues for trade unions affiliating with the New Party should be 5c per month. Since the trial of this action, which took place at the end of June, I have noticed in the press reports of the founding of the New Party under the new name "New Democratic Party"' (*Oil, Chemical and Atomic Workers' International Union, Local No. 16-601* v. *Imperial Oil Ltd.* (1962) 30 DLR (2d) 657, at pp. 660–1.

TABLE 29. *Annual contribution income of the Progressive Conserva-tive, Liberal and New Democratic Parties, 1985–1988 ($)*

Year	Progressive Conservative	Liberal	NDP
1985	14,565,652	5,570,822	5,609,412
1986	15,177,750	10,619,007	6,461,460
1987	12,761,155	8,832,377	6,174,903
1988	24,542,036	13,211,364	10,914,220
TOTAL	67,046,593	38,233,570	29,159,995

Note: This includes contributions from individuals, businesses and commercial organizations, governments, trade unions, and other organizations (except in the case of the NDP for this last category).

Source: Chief Electoral Officer of Canada 1989*b*.

thus very similar to that in the earlier period 1981–4. It is important to be reminded again of the fact that not all the money raised by the NDP federal office will be available for use for federal purposes.

If we turn to the numbers of donors to each of the parties, the NDP was the best supported in terms of the number of individual donors in the period 1985–8. The number of con-tributions by individuals to the NDP rose to 394,168, while the Liberals increased to 123,528 only and the Conservatives actually declined to 221,116. Perhaps the most remarkable fea-ture of this is that despite having more than three times as many donors as the Liberals and more than one and a half times as many donors as the Conservatives, the NDP had only three-quarters (76%) and less than half (43%) the income of these parties respectively in the four-year period. This can be explained partly by the size of the donations to the parties. So while the average NDP donation was a mere $56, the average Conservative and Liberal donations were $145 and $139. But this is not the whole story, with corporate support being another factor helping to explain the gulf between the parties. NDP income of $6.7 million from trade unions and businesses combined pales alongside the $21 million received by the

Liberals and the $35 million received by the Conservatives from corporations. If we remove corporate and trade union funding and look only at contributions from individuals in the period 1985–8, the total contribution income of the Conservatives would have been $31,993,445, the Liberals $17,102,371, and the NDP $22,274,788. This would mean that Liberal income would be 53% that of the Conservatives; NDP income would be 70% that of the Conservatives; and Liberal income would be 77% that of the NDP. There would thus still be a gap between the parties, and indeed the Liberals would be disadvantaged relative to both the others. But the effect of a ban on corporate funding is that it would at least benefit the party which appears to be best supported in terms of numbers of donors. So a ban on corporate funding may be justifiable at least in the Canadian context as a means of equalizing electoral opportunity. But if such a step were to be taken, important lessons about enforcement would have to be learned from the experience of the Dominion Elections Act 1908 in particular. This was discussed in Chapter 1.

Given the financial dependence of all of the parties on institutional money, it is difficult to see how they could seriously contemplate any significant restrictions on this source of funding unless the shortfall was to be made up at least on an interim basis by a major infusion of public money. But the only party which has seemed seriously committed to an initiative of this kind is the NDP, though it has to be said that the NDP believes such an infusion should be additional to rather than in place of any institutional funding. In its submission to the Royal Commission, the party identified three areas where the level of state support could be increased. The first related to the tax credit which the party complained had never been increased, despite the rise in the cost of living since 1974 when it was introduced. As a result, 'the salutary effect of this legislation 16 years ago, in encouraging public participation in the political process and broadening the financial base of registered parties and candidates, has been largely eroded'. It was proposed that the existing limits should be doubled, and revised every few years. A second concern related to the election expenses rebate, with the party arguing that the rebate of 22.5% of expenses of parties should be increased to 50%;

(again) that the reimbursement to candidates should apply to those receiving 10% or more of the popular vote in place of the 15%; and that the reimbursement to parties should not be confined to those which spend more than 10% of their permitted limit. Thirdly, and perhaps more controversially, the NDP proposed the introduction of annual public funding, along the lines of that operating in Quebec, arguing that such arrangements are 'administratively efficient, not subject to abuse and help to restore public confidence in the political process'; in the last sense this is by addressing 'public concerns about the potential for abuse of political influence by large contributors' (NDP, 1990*b*). There is, however, little support for this last proposal in particular. So while the Conservatives are strongly committed to the existing public funding provisions (which they believe have made a positive contribution to Canada's democratic process) and while they are in favour of increasing the tax credit, they are also against annual public funding as well as any significant increase in election expense reimbursements. That being so, the case for restricting private funding will be hard to sustain.

IV. Equality of Electoral Opportunity

If we turn from the income of the parties to expenditure, details of the operating expenses of the three parties are presented in Tables 30, 31 and 32. The first point to note is that although the operating expenses of the parties continued to grow in the period 1985–8, in the case of at least the Tories and the Liberals this was at nothing like as fast a rate as in 1981–4. Thus Tory operating expenses increased by only 17% (compared with 210% in the previous period), while the Liberals saw an increase of 35%. The real surprise was the NDP, with operating expenses increasing by more than 121% on the previous period. The second point to note is that in some respects the gap between the parties appears to have closed on the 1981–4 period, though again it is important to be reminded of the fact that unlike the other parties, the NDP expenditures include those by both the federal and provincial sections. So in the period 1985–8, looking at operating expenses only, Liberal operating expenses were 62% of the Conservatives;

TABLE 30. *Operating expenses of the Progressive Conservative Party, 1985–1988* ($)

Details of operating expenses	1985	1986	1987	1988	Total
Salaries, wages, and benefits	3,369,243	4,001,119	4,299,462	4,961,613	16,631,437
Travelling expenses	1,426,567	1,325,251	1,804,053	2,712,842	7,268,713
Party conventions and meetings	157,996	953,010	0	0	1,111,006
Rent, light, heat, and power	430,475	497,330	578,719	841,046	2,347,570
Advertising	31,232	57,052	49,466	220,009	357,759
Broadcasting	—	—	—	—	—
Printing and stationery	3,108,819	3,111,199	3,102,224	6,547,772	15,870,014
Telephone and telegraph	515,387	546,324	519,122	975,815	2,556,648
Legal and audit fees	112,123	93,428	34,198	74,626	314,375
Miscellaneous expenses	761,367	922,932	1,101,126	1,434,789	4,220,214
TOTAL EXPENDITURE	9,913,209	11,507,645	11,488,370	17,768,512	50,677,736

Source: Chief Electoral Officer of Canada, 1989*b*.

TABLE 31. *Operating expenses of the Liberal Party, 1985–1988* ($)

Details of operating expenses	1985	1986	1987	1988	Total
Salaries, wages, and benefits	2,046,729	3,069,879	3,012,859	2,843,060	10,972,527
Travelling expenses	484,714	718,280	733,292	547,826	2,484,112
Party conventions and meetings	1,013,969	1,766,669	200,886	183,984	3,165,508
Rent, light, heat, and power	300,465	429,458	477,233	351,528	1,558,684
Advertising	889,227	1,156,658	881,521	760,174	3,687,580
Broadcasting	—	—	3,509	8,776	12,285
Printing and stationery	382,292	268,846	344,588	218,121	1,213,847
Telephone and telegraph	273,329	184,490	249,323	230,151	937,293
Legal and audit fees	186,992	67,402	56,153	82,160	392,707
Miscellaneous expenses	1,676,134	1,946,560	1,680,562	1,723,739	7,026,995
TOTAL EXPENDITURE	7,253,851	9,608,242	7,639,926	6,949,519	31,451,538

Source: Chief Electoral Officer of Canada, 1989b.

TABLE 32. *Operating expenses of the New Democratic Party, 1985–1988 ($)*

Details of operating expenses	1985	1986	1987	1988	Total
Salaries, wages, and benefits	3,413,013	3,837,428	4,056,667	3,694,346	15,001,454
Travelling expenses	972,566	1,174,490	930,467	1,014,335	4,091,858
Party conventions and meetings	687,974	596,032	1,155,382	834,788	3,274,176
Rent, light, heat, and power	197,637	226,498	279,904	355,065	1,059,104
Advertising	1,579,936	1,276,583	1,217,215	340,794	4,414,528
Broadcasting	319,564	2,040,481	150,192	454,050	2,964,287
Printing and stationery	1,176,565	1,139,747	1,208,181	1,297,306	4,821,799
Telephone and telegraph	296,597	331,029	310,961	319,193	1,257,780
Legal and audit fees	145,132	180,297	142,127	150,828	618,384
Miscellaneous expenses	1,336,293	1,680,463	3,268,984	3,631,427	9,917,167
TOTAL EXPENDITURE	10,125,277	12,483,048	12,720,080	12,092,132	47,420,537

Source: Chief Electoral Officer of Canada, 1989b.

Conclusion

TABLE 33. *Party expenditures at the federal election, 1988* ($)

	Progressive Conservative	Liberal	NDP
Advertising	721,557	812,365	155,872
Broadcasting			
Radio	1,554,677	1,023,465	476,998
TV	2,440,503	2,024,456	2,495,316
Rent, heat, and light	7,218	28,378	40,094
Salaries and benefits	73,179	483,623	906,952
Professional services	920,625	332,321	226,765
Leader's tour (net)	1,353,932	1,066,972	766,789
Travel and rental of vehicles (other than Leader's tour)	197,526	151,766	270,196
Fund-raising	108,880	27,353	419,439
Administration expenses	148,380	667,557	908,536
National Office expenses	394,943	221,619	389,124
Miscellaneous expenses	318	0	4,482
Total election expenses	7,921,738	6,839,875	7,060,563
Limit of election expenses	8,005,799	7,977,679	8,005,799
Reimbursement	1,782,391	1,538,972	1,588,627

Source: Chief Electoral Officer of Canada, 1989*b*.

NDP operating expenses were 94% of the Conservatives; and Liberal operating expenses were 66% of the NDP. The third point to note, however, is the continuing difficulty about when these expenditures are incurred. As we saw in Chapter 5, in the period 1981–4, there was a significant increase in the level of operating expenses in the election year: 42% of all Conservative operating expenses in the period and 48% of all Liberal operating expenses were incurred in 1984. In 1985–8 this was less marked, with the operating expenses of both the NDP and the Liberals showing a decline in 1988 on their 1987 level. Indeed Liberal operating expenses fell from $9.6 million in 1986 to $7.6 million in 1987 to $6.9 million in 1988. In the case of the Conservatives, however, an increase in operating costs during

217

the election year was noticeable with operating expenses rising from $11.4 million in 1987 to $17.7 million in 1988, an increase of 55%. In fact 35% of Tory operating costs over a four-year period were incurred in the election year, in contrast to the 25% incurred by the NDP and the 22% incurred by the Liberals.

In 1988 the permitted election expenses of the parties rose, but the difference in the election expenditure of the parties was very slight, as is shown in Table 33. At the 1988 general election Liberal spending was 86% of Conservative spending; NDP spending was 89% of Conservative spending; and Liberal spending was 97% of NDP spending. This in fact was the most evenly fought election yet in terms of expenditure between the parties. Clearly there is a danger, however, that this equality will be undermined and disturbed by the practice of inflating operating costs to include items which might be electorally significant and incurred with a view to the election. If, instead of looking at election expenses, we look at total expenditures for the parties in 1988, we find that the Conservatives spent $25.6 million, the NDP $19.1 million, and the Liberals $13.7 million. Thus subject to the standard qualification in the case of the NDP, in 1988 Liberal total expenditure was 54% of Conservative spending; NDP total expenditure was 75% of Conservative spending; and Liberal total expenditure was 72% of NDP spending. It is perhaps inevitable that there should be some gap in the spending levels of the parties in view of the fact that their income shows such wide variations. Liberal contribution income, for example, remains stuck at 57% of the Conservatives'. The purpose of the legislation, however, is to promote electoral equality, which will be seriously undermined if well-financed parties increase their general expenditures in an election year. Although this expenditure may not constitute election expenses within the legal definition, it may be difficult to argue that it would not have any electoral impact.

This is rightly regarded as a serious problem and has given rise to proposals for a broader definition of election expenses to catch a wider range of expenditures. As already pointed out, the 1974 Act defines election expenses as meaning costs incurred 'for the purpose of promoting or opposing, directly and during an election, a particular registered party . . .' and continues by providing that without limiting the generality of the foregoing this includes matters such as advertising expenses and the mailing of objects of a promotional nature.[6] This is a definition which is thought by many not only to be too narrow, but by most to be too confusing and uncertain, inspiring 'almost theological debates as to its real meaning' (NDP, 1990*b*). Both the Liberal Party and the NDP have proposed that the definition should be replaced by a new formula. Thus, in a position agreed between the two parties, it was proposed that 'Election expenses should include every expense incurred between the issuance of the writ and the close of polls except for those items specifically excluded in the Act' (Liberal Party of Canada, 1990*b*). The definition would thus read:

Election expenses means any expense incurred by a registered party or candidate in respect of the conduct or management of an election, including amounts paid, liabilities incurred, the commercial value of goods and services donated or provided, other than volunteer labour, and any discounts on donated goods or services, other than for:

(a) Office and equipment rental expenses for the period following the close of the polls;
(b) Expenses incurred by a candidate seeking nomination, as allowed by this Act;
(c) Auditor and accounting fees;
(d) A candidate's deposit on nomination;
(e) Expenses incurred in holding a fund-raising function, which must make a profit;
(f) Expenses incurred for parties or advertising taking place after the close of the polls;
(g) Transfers between registered parties, candidates and local associations;
(h) Expenses relating to a recount; and
(i) Interest on loans for the period after polling day.

But although this might go some way towards dealing with the problem, it is open to question whether it is an adequate or an appropriate solution. In terms of its adequacy, the difficulty relates to the fact that electoral expenditure might be incurred in the pre-writ period. As the time for an election draws nearer, so the likelihood of election-related expenditure may

[6] Election Expenses Act, SC 1973–4, c.51, s.2, amending Canada Elections Act, RSC 1970, c.14 (1st Supp). See now Canada Elections Act, RS, c.14 (1st Supp), s.2.

increase. It is possible, for example, that literature and television commercials would be prepared in anticipation of the election, with the costs being incurred before the writ is issued. Such expenditure would not be caught by the above definition, so that it would be necessary to include a proviso similar to that contained in the NDP submission whereby election expenses are 'deemed to include the value of any goods held in inventory which have been used in whole or in part during the period commencing with the issue of the writ for an election and terminating on election day' (NDP, 1990*b*). But although necessary in principle, it is uncertain whether this would be wide enough in practice to include all electorally related pre-writ expenditures which could conceivably include promotional activity. Yet while the new definition proposed by the Liberals and the NDP suffers from these problems of potential under-inclusion, there may also be problems of over-inclusion during the election period itself. This is a point which troubled the Conservatives who, while accepting the need for a new, simpler, and clearer 'user-friendly' definition, were concerned about the details of this particular proposal. As drafted, the measure could apply to expenses incurred by a party during the election period which are genuine operating costs which would have occurred regardless of the election. The Conservatives, perhaps rightly, pointed out that a modern political party does not operate only at election periods, but as a continuing business entity, making long-term commitments for the leasing of office space and sophisticated and costly equipment, as well as engaging the services of permanent staff and other professionals. Many of these expenditures, it was claimed, do not 'contribute directly to the winning of an election' (Progressive Conservative Party of Canada, 1990*b*).

V. Third-Party Expenditures

A major weakness of the current legislation relates to the question of third-party or interest-group expenditures. As we saw in Chapter 6, the problems here have arisen largely because of the Charter-inspired decision in the *National Citizens' Coalition* case.[7] The case is all the more significant in its uncritical adoption of *Buckley* v. *Valeo*[8] for the fact that the decision of the US Supreme Court had been universally condemned in a quite unprecedented fashion (by politicians, judges, and scholars, and by liberals and radicals alike) and for the fact also that the structural differences between the Charter and the First Amendment would easily have permitted the Canadian court to have ploughed its own furrow. This is not to deny that there may have been some substance in the case against the imposition of any restrictions on third-party advertising in Canada. Thus, when asked how many occurrences there were of substantial third-party advertising during the 1984 election, the Chief Electoral Officer replied that 'on the national level, there was practically none, or very little'.[9] There was, however, some at local level, though he was unable to indicate the precise scale of the problem. It may be thought that this evidence—together with the rather limited examples provided during the Alberta litigation—gives some credence to the decision in that case. In other words, there is not yet a mischief and not yet a problem which needs to be tackled. On the other hand, however, it may be that the reason why there is not yet a problem and why the excesses of the US campaigns had not come to Canada is simply because the problem was tackled early enough. It may be that there is not a problem because the legislation effectively prevented it from erupting. At any rate it does not take much imagination to anticipate some of the problems which could easily arise if the restrictions are lifted.

The potential difficulties caused by the *NCC* decision were soon realized by the experience of the 1988 general election, which saw third-party expenditures on a 'lavish' scale (Gray, 1989). The major costs were consumed by the issue which was central to the 1988 election, the Free Trade Agreement with the USA. The Conservatives were in favour, and were supported in their campaign by the Canadian Alliance for Trade and Job Opportunities, a 'blue-ribbon corporate lobby' which sprang to life as 'a non-partisan advocacy group to build national support

[7] (1985) 11 DLR (4th) 481.
[8] 424 US 1 (1976).
[9] Minutes of Proceedings and Evidence of the Standing Committee on Privileges and Elections, 18 Dec. 1984, p. 20.

for the Free Trade Agreement' (ibid.). Both the Liberals and the New Democrats were against it and were supported by the much less well-financed Pro-Canada Network, a 'nationalist coalition of thirty-five unions and women's, cultural and church groups' (ibid.) which had been formed to oppose free trade. But although these were the principal protagonists, there were others, with the National Citizens' Coalition and individual companies incurring advertising expenses, not to mention the government of Alberta, which advertised in each of the daily newspapers in the province and delivered to every household a report on the alleged benefits of free trade. According to the Alberta government, the campaign cost about $500,000,[10] though this was disputed by the provincial opposition which believed that more had been spent. Although free trade appeared thus to dominate the campaign, it was not the only cause to attract third-party attention, with advertisements from anti-abortion groups also being prominent. Voters were encouraged to abandon party loyalties and to reject candidates who supported abortion. Much of this advertising appeared to take place in local papers (the *Regina Leader-Post*, the *Sudbury Star*, and the *Saint John Telegraph Journal*) and often identified candidates who were 'pro-life'.

Quite how much was spent by these different groups is difficult to know in the absence of reporting and disclosure requirements applicable to persons or organizations other than candidates or political parties. There are, however, a number of studies which have been done, and although apparently reliable they reach different conclusions, perhaps because the basis of calculation is different in each case. But if we look first at the study by Charlotte Gray, she claims that the 'cost of advertising campaigns by groups for and against the [free] trade deal probably topped $10-million during the campaign' (Gray, 1989), it being suggested further that the Canadian Alliance for Trade and Job Opportunities spent $2.5 million to promote free trade before the campaign began and another $2 million during the campaign. The same study also estimated that the NCC 'plunged into the 1988 election with its own $842,000 campaign' promoting free trade, and noted (without

---

[10] *Globe and Mail*, 4 Nov. 1988.

quantifying the cost) the advertising in favour of the agreement incurred by a large number of others which included 'organizations' such as 'Canadians Committed To a Better Canada', 'Concerned Citizens of Canada', and 'Canadians for a Strong Canada' as well as specific interests as diverse and varied as steel companies, farmers, physicians, home builders, and furriers. Other costs included the 'internal lobbying efforts' of companies, such as letters to employees and 'educational sessions' which one source claimed could have cost as much as $4 million. In contrast to these large expenditures by business interests in favour of the agreement, the campaign on the other side had relatively little money. Thus, while the Pro-Canada Network was able to match the pre-election lobbying of those in favour of free trade, its 'war-chest for the election period was only $750,000' which it had effectively used up after 'it papered the country with 2.2 million comic books early in the campaign' (ibid.). Although there was newspaper advertising, nationally and provincially, by other groups (the Council of Canadians, the agrifood industry, the Manitoba Coalition Against Free Trade, and Borowski's Foods) it was no match for what was being churned out by supporters of the agreement.

Hiebert's (1991) study undertaken for the Royal Commission reaches different conclusions. She estimates that the total amount spent by third parties (interest groups, individuals, corporations, and unions) exceeded $4.7 million. This, however, probably underestimates what was actually spent, for in her words it is 'an approximation based on independent research, monitoring of 13 newspapers across the country, and interviews with the principal interest groups involved in the election' (ibid.). It is unclear whether this figure applies to expenditures incurred before the election, though presumably it does not in view of the fact that the Canadian Alliance for Trade and Job Opportunities is reported as having spent at least $4.5 million before and during the election. Secondly, it appears that the $4.7 million applies only to the newspaper advertising costs of the different groups. It thus excludes the value of voluntary labour, but more importantly perhaps also 'internal organisation [and] administrative costs' (ibid.) which in the case of the Alliance exceeded $500,000. Thirdly, the $4.7 million does not cover all advertising costs. Specifically, it appears to exclude 'smaller groups or individuals who incurred expenses' in what may have been local newspapers. It also excludes radio and television advertising. Yet even this very conservative estimate of what was actually spent nevertheless makes rather disturbing reading. For of the total advertising of $4.7 million, no less than $3.6 million of this was spent promoting free trade, with only $799,321 being spent by those opposed. As Hiebert points out, the benefits of this advertising disproportionality accrued to one party to the extent that the Conservatives 'received almost four times the independent financial support promoting free trade, the central issue in the party's campaign plank, than the Liberal or NDP parties received from anti-free trade groups'. Although it is true that most (though by no means all) of the advertising merely presented the issues without exhorting the electors to endorse any particular candidate or party, the message would normally have been clear enough, unless the electors were abnormally stupid.

Little wonder then that both the opposition parties should have raised the question of interest-group expenditures in their submissions to the Royal Commission. For its part the NDP referred to the Medhurst judgment in the *NCC* case where it will be recalled he said that 'Fears or concerns of mischief that may occur are not adequate reasons for imposing a limitation. There should be actual demonstration of harm or a real likelihood of harm to a real society value before a limitation can be said to be justified.'[11] Following the 1988 general election and the 'alarming' practices of advocacy groups during that campaign, it was submitted that there was now enough evidence of harm to justify controls and ample evidence that the fears or concerns of mischief had been fully realized. Consequently it was proposed by the NDP—and by the Liberals—that section 70.1 of the Elections Act should be referred by the government to the Supreme Court of Canada for a definitive ruling as to whether it is consistent with the requirements of the Charter. Again, however, it is questionable whether this would go far enough to meet the problem. Section 70.1 makes it an offence for anyone other than a political party or can-

---

[11] (1985) 18 DLR (4th) 481, at p. 496.

didate to incur an election expense, a term defined to mean costs incurred 'for the purpose of promoting or opposing, directly and during an election', a particular party or candidate. It is strongly arguable that much (indeed the overwhelming bulk) of the free trade advertising was not unlawful on this ground, for as it was confined to the issues and avoided any mention of the parties it could be said not to be promoting *directly* the election of any party or candidate. In other words, if s.70.1 is to meet the full extent of the problem it may have to be redrafted and extended before it is put up to the Supreme Court for reconsideration. Until that is done any reference would be premature, even if the government was willing to accept the case for a reference, which seems unlikely in view of the Conservative Party's submission to the Royal Commission that 'Advocacy groups play a vital and important role in the development of public policy in Canada' and that as a result Parliament should not impose undue restrictions or regulations upon the fundamental right of these groups to advance their cause (Progressive Conservative Party of Canada, 1990*b*).

VI. Enforcement

In addition to the substantive questions discussed above, some concern has been expressed about enforcement. Under the present law, the CEO has limited powers to investigate alleged violations of the Act. When a complaint is made, it may be possible for the Commissioner of Canada Elections (who as we said in Chapter 4 carries out duties under the general supervision of the CEO) to take no further action if the Commissioner's inquiries establish that they are unfounded 'or the evidence available . . . so marginal as to make further action unjustified' (Chief Electoral Officer of Canada, 1984: 22). Otherwise, however, the matter must be referred to the Royal Canadian Mounted Police (RCMP) for investigation. This has given rise to some difficulty, with the Chief Electoral Officer pointing out that:

'Complaints received during an election alleging that a candidate has committed an offence must be handled judiciously, as that candidate's chances of being elected could be adversely affected if it became known that he or she was under police investigation. The same care must be taken outside the election period to protect the reputation of individuals. The possibility that the investigation may prove the complaint to be unfounded adds to my concerns.

Apart from the factors mentioned in the preceding paragraph, experience has shown that not all cases where there may be a violation of the *Act* require the full weight of a police investigation. Some of them, including many of those which must be investigated during an election, could be handled quite properly and more expeditiously by investigators appointed by the Commissioner, providing they had the necessary powers to obtain relevant information and documents'. (Chief Electoral Officer of Canada, 1985*a*: 5)

It is to be noted that although investigations are conducted by the RCMP, the Commissioner of Canada Elections remains in a crucial position to determine whether or not to prosecute. The CEO must give his consent to a prosecution[12] and will do so only in those cases where he believes that the prosecution is likely to succeed (Chief Electoral Officer of Canada, 1984: 21). The concern now is to improve the investigative powers by allowing the office to discharge this function without the need for police involvement in cases where discretion may be important.

In a White Paper in 1986 the government appeared to accept the CEO's need for more flexibility and discretion in enforcement (Hnatyshyn, 1986: 32). But without making any commitment, the government also raised the possibility of creating an Election Commission to which would be transferred the powers of the Commissioner of Canada Elections (ibid. 24). This effectively reopens the debate which surfaced in the Barbeau and Chappell reports, with the former arguing the need for a separate enforcement commission and the latter suggesting that for practical reasons the work of enforcement should be vested in the Chief Electoral Officer. Following the White Paper the government proposed in Bill C-79[13] the creation of a new independent agency—some twenty years after

[12] Canada Elections Act, SC 1977–8, c.2, s.45, amending Canada Elections Act, RSC 1970, c.51, s.70. See now Canada Elections Act, RS, c.14 (1st Supp), s.256.
[13] Bill C-79, 2nd session, 33rd Parliament, 35–36 Eliz. II, 1986–7.

Barbeau—but one with very tough powers. The Canada
Election Enforcement Commission was to consist of a number
of people representing different interests: a chairman to be
appointed by resolution of the House of Commons, a member
to represent the public, and a member to represent every party
having at least twelve members in the House of Commons at
the time of appointment. The last two categories of members
were to be appointed by the Governor in Council. Appointment was to be for fixed terms of up to seven years in the case
of the chairman, up to five years in the case of the member
representing the public, and up to three years for all other
members. Members would not be removed during their period
of tenure, save for cause (by the Governor-General following
an address of the House of Commons).

The Commission's function would be to ensure that the
provisions of the Act were enforced. To this end, it would be
empowered to make by-laws for the conduct of its affairs, and
might, for example, make by-laws respecting the conduct of
investigations. In addition, the Commission would be empowered (after consultations with the CEO) to issue directives
prescribing how the Act was to be enforced, and any such
directives would be binding on the Commission, candidates,
and political parties. Wide powers would be given to the Commission to investigate complaints. It might obtain the assistance of the RCMP, or designate a person to be an investigator.
A person so designated would conduct a complaint in accordance with the Commission's by-laws. Under the Bill, such a
person would have power to enter and search premises to
carry out investigations, provided that a warrant had first been
issued by a judge (on an ex-parte application). Once on the
premises an investigator could require an individual to produce
for inspection any matter relevant to the conduct of the investigation. At the end of an investigation, the investigator would
have to report his or her findings to the Commission. It was
expressly provided that only the Commission could prosecute
under the Act, in the Trial Division of the Federal Court. It will
be noted that the consent of the Attorney-General would not
be necessary. Finally important measures were included to
protect the confidentiality of alleged violators of the Act. Thus,
until a prosecution had commenced, no person could disclose

the name of any person alleged to have committed the offence. There was also a more general prohibition on the Commission, and every person acting on its behalf or under its direction, not to disclose any information that came to their knowledge in the performance of their duties and functions.

Bill C-79 died on the order-paper with the calling of the general election in 1988. Since then the debate has moved on, with some very interesting proposals on enforcement being made by the CEO. These reflect a desire to move away from an enforcement regime based on the criminal law to one based on the imposition of civil and administrative sanctions. There seems some cause to believe that this may be inspired partly by the difficulty of using criminal sanctions effectively. The burden of proof is higher and convictions are difficult to secure, with many judges apparently reluctant to regard much of this area as being suitable for the criminal law. This is not to say that the CEO wholly denied that the criminal law had a role to play. In his view conduct involving electoral fraud would continue to be subject to criminal proceedings, though he did suggest that such cases should be dealt with only by the police without any involvement by his office. The real novelty of his proposal, however, related to the replacement of the criminal law by proposed new civil and administrative penalties. This would happen in two ways. In the first place, for offences such as a failure to submit an election expenses report on time the CEO thought it appropriate to impose civil penalties in the form of reasonable fines. These would be imposed by the CEO himself, with a right of defendants to contest the imposition of the fine in the federal court. Secondly, so far as other non-compliance is concerned, such as violations of the campaign financing rules, the CEO proposed the use of administrative tribunals and the creation of a new electoral dispute tribunal. Investigations would be carried out by his office, which would be responsible for reviewing the cases and determining whether to refer them to the tribunal, with a right of appeal to the Federal Court of Appeal being possible. Tribunal decisions would be filed with the Federal Court and, once filed, would become court orders for the purposes of execution. Failure to comply would thus be a contempt and presumably would be punishable as such.

There are thus two substantive proposals on the agenda for reforming the enforcement procedures, both involving a fairly radical change of direction. As such, it is open to question whether they meet the criteria for effective enforcement identified by the Ontario Commission on Election Contributions and Expenses, referred to in Chapter 2. So far as relevant for present purposes, the first of these is that the enforcement agency should be independent, and secondly that the penalties for breach of the legislation should be severe. Reservations have been expressed on the first count with regard to the creation of a new agency which would perform the enforcement powers presently undertaken by the Chief Electoral Officer and the police. Although it appears to be accepted that there is a need to reduce the investigative powers of the police, the NDP in particular 'have not been persuaded that a Commission composed of political appointments, will better ensure the active and impartial application of the *Canada Elections Act*' (NDP, 1990*b*). The party was particularly concerned about the methods of appointment proposed by the government in its White Paper and subsequent bill. In the view of the NDP, 'the appointment system proposed would guarantee the nomination of partisans. The appointment of the member "to represent the public" would encourage abuse by the Government, and the entire process would offend a discerning and discriminating public.' It seems that there is as much suspicion in Canada about the misuse of executive patronage as there is in Britain. But while this first proposal of the government has excited some adverse reaction it is perhaps too early at the time of writing to have expected much response to the Chief Electoral Officer's proposal for different methods of enforcement—by administrative penalties rather than criminal sanctions. However, such a proposal gives rise to serious questions as to whether the legislation is likely to be adequately policed by strong enough sanctions. It is arguable, on the other hand, that the proposed changes are likely to lead to more rather than less vigorous enforcement of the legislation. Non-disclosure would lead to an automatic penalty which would accumulate on a daily basis, while over-spending would lead to penalties being imposed by an administrative tribunal. If the tribunal was appointed partly because of the commitment of its members to the legislation, it is hoped that the reluctance of the ordinary criminal courts to convict could thus be overcome. At the end of the day, however, effective and severe sanctions are not the province of the criminal law only. Potentially more significant would be powers to prevent individuals from standing for election, to prevent them from taking their seats when elected, and to have a political party deregistered. Although the last is unlikely ever to be used in the case of the large parties, there are no doubt other sanctions which could be employed, such as the refusal of election expense rebates or the denial of income tax credits for contributions to their funds.

VII. Conclusion

As pointed out in Chapter 3, in introducing what was to become the Election Expenses Act 1974, Mr Allan MacEachen said that the measure would give Canada 'one of the most democratic and open electoral systems in the world'.[14] Compared with a number of other parliamentary democracies this was almost certainly true. The 1974 Act is much more detailed and sophisticated than the legislation of probably all other non-Canadian parliamentary democracies. It has indeed been influential in shaping the laws of other countries (with Australia and New Zealand being guided in part by the Canadian experience), and it would be a valuable and relevant model for adoption in Britain. Yet all is far from perfect, with the legislation failing to serve its original purposes as fully as it might. But as the evidence to the Royal Commission has shown, these problems are not fatal, though it is not altogether clear that all of the proposals for reform will be sufficient or appropriate to deal with the problems at hand. In the end, however, the problems will be resolved only if there is the political will to deal with them. Given that any major changes in the direction of greater electoral equality of opportunity will tend to prejudice the present governing party, it would

[14] House of Commons Debates, 1st session, 29th Parliament, vol. v, 10 July 1973, p. 5476.

be unrealistic to expect the speedy implementation of any recommendations which may be made by the Lortie Royal Commission.

Legislation of this kind can never by itself create a level playing-field for election campaigns. The financing of a political party depends on a wide range of factors, not the least of which is the electoral popularity of the party. But the law can help, and in particular it can help to regulate the influence of big money. Yet it can do so only if three conditions are satisfied. The first is that there should be constant review of the legislation to monitor its effectiveness and to identify new problems as they arise. Secondly, there should be an effective response to these problems to ensure that the underlying goals of the legislation continue to be met. And thirdly there must be a commitment from all the main players in the electoral game to these underlying goals, reinforced by a desire to enforce the legislation with effective sanctions. But above all, perhaps, the operation of legislation of this kind depends on its winning judicial approval and acceptance. This has not yet been secured in Canada. It is of course paradoxical that legislation designed to improve the quality of representative and accountable government should be frustrated by people who are neither representative nor accountable. Yet whatever criticisms can be made of the judges (and there are many), it remains the case that if campaign finance goals of the type embodied in the 1974 Act are to succeed in Canada, the judges will be required to break free from the crippling consequence of *Buckley* v. *Valeo*[15] and its progeny. Given the ideological commitment of the courts to liberty rather than equality this may be more difficult than is sometimes imagined. But unless it is done, the case for exporting one of Canada's other recent initiatives—the Charter of Rights and Freedoms—will become much less persuasive. For, rather than protect and promote democratic principles, the Charter, like the US Bill of Rights, could serve ultimately to frustrate them.

---

[15] 424 US 1 (1976).

Appendix

The Purposes, Aims, and Principles of the Political Parties

THE three major political parties in Canada correspond roughly with the three major political parties in Britain. The Progressive Conservatives would be close in spirit and ideology to the Conservative Party in Britain, while the Liberal Party of Canada is the counterpart of the Liberal Democrats in Britain and the New Democratic Party is the counterpart of the Labour Party. The following statements of the purposes, aims and principles of the parties are extracted from their respective constitutions.

I. The Progressive Conservative Party of Canada

'The aims and principles of the Party as set forth in the following words at the National Convention on 14 December 1956 are:

We believe in freedom of worship, speech and assembly; loyalty to the Queen of Canada; and the rule of law. Believing these things, we hold, with history, that vigilance over such parliamentary institutions is the best guarantee of such traditional freedoms.

We believe that the state should be the servant of the people and that our national progress depends on a competitive economy, which, accepting its social responsibilities, allows to every individual freedom of opportunity and initiative and the peaceful enjoyment of the fruits of his labour.

We believe that progress and stability can best be achieved by building on the firm foundation of those things proved good by experience.

We believe in Canada, founded on these principles, a nation of many creeds and many cultures, united in its aims and accepting its obligations among the nations of the world.

We further believe that the quality of the environment is a vital part of our heritage to be protected by each generation for the next.' (Progressive Conservative Party of Canada, 1990*a*)

II. The Liberal Party of Canada

'The Liberal Party of Canada is committed to the view that the dignity of each individual man and woman is the cardinal principle of

232

democratic society and the primary purpose of all political organization and activity in such a society.

The Liberal Party of Canada is dedicated to the principles that have
historically sustained the Party: individual freedom, responsibility and
human dignity in the framework of a just society, and political freedom in the framework of meaningful participation by all persons. The
Liberal Party is bound by the Constitution and the Charter of Rights
and Freedoms and is committed to the pursuit of equality of opportunity for all persons, to the enhancement of our unique and
diverse cultural community, to the recognition that English and French
are the official languages of Canada, and to the preservation of the
Canadian identity in a global society.

In accordance with this philosophy, the Liberal Party of Canada
subscribes to the fundamental rights and freedoms of persons under
the rule of law and commits itself to the protection of these essential
values and their constant adoption to the changing needs of modern
Canadian society.

The Liberal Party of Canada recognizes that human dignity in a
democratic system requires that all citizens have access to full information concerning the policies and leadership of the Party; the
opportunity to participate in open and public assessment of such
means, such modifications of policies and leadership as they deem
desirable to promote the political, economic, social, cultural and
general well being of Canadians.

To realize this objective, the Liberal Party of Canada strives to
provide a flexible and democratic structure whereby all Canadians can
obtain such information, participate in such assessment and militate
for such reform through open communications, free dialogue and
participatory action both electoral and non-electoral.'
(Liberal Party of Canada, 1990*a*)

III. The New Democratic Party

'The New Democratic Party believes that the social, economic and
political progress of Canada can be assured only by the application of
democratic socialist principles to government and the administration
of public affairs.

The principles of democratic socialism can be defined briefly as:

That the production and distribution of goods and services shall be
directed to meeting the social and individual needs of people within a
sustainable environment and economy and not to the making of
profit;

To modify and control the operations of the monopolistic productive and distributive organizations through economic and social planning. Towards these ends and where necessary the extension of the principle of social ownership;

The New Democratic Party holds firm to the belief that the dignity and freedom of the individual is a basic right that must be maintained and extended; and

The New Democratic Party is proud to be associated with the democratic socialist parties of the world and to share the struggle for peace, international co-operation and the abolition of poverty.'
(New Democratic Party, 1990*a*)

Bibliography and
Further Reading

ADAMANY, D. W. (1972), *Campaign Finance In America* (Belmont, Calif.: Duxbury Press).

—— (1981), 'PACs and the Democratic Financing of Politics', *Arizona Law Review*, 22, 569.

—— (1983*a*), 'Political Action Committees and Democratic Politics', *Detroit College of Law Review*, 1013.

—— (1983*b*), 'Political Finance and the American Political Parties', *Hastings Constitutional Law Quarterly*, 10, 497.

—— and AGREE, G. E. (1975), *Political Money: A Strategy for Campaign Financing in America* (Baltimore: Johns Hopkins University Press).

ALEXANDER, H. E. (1961), *Tax Incentives for Political Contributions?* (Princeton, NJ: Citizens' Research Foundation).

—— (1972), *Money in Politics* (Washington, DC: Public Affairs Press).

—— (ed.) (1979), *Political Finance* (Beverly Hills, Calif.: Sage Publications).

—— (1981), 'The Obey–Railsback Bill: Its Genesis and Early History', *Arizona Law Review*, 22, 653.

—— (1983), 'The Future of Election Reform', *Hastings Constitutional Law Quarterly*, 10, 721.

ANON. (1949), 'Backstage at Ottawa', *MacLean's*, 62, Aug., 15.

ANON. (1974), 'The Constitutionality of Restrictions on Individual Contributions to Candidates in Federal Elections', *University of Pennsylvania Law Review*, 122, 1609.

ANON. (1975), 'Corporate Democracy and the Corporate Political Contribution', *Iowa Law Review*, 61, 545.

ANON. (1977), 'The Unconstitutionality of Limitations on Contributions to Political Committees in the 1976 Federal Election Campaign Act Amendments', *Yale Law Journal*, 86, 953.

ANON. (1978), 'Campaign Contributions and Federal Bribery Laws', *Harvard Law Review*, 92, 451.

ANON. (1981), 'Independent Political Committees and the Federal Election Laws', *University of Pennsylvania Law Review*, 129, 955.

ATKEY, R. G. (1985), 'Corporate Political Activity', *University of Western Ontario Law Review*, 23, 129.

Australian Electoral Commission (1984), 'Election Funding and

Financial Disclosure. Guidelines for Political Parties' (Canberra: as author).

BARBEAU, A. (1966), *Report of the Committee on Election Expenses* (Ottawa: Queen's Printer).

BEATTY, D. M. (1987), *Putting the Charter to Work: Designing a Constitutional Labour Code* (Kingston: McGill-Queen's University Press).

BERTOU, P. (1976), 'The Pacific Railway Scandal', in Gibbons and Rowat, 1976, q.v.

BEVIER, L. R. (1985), 'Money and Politics: A Perspective on the First Amendment and Campaign Finance Reform', *California Law Review*, 73, 1045.

BLUM, J. M. (1983), 'The Divisible First Amendment: A Critical Functionalist Approach to Freedom of Speech and Electoral Campaign Spending', *New York University Law Review*, 58, 1273.

BOLTON, J. R. (1981), 'Constitutional Limitations on Restricting Corporate and Union Free Speech', *Arizona Law Review*, 22, 373.

BOYER, J. P. (1978), 'The Legal Status of Union Political Contributions in Canada Today', *Business Quarterly*, 43, (3) 20.

—— (1979), 'Legal Aspects of the Corporate Political Contributions in Canada', *Canadian Business Law Journal*, 3, 161.

—— (1982), 'Political Rights and the Charter', *Canadian Lawyer*, 6, (4) 30.

—— (1983), *Money and Message: The Law Governing Election Financing, Advertising, Broadcasting and Campaigning in Canada* (Toronto: Butterworths).

British Columbia (1978), *Royal Commission on Electoral Reform*, vol. iv (as author).

BROWN, D. V. (1977), 'Corporate Political Action Committees: Effect of the Federal Election Campaign Act Amendment of 1976', *Catholic University Law Review*, 26, 756.

BUCKSBAUM, A. P. (1983), 'Campaign Finance Re-Reform: The Regulation of Independent Political Committees', *California Law Review*, 71, 673.

BUDDE, B. A. (1981), 'The Practical Role of Corporate PACs in the Political Process', *Arizona Law Review*, 22, 553.

CAMP, D. (1974), *Ontario Commission on the Legislature: Third Report* (Toronto).

CHAPPELL, H. (1971), *Minutes of Proceedings and Evidence of the Special Committee on Election Expenses* (3rd Session, 28th Parliament, 1970–1, 1 June 1971).

Chief Electoral Officer of Canada (1979a), *Statutory Report* (Ottawa: as author).

—— (1979*b*), *Report of the Chief Electoral Officer Respecting Election Expenses* (Ottawa: as author).

—— (1980*a*), *Statutory Report* (Ottawa: as author).

—— (1980*b*), *Report of the Chief Electoral Officer Respecting Election Expenses* (Ottawa: as author).

—— (1983), *Statutory Report* (Ottawa: as author).

—— (1984), *Statutory Report* (Ottawa: as author).

—— (1985*a*), *Report of the Chief Electoral Officer of Canada on Proposed Legislative Changes* (Ottawa: as author).

—— (1985*b*), *Report of the Chief Electoral Officer Respecting Election Expenses* (Ottawa: as author).

—— (1986), *Statutory Report* (Ottawa: as author).

—— (1989*a*), *Statutory Report* (Ottawa: as author).

—— (1989*b*), *Report of the Chief Electoral Officer Respecting Election Expenses* (Ottawa: as author).

—— (1991), *Statutory Report* (Ottawa: as author).

CHILES, L. (1984), 'PAC's: Congress on the Auction Block', *Journal of Legislation*, 11, 193.

CLAGETT, B. M., and BOLTON, J. R. (1976), 'Buckley v. Valeo, Its Aftermath, and Its Prospects: The Constitutionality of Government Restraints on Political Campaign Financing', *Vanderbilt Law Review*, 29, 1327.

CLANCY, J., ROBERTS, W., SPENCER, D., and WARD, J. (1986), *All for One: Arguments From the Labour Trial of the Century on the Real Meaning of Trade Unionism* (Toronto: Ontario Public Service Employees Union).

CLIFTON, J. R. (1973–4), 'Corporate Campaign Funding', *Cumberland-Samford Law Review*, 544.

CLYDE, H. M. (1977), 'Corporate and Union Political Contributions and Expenditures Under 2 U.S.C. s.441b: A Constitutional Analysis', *Utah Law Review*, 291.

COATES, B., COOK, C., MALONE, A., and REID, J. (1981), 'The Canada Elections Act Revisited: Assessing the 1974 Reforms', *Parliamentary Government*, 2, (2) 3.

COURTNEY, J. C. (1978), 'Recognition of Canadian Political Parties in Parliament and in Law', *Canadian Journal of Political Science*, 11, 33.

COX, A. (1982), 'Constitutional Issues in the Regulation of the Financing of Election Campaigns', *Cleveland State Law Review*, 31, 395.

DEBBASCH, C., and PONTIER, J. M. (1983), *Les Constitutions de la France* (Paris: Dalloz).

'Defunct Politician' (1931), 'Campaign Funds—The Remedy', *MacLean's*, 44, Nov., 15.

DICKERSON, R. W. V., and NADEAU, P. A. (1978), *Royal Commission on Corporate Concentration: Report* (Ottawa: Minister of Supply and Services).

DONOVAN, S. J., and WINMILL, R. B. (1976), 'The Beauharnois Power Scandal', in Gibbons and Rowat, 1976, q.v.

DOUBLET, Y.-M. (1990), *Le Financement de la vie politique* (Paris: Presses Universitaires de France).

Economist (1986), 'Give Early, Give Often', 1 Mar.

ELLIOTT, L. A. (1981), 'Political Action Committees—Precincts of the '80's', *Arizona Law Review*, 22, 539.

EMERSON, T. (1964), 'Freedom of Association and Freedom of Expression', *Yale Law Journal*, 74, 1.

EPSTEIN, E. M. (1980), 'Business and Labor under the Federal Election Campaign Act of 1971', in Malbin, 1980, q.v.

EPSTEIN, E. (1981), 'The PAC Phenomenon—An Overview', *Arizona Law Review*, 22, 355.

ERVIN, S. J. (1974), 'Campaign Practices and the Law: Watergate and Beyond', *Emory Law Journal*, 23, 1.

ESCH, M. D. (1978), 'Minor Political Parties and Campaign Disclosure Laws', *Harvard Civil Rights—Civil Liberties Law Review*, 13, 475.

ETHERINGTON, B. (1987), 'Freedom of Association and Compulsory Union Dues: Towards A Purposive Conception of a Freedom not to Associate', *Ottawa Law Review*, 19, 1.

EWING, K. D. (1982a), 'Campaign Funding: A Dilemma for Liberal Democracy'. Osgoode Hall Law School of York University, Public Law Workshops.

—— (1982b), *Trade Unions, the Labour Party and the Law: A Study of the Trade Union Act 1913* (Edinburgh: Edinburgh University Press).

—— (1984), 'Trade Union Political Funds: The 1913 Act Revised', *Industrial Law Journal*, 13, 227.

—— (1987a), *The Funding of Political Parties in Britain* (Cambridge: Cambridge University Press).

—— (1987b), 'Freedom of Association in Canada', *Alberta Law Review*, 25, 437.

—— (1989), 'The Funding of Political Parties in Ontario', *Osgoode Hall Law Journal*, 27, 27.

FIRMAGE, E. B., and CHRISTENSEN, K. (1980), 'Speech and Campaign Reform: Congress, the Courts and the Community', *Georgia Law Review*, 14, 195.

FLEISHMAN, J. L. (1973), 'Freedom of Speech and Equality of Political Opportunity: The Constitutionality of the Federal Election Campaign Act of 1971', *North Carolina Law Review*, 51, 389.

FORRESTER, R. (1983), 'The New Constitutional Right to Buy Elections',

American Bar Association Journal, 69, 1078.

FRANCIS, D. (1987), *Controlling Interest: Who Owns Canada?* (Toronto: Seal Books).

FRASER, B. (1945), 'Shakedown', *MacLean's*, Nov., 15.

—— (1953), 'Our Illegal Federal Elections', *MacLean's*, Apr., 15.

FREEMAN, J. (1984), 'Political Party Contributions and Expenditures Under the Federal Election Campaign Act: Anomalies and Unfinished Business', *Pace Law Review*, 4, 267.

FRIEDMAN, R. D. (1976), 'A New Approach to the Dilemma of Campaign Finance Reform', *American Bar Association Journal*, 62, 72.

GEDE, T. F. (1981), 'Comparative Study of U.S. and West German Political Finance Regulation: The Question of Contribution Controls', *Hastings International and Comparative Law Review*, 4, 543.

GIBBONS, K. M., and ROWAT, D. C. (eds.) (1976), *Political Corruption in Canada: Cases, Causes and Cures* (Toronto: McClelland and Stewart).

GILLEN, D. M. (1977), 'Buckley v. Valeo: Federal Election Campaign Reform at the Expense of First Amendment Rights', *Ohio Northern University Law Review*, 4, 77.

Globe and Mail, 4 Nov. 1987, 12 Jan. 1988, 4 Nov. 1988.

GOTTLIEB, S. E. (1976–7), 'Election Law and Election Reform: Strategy for the Long Run', *West Virginia Law Review*, 79, 237.

—— (1985), 'Fleshing Out the Right of Association: The Problem of the Contribution Limits of the Federal Election Campaign Act', *Albany Law Review*, 49, 825.

GRAY, C. (1989), 'Purchasing Power', *Saturday Night*, 15 Mar.

GROSSBERG, D. A. (1974), 'The Constitutionality of the Federal Ban on Corporate and Union Campaign Contributions and Expenditures', *University of Chicago Law Review*, 42, 148.

HAY, J. (1980), 'Election 1980: How They Make Money Talk', *MacLean's*, 93, Feb., 4.

HEARD, A. (1960), *The Costs of Democracy* (Chapel Hill, NC: University of North Carolina Press).

HEIDENHEIMER, A. (ed.) (1970), *Comparative Political Finance: The Financing of Party Organizations and Election Campaigns* (Lexington, Ky.: D. C. Heath & Company).

HIEBERT, J. (1991), 'Interest Groups and Canadian Federal Elections Research'. Paper for Royal Commission on Electoral Reform and Party Financing (Ottawa).

HNATYSHYN, R. (1986), *White Paper on Election Law Reform* (Ottawa: Queen's Printer).

HOGG, P. W. (1986), *Constitutional Law of Canada* (2nd edn., Toronto: Carswell).

HOPKINS, C. (1931), *The Canadian Annual Review of Public Affairs* (Toronto: Canadian Review Company).

HOY, C. (1987), *Friends in High Places. Politics and Patronage in the Mulroney Government* (Toronto: Key Porter Books).

IFSHIN, D. M. (1980), 'Resolving Constitutional Issues Under the Federal Election Campaign Act: A Procedural Labyrinth', *New York University Review of Law and Social Change*, 10, 101.

ILGENFRITZ, S. (1983), 'The Unconstitutionality of Limits on Contributions to Independent Expenditure Committees', *University of Florida Law Review*, 35, 316.

ISENBERG, S. (1980), 'Can You Spend Your Way into the House of Commons?' *Optimum*, 11, 28.

—— (1981), 'Spend and Win? Another Look at Federal Election Expenses', *Optimum*, 12 (4), 5.

KATSKEE, M. R. (1979), 'Political Action Committees: Should National Banks Stay Away?' *Banking Law Journal*, 96, 738.

KENSKI, H. C. (1981), 'Running With and From the PAC', *Arizona Law Review*, 22, 627.

KINGSLEY, J.-P. (1990), 'Brief Presented to the Royal Commission on Electoral Reform' (Ottawa).

KILEY, T. R. (1981), 'PACing the Burger Court: The Corporate Right to Speak and the Public Right to Hear after First National Bank v. Bellotti', *Arizona Law Review*, 22, 427.

LACALAMITA, J. (1984), 'The Equitable Campaign: Party Political Broadcasting Regulation in Canada', *Osgoode Hall Law Journal*, 22, 543.

Liberal Party of Canada (1990*a*), *Constitution* (Ottawa: as author).

—— (1990*b*), 'Presentation to the Royal Commission on Electoral Reform and Party Financing'.

MCCARTHY, M. (1972), *Elections for Sale* (Boston: Houghton Mifflin).

MACDONALD, D. C. (1986), 'Revised Ontario Act Balances Election Spending', *Globe and Mail*, Sept., 23.

MACDONALD, D. S. (1985), *Royal Commission on the Economic Union and Development Prospects for Canada*, vols. i, ii, iii (Ottawa: Minister of Supply and Services).

MCINTOSH, F. W. (1976), 'A Comparative Study of Legislative Control of Union Political Activity in England, United States and Canada', *Queen's Law Journal*, 3, 58.

MACKAY, R. A. (1931), 'After Beauharnois—What?' *MacLean's*, 44, Oct., 15.

MCLEAY, E. (1987), 'Towards a Better Democracy?' Review Essay of the *Report of the Commission on the Electoral System*, *Political Science*, 39, 80.

McWHINNEY, E. (1989), 'Electoral Laws in Free and Democratic Countries: Political Questions and Judicial Review', *Journal of the Indian Law Institute*, 31, 318.

MAGER, R. T. (1976), 'Past and Present Attempts by Congress and the Courts to Regulate Corporate and Union Campaign Contributions and Expenditures in the Election of Federal Officials', *Southern Illinois University Law Journal*, 338.

MALBIN, M. J. (1980), *Parties, Interest Groups, and Campaign Finance Laws* (Washington, DC: American Enterprise Institute).

—— (ed.) (1984), *Money and Politics in the United States. Financing Elections in the 1980's* (Chatham, NJ: Chatham House).

Manitoba Law Reform Commission (1977), *Working Paper on Political Financing and Election Expenses* (Winnipeg: as author).

MEIKLEJOHN, A. (1965), *Political Freedom: The Constitutional Powers of the People* (New York: Oxford University Press).

MILLER, A. S. (1981), 'On Politics, Democracy, and the First Amendment: A Comment on First National Bank of Boston v. Bellotti', *Washington and Lee Law Review*, 38, 21.

MONAHAN, P. J. (1987), 'Judicial Review and Democracy: A Theory of Judicial Review', *University of British Columbia Law Review*, 21, 87.

MORISON, S. E., and COMMAGER, S. E. (1950), *The Growth of the American Republic* (4th edn., New York: Oxford University Press).

MURRAY, G. G. (1975), 'Canada's New Election Laws: Counting the Dollars and Making Them Count', *Canadian Business Review*, 2, 41.

MURRAY, G. M. (1931), 'The Campaign Fund Racket', *MacLean's*, 44, Nov., 1.

MYERS, G. (1976), 'The Distribution of Railway Subsidies', in Gibbons and Rowat, 1976, q.v.

New Democratic Party (1981), *Constitution* (Ottawa: as author).

—— (1990*a*), *Constitution* (Ottawa: as author).

—— (1990*b*), 'Submission to the Royal Commission on Electoral Reform and Party Financing' (Ottawa).

NEWMAN, P. C. (1961), 'Who'll Pay the Record Shot for Our Next Election?' *MacLean's*, 74, May, 6.

New York Times, 3 Apr. 1982, 3 Feb., 3 and 19 Apr. 1983, 7 June 1987, 23 May 1991.

NICHOLS, D. (1974), *Financing Elections: The Politics of an American Ruling Class* (New York: New Viewpoints).

NICHOLSON, M. A. (1974), 'Campaign Financing and Equal Protection', *Stanford Law Review*, 26, 815.

—— (1977), 'Buckley v. Valeo: The Constitutionality of the Federal Election Campaign Act Amendments of 1974', *Wisconsin Law Review*, 323.

NICHOLSON, M. A. (1980), 'The Constitutionality of the Federal Restrictions on Corporate and Union Campaign Contributions and Expenditures', *Cornell Law Review*, 65, 945.

—— (1983), 'Political Campaign Expenditure Limitations and the Unconstitutional Condition Doctrine', *Hastings Constitutional Law Quarterly*, 10, 601.

OLDAKER, W. C., and PICARD, D. S. (1983), 'Broadcasters Rights: Whether to Air Independent Political Committee Advertisements', *Hastings Constitutional Law Quarterly*, 10, 49.

Ontario Commission on Election Contributions and Expenses (1976), *The First Report of the Commission on Election Contributions and Expenses. For the Period May 7th to December 31st 1975* (Toronto: as author).

—— (1977), *Second Annual Report* (for the year 1976) (Toronto: as author).

—— (1978*a*), *Third Annual Report* (for the year 1977) (Toronto: as author).

—— (1978*b*), *A Comparative Survey of Election Finance Legislation* (Toronto: as author).

—— (1979), *Fourth Annual Report* (for the year 1978) (Toronto: as anthor).

—— (1980), *Fifth Annual Report* (for the year 1979) (Toronto: as author).

—— (1981), *Sixth Annual Report* (for the year 1980) (Toronto: as author).

—— (1982), *Seventh Annual Report* (for the year 1981) (Toronto: as author).

—— (1983), *Eighth Annual Report* (for the year 1982) (Toronto: as author).

—— (1984), *Ninth Annual Report* (for the year 1983) (Toronto: as author).

—— (1985*a*), *Tenth Annual Report* (for the year 1984) (Toronto: as author).

—— (1985*b*), *The Commission: Ten Years Later 1975–1985. Reflections on Political Financing in Ontario* (Toronto: as author).

—— (1986), *Eleventh Annual Report* (for the year 1985) (Toronto: as author).

OVERACKER, L. (1932), *Money in Elections* (New York: Macmillan).

PACKWOOD, B. (1983), 'Campaign Finance, Communications and the First Amendment', *Hastings Constitutional Law Quarterly*, 10, 745.

PALTIEL, K. Z. (1970), *Political Party Financing in Canada* (Toronto: McGraw Hill).

—— (1974), 'Party and Candidate Expenditures in the Canadian General Election of 1972', *Canadian Journal of Political Science*, 7, 341.

—— (1975), 'Campaign Financing in Canada and Its Reform', in Penniman, 1975, q.v.

—— (1976*a*), *Royal Commission on Corporate Concentration. Study No. 22. Party, Candidate and Election Finance* (Ottawa: Minister of Supply and Services).

—— (1976*b*), 'Improving Laws on Financing Elections', in Gibbons and Rowat, 1976, q.v.

—— (1976*c*), 'Federalism and Party Finance', in Gibbons and Rowat, 1976, q.v.

—— (1979), 'The Impact of Election Expenses Legislation in Canada, Western Europe and Israel', in Alexander, 1979, q.v.

—— (1980), 'Public Financing Abroad: Contrasts and Effects', in Malbin, 1980, q.v.

PENNIMAN, H. (ed.) (1975), *Canada at the Polls: The General Election of 1974* (Washington, DC: American Enterprise Institute).

PETERSEN, D., and RAE, B. (1975), 'An Agenda for Reform: Proposals for Minority Parliaments' (Toronto).

PETTER, A. (1986), 'The Politics of the Charter: Lessons from the Early Charter Decisions of the Supreme Court of Canada', *Supreme Court Law Review*, 8, 473.

PINTO-DUSCHINSKY, M. (1989), 'Trends in British Party Funding 1913–87', *Parliamentary Affairs*, 42, 197.

POLSBY, D. D. (1976), 'Buckley v. Valeo: The Special Nature of Political Speech', *Supreme Court Review*, 1.

POWER, C. G. (1949), 'Wanted: A Ceiling on Election Spending', *McLean's*, 62, Feb., 1.

Progressive Conservative Party of Canada (1990*a*), *Constitution* (Ottawa: as author).

—— (1990*b*), 'Presentation to the Royal Commission on Electoral Reform and Party Financing' (Ottawa).

RAWLS, J. (1971), *A Theory of Justice* (Cambridge, Mass.: Harvard University Press).

REAVES, L. (1983), 'Campaign Financing Reform: Is Congress Ready?' *American Bar Association Journal*, 69, 715.

ROSS, J. L. (1983), 'Regulation of Campaign Contributions: Maintaining the Integrity of the Political Process through an Appearance of Fairness', *Southern California Law Review*, 56, 669.

SABATO, L. J. (1985), *PAC Power: Inside the World of Political Action Committees* (New York: W. W. Norton).

SCHNEIDER, W. (1976), '*Buckley v. Valeo*: The Supreme Court and Federal Campaign Reform', *Columbia Law Review*, 76, 852.

SCOTT, J. (1961), 'Political Slush Funds Corrupt All Parties', *MacLean's*, 74, Sept., 9.

SEEGER, C. M. (1976), 'Free Speech and Political Contributions'

Connecticut Bar Journal, 50, 33.

SEIDLE, F. L. (1980), 'Electoral Law and its Effects on Election Expenditure and Party Finance in Great Britain and Canada' (Oxford: D.Phil. thesis).

—— and PALTIEL, K. Z. (1981), 'Party Finance, the Election Expenses Act, and Campaign Spending in 1979 and 1980', in H. Penniman (ed.), *Canada at the Polls, 1979 and 1980: A Study of the General Elections* (Washington, DC: American Enterprise Institute).

SENDROW, S. G. (1981), 'The Federal Election Campaign Act and Presidential Election Campaign Fund Act: Problems in Defining and Regulating Independent Expenditures', *Arizona State Law Journal*, 4, 977.

SHOCKLEY, J. S. (1983), 'Money in Politics: Judicial Roadblocks to Campaign Finance Reform', *Hastings Constitutional Law Quarterly*, 10, 679.

SORAUF, F. J. (1981), 'Political Parties and Political Action Committees: Two Life Cycles', *Arizona Law Review*, 22, 445.

—— (1986), 'Caught in a Political Thicket: The Supreme Court and Campaign Finance', *Constitutional Commentary*, 3, 97.

SPROUL, J. M. (1981), 'Corporations and Unions in Federal Politics: A Practical Approach to Federal Election Law Compliance', *Arizona Law Review*, 22, 465.

STANBURY, W. (1986), 'The Mother's Milk of Politics: Political Contributions to Federal Parties in Canada 1974–1984', *Canadian Journal of Political Science*, 19, 795.

SYLVESTER, J. M. (1982), 'Equalizing Candidates' Opportunities for Expression', *George Washington Law Review*, 51, 113.

TARNOPOLSKY, W. S. (1978), *The Canadian Bill of Rights* (2nd edn., rev., Toronto: McClelland and Stewart).

TAYLOR, A. R. (1991), 'Business, Politics and Politicians', 8th Annual James C. Taylor Distinguished Lecture in Finance, School of Business Administration, University of Western Ontario (London, Ont.).

THAYER, G. (1973), *Who Shakes the Money Tree?* (New York: Simon and Shuster).

Time (1982), 'The PAC Men: Turning Cash into Votes', 25 Oct.

TOCQUEVILLE, A. C. H. M. C. (1946), *Democracy in America*, trans. Henry Reeve (London: Oxford University Press).

TUSHNET, M. (1982), 'Corporations and Free Speech', in D. Kairys (ed.) *The Politics of Law* (New York: Pantheon Books).

URQUHART, I. (1976), 'How Big Oil Provides for its Friends in High Places', *MacLean's*, 89, Feb., 9.

VANDEGRIFT, B. M. (1980), 'The Corporate Political Action Committee',

New York University Law Review, 55, 422.

WADE, E. C. S., and BRADLEY, A. W. (1985), *Constitutional and Administrative Law* (10th edn. by A. W. Bradley, London: Longman).

WANCZYCKI, J. K. (1966), 'Union Dues and Political Contributions, Great Britain, United States, Canada: A Comparison', *Relations industrielles*, 21, 143.

WARD, N. (1972), 'Money and Politics: the Costs of Democracy in Canada', *Canadian Journal of Political Science*, 5, 335.

WEARING, J. (1981), *The L-Shaped Party: The Liberal Party of Canada 1958–1980* (Toronto: McGraw-Hill Ryerson).

—— and WEARING, P. (1990), 'Mother's Milk Revisited: The Effect of Foreign Ownership on Political Contributions', *Canadian Journal of Political Science*, 23, 116.

WERTHEIMER, F. (1981), 'The PAC Phenomenon in American Politics', *Arizona Law Review*, 22, 603.

—— and HUWA, R. (1980), 'Campaign Finance Reforms: Past Accomplishments, Future Challenges', *New York University Review of Law and Social Change*, 10, 43.

WINTER, R. K. (1973), *Campaign Financing and Political Freedom* (Washington, DC: American Enterprise Institute).

WISHART, D. H. (1974), 'The Election Expenses Act', *Canadian Chartered Accountant*, 104, (3) 32.

WRIGHT, J. R. (1985), 'PACs, Contributions, and Roll Calls: An Organizational Perspective', *American Political Science Review*, 79, 400.

WRIGHT, J. SKELLY (1976), 'Politics and the Constitution: Is Money Speech?' *Yale Law Journal*, 85, 1001.

—— (1982), 'Money and the Pollution of Politics: Is the First Amendment an Obstacle to Political Equality?' *Columbia Law Review*, 82, 609.

WRIGHT, S. F. (1982), 'Clipping the Political Wings of Labor Unions: An Examination of Existing Law and Proposals for Change', *Harvard Journal of Law and Public Policy*, 5, 1.

Index

advertising:
  amount spent on 222–4
  candidates, by 89
  Chief Electoral Officer,
    recommendations of 143
  third-party restrictions,
    challenge to 132–3
  US, control in 190
  voting records, of 176–7
agency:
  doctrine of 34–5, 37, 53

Barbeau Committee:
  recommendations of 47–52
Bill of Rights:
  judicial review of legislation,
    introduction of 134–5
broadcasting:
  access to 19–20
  allocation of time 74–7
  Bill C-211, provisions of 62
  Broadcasting Arbitrator 75–6
  Election Expenses Act 1974,
    provisions of 74
  expenses, reimbursement of 76
  federal elections, at 89
  law reforms, proposed 52
  limit on access to 48–9
  reforms relating to 75–6
  US, expenditure in 177–8

campaign finance, see political
    finance
campaign funds:
  Liberal and Progressive
    Conservative parties, of 6

campaigns:
  costs of 122; reduction of 55
  individual candidates, by,
    regulation of 34; period:
    duration of 77–8;
    shortening 50
  United States, legislation in, see
    United States
Canada:
  federal structure, creation of 1
  governance of 5–8
  state, legal basis of 1
Canada Election Enforcement
    Commission:
  function of 227
  members 227
  proposal for creation of 226–7
candidates:
  advertising by 89
  financial assistance to: Bill
    C-211, provisions of 63–4;
    Election Expenses Act 1974,
    provisions of 73–4;
    qualification for 54, 69
  spending limits 65
Chappell Committee:
  recommendations of 52–8
Charter of Rights and Freedoms:
  collective goals, advancement
    of 160
  democratic principles, effect
    on 231
  effect of 3
  federal law on campaign
    finance, impact on 126
  freedom not to associate, no